CHINA: THE IMPACT OF THE CULTURAL REVOLUTION

CHINA
THE IMPACT OF THE CULTURAL REVOLUTION

EDITED BY BILL BRUGGER

CROOM HELM   LONDON

BARNES & NOBLE BOOKS · NEW YORK
(a division of Harper & Row Publishers, Inc.)

© 1978 Bill Brugger
Croom Helm Ltd, 2-10 St John's Road, London SW11
ISBN 0-85664-691-1

British Library Cataloguing in Publication Data

Revolution and consolidation.
   1. China – Social conditions
   I. Brugger, William
   309.1'51'05   HN733.5

   ISBN 0-85664-691-1

Published in the USA 1978 by
HARPER & ROW PUBLISHERS, INC.
BARNES & NOBLE IMPORT DIVISION
ISBN 0-06-490760-0

Library of Congress Cataloging in Publication Data

Main entry under title:

China.

   Includes index.
   1. China – History – 1949-1976 – Addresses,
essays, lectures. I. Brugger, Bill.
DS777.55.C4486   951.05   77-28197
ISBN 0-06-490760-0

Printed in Great Britain by
Biddles Ltd, Guildford, Surrey

CONTENTS

ABBREVIATIONS

CB	*Current Background*
CC	Central Committee
CCP	Chinese Communist Party
CPSU	Communist Party of the Soviet Union
CQ	*China Quarterly*
EEC	European Economic Community
FBIS	*Federal Broadcast Information Service*
FEER	*Far Eastern Economic Review*
GMRB	*Guangming Ribao*
HK	Hong Kong
JPRS	*Joint Publications Research Service*
KMT	Kuomintang
NCNA	*New China (Hsinhua) News Agency*
PFLP	Peking Foreign Languages Press
PLA	People's Liberation Army
PR	*Peking Review*
RMRB	*Renmin Ribao*
SC	State Council
SCMM	*Selections from China Mainland Magazines* (later *Selections from People's Republic of China Magazines*)
SCMP	*Survey of China Mainland Press* (later *Survey of People's Republic of China Press*)
SW	*Selected Works*
SWB	*Summary of World Broadcasts* (British Broadcasting Corporation) *Pt. 3, The Far East*
UN	United Nations
URI	Union Research Institute
Wansui	*Mao Zedong Sixiang Wansui*

ACKNOWLEDGEMENTS

To Neale Hunter and Steve Reglar for their invaluable advice on all chapters in this book. To Andrew Little for map work. To Suzanne Brugger for putting up with a frequently ill-tempered editor. To Marie Baker, Anne Gabb, Jenifer Jefferies and Linda Kelly for typing the manuscript. To Ron Slee for preparing the index.

ACKNOWLEDGEMENTS

PREFACE

After a ten-year hiatus, the Chinese National People's Congress met in
early 1975. Observing that the aim of that congress was to legitimise
the new state structure which had emerged from the Cultural
Revolution, the contributors to this book considered it an appropriate
time to evaluate the achievements of that revolution. Collective
works, however, take a long time to put together and it was not until
mid-1977 that a final version began to appear. In the meantime, a
major campaign to Criticise Lin Piao and Confucius had given way to
another campaign to Study the Theory of the Dictatorship of the
Proletariat which, in turn, developed into an onslaught on the newly
rehabilitated Vice Premier and Communist Party Vice Chairman —
Teng Hsiao-p'ing. Then, in the autumn of 1976, the proponents of
this campaign were themselves subjected to bitter attack and Teng was
rehabilitated once again. In each of these campaigns, the Chinese
attempted to re-evaluate immediate past history and it proved
difficult to bring the work up to date and still maintain scholarly
integrity. We decided, therefore, to focus on the period 1969-73 and to
incorporate subsequent evaluations only where absolutely necessary.

For Young, who in Chapter 1 discusses the reconstruction of the
Communist Party after the Cultural Revolution, the task was
relatively easy for this process was completed before 1973 and the
subsequent movements were all carried out under Party leadership.
Similarly, Woodward, who in Chapter 2 discusses the phasing out of
the Army from civilian administration, does not have to confront any
military problems after 1973 and has not felt obliged to extend his
argument. The same author, in Chapter 5, confronts the problem of
'ultra-leftism' in agriculture which was, as far as we know, a
temporary phenomenon and was not involved in the polemics of
1973-7. O'Leary, who in Chapter 7 analyses in detail the shift in
foreign policy orientation which came as a result of a changing world
situation, does not have to deal with any significant new developments
after 1973 and the veiled opposition to the post-Lin Piao foreign
policy stance, which emerged in 1974-6, was probably not very
significant.

Cheng, who surveys the economy after the Cultural Revolution,
however, does not stay within the bounds of the 1969-73 period, not

because he is obliged to re-evaluate his position in the light of subsequent evidence but because he feels that the major political movements, throughout the period since 1969, had little impact on the overall economic strategy and there is not much point taking 1973 as a cut-off date. With the possible exception of the movement to criticise Lin Piao after 1971, he is probably correct; though it cannot be denied that the subsequent polemics could potentially have a considerable effect on development strategy. Watson, who in Chapter 6 discusses industrial management, adopts a similar position to Cheng and traces a consistent trend of development in management methods from 1969 onwards. He does, however, note a change of emphasis between the pre- and post-Lin Piao periods, and points out that attempts to resist the overall trend during 1973 and 1974 led to some confusion and disruption and contributed to the crisis after the death of Mao.

Chapter 3, in which Chan focuses on higher education, poses the most problems, since education was at the heart of the major movements of 1973-7. Chan could not ignore the polemics and counter polemics of those years and has made a tentative incorporation.

The fact that most of the chapters have confined their argument to the 1969-73 period should not detract from their contemporary relevance. The heated polemics of the past four years have been concerned with exactly the same issues as those of the preceding four years. There is, however, one possible exception. In 1975, an attempt was made to explicate a generative view of class which in the period 1969-75 had remained latent. To accommodate this, I have traced the antecedents of this view in an historical introduction and have tried to relate it to the arguments of this book in a concluding chapter which gives a summary of the post-1973 movements. This generative view of class is currently the subject of the bitterest polemic and the position of its recent proponents has been subjected to considerable distortion. But, even if they have phrased the problem wrongly in terms of Marxist theory, we can only come to a satisfactory view of the dynamics of Chinese society once we have been able to analyse its class structure. At this stage we can only speculate and thus this book, like all other current publications on China, is only tentative — an essay in the literal sense of the word.

THE PEOPLES REPUBLIC OF CHINA
Provincial Boundaries, 1974

N

0   300   600   900 km

Boundary of China
International Boundary
Provincial Boundary
AR Autonomous Region
KIRIN Province
Hofei Town

Source: Zhongguo Dituce.
Peking Ditu Chubanshe 1974 p.1

HEILUNGKIANG

●Harbin

KIRIN

●Changchun

Shenyang

LIAONING

MONGOLIAN PEOPLES REPUBLIC

INNER MONGOLIA AR

●Huehot

●Urumchi

SINKIANG UIGHUR AR

NINGSIA HUI AR

●Yinchuan

KANSU

●Lanchow

●Sining

CHINGHAI

TIBET AR

●Lhasa

NEPAL

BHUTAN

BANGLA DESH

INDIA

HOPEI

PEKING●
TIENTSIN●

Shihchiachuang

SHANSI

●Taiyuan

SHENSI

●Yenan

●Sian

SZECHWAN

●Chengtu
●Chungking

KWEICHOW

●Kweiyang

YUNNAN

●Kunming

BURMA

LAOS

THAILAND

VIETNAM

S KOREA
N KOREA
Lushun & Talien

JAPAN

Tsingtao

SHANTUNG

●Tsinan

HONAN

●Chengchow

HUPEH

●Wuhan

HUNAN

●Changsha

KWANGSI CHUANG AR

●Nanning

KIANGSU

●Nanking

ANHWEI

Hofei●

CHEKIANG

●Hangchow

KIANGSI

●Nanchang

FUKIEN

●Foochow

●Taipeh

TAIWAN

KWANGTUNG

●Kwangchow
Hong Kong
Macao

Hainan Is.

PHILIPPINES

INTRODUCTION: THE HISTORICAL PERSPECTIVE

Bill Brugger

The 1950s

When the People's Liberation Army entered China's cities in 1948-9, the primary concern of the Chinese Communist Party was not 'socialist revolution' but the establishment of a 'New Democratic State'.[1] This state was to be based on an alliance of workers, peasants, petty bourgeoisie and national capitalists united in their opposition to landlords, foreign imperialism and the domestic 'comprador' class.[2] The New Democratic Revolution was seen as a bourgeois democratic revolution in which forms of capitalism (small private business and a peasant market economy) were to thrive. The policy of maintaining a mixed economy was a continuation of that carried out in the wartime base areas where political and economic moderation was combined with organisational and ideological radicalism.[3] The 'Yenan spirit' of collectivism, anti-bureaucratism, Mass Line leadership and concern for the people's livelihood had served the Party well for many years but came under attack in the new situation. It was very difficult to maintain good relations between Party and masses when Party organisations barely penetrated the vast ocean of individual peasant proprietors created by land reform. It was even more difficult to adapt the characteristic Yenan 'cadre' style of leadership (the promotion of change within a network of human solidarity)[4] to the requirements of heavy industry confiscated from the Nationalist (Kuomintang) government and comprador capitalists.

In the early 1950s, most of the Party's efforts were directed to immediate problems of economic development. Lack of experience in running modern industry in the face of Cold War blockade caused the Party to turn to the Soviet Union for help and, in 1953, a five-year plan of Soviet inspiration was instituted. Priority was given to industry over agriculture and heavy industry over light industry. Within heavy industry, early attempts to promote worker participation gave way to the Soviet system of one-man management which negated the Yenan collectivist tradition.[5] In agriculture, a lack of sustained attention after the first co-operativisation campaign was launched in December 1951[6] resulted in sporadic campaigns of differing pace and intensity interspersed with periods when co-operatives were dissolved and gradualist policies pursued.[7]

Behind this Soviet model lay a view of socialism which tended to see ownership of the means of production in a deterministic sense. Thus, when the socialisation of the Soviet economy had been completed in 1936, Stalin could claim that socialism had been achieved and exploiting classes had been overthrown. Since the new workers' state could not, by definition, exploit workers the only classes which continued to exist were merely residues of the past society. Thus, Stalin was hard put to it to explain the intensification of class struggle in the 1930s and could only do so by invoking foreign influence and by suggesting that the weaker classes became, the harder their struggles.[8] Such an unsatisfactory explanation was eventually to cause Stalin to begin to modify his position in 1952[9] but his death in 1953 ossified Soviet thought once again. Thus, it was an almost economistic view of socialism with a residual notion of class which was transmitted to China in the 1950s. Since the Soviet Union had 'achieved' socialism, there was a model for which the Chinese Communist Party might strive.

The above is not to argue that the Soviet model was accepted uncritically, I have argued elsewhere that there was marked disquiet with a developmental strategy which negated much of the Yenan spirit.[10] At the same time, the Soviet model led to very serious economic problems which required a change in course, and by 1955, the Party had already begun to consider ways of dealing with them. Agricultural policy, which envisaged the gradual transformation of mutual aid teams into elementary co-operatives and eventually 'higher stage' co-operatives, was too slow to prevent the concentration of land in the hands of richer peasants whilst poorer peasants fell into debt.[11] Secondly, the fact that much of light industry was still in private hands made the channelling of investment funds from agriculture into heavy industry less than efficient. Thirdly, excessive vertical control in heavy industry relegated the Party structure to merely 'staff' status in a situation where all key decisions were taken by line management.[12] A whole series of measures was taken, therefore, to effect the 'socialist transformation' of agriculture and light industry and to restore Party authority in heavy industry. In mid 1955, Mao Tsetung announced an acceleration of the movement to establish co-operatives,[13] flying in the face of those who felt that co-operativisation should wait upon agricultural mechanisation. At the same time, private businesses were reorganised as 'joint public and private' enterprises with former proprietors, now employed as managers, receiving not only a salary but up to 5 per cent per annum on the estimated value of their former property.[14] Thirdly, the one-man management system in industry was replaced by a system known as 'managerial responsibility under the unified leadership of the enterprise Party committee'.[15]

With the completion of 'socialist transformation', one might assume that the period of 'New Democracy' was over. Chinese sources, however, do not draw such a clear line. Sometimes the term 'New Democracy' refers only to the period 1949-53. At other times essential categories of the 'New Democratic' formula are applied to the late 1950s.[16] To add to the confusion, Mao Tsetung, in the early 1960s, declared that the 'bourgeois democratic revolution' had basically come to an end in 1949.[17] Despite the confusion, however, there does seem to have been a general awareness that a new socialist stage had been embarked on in the mid 1950s. This was not to say that socialism had been achieved (as in the Soviet U   merely that the construction of socialism had begun and would be achieved at some stage in the future along with 'ownership by the whole people'.

The rejection of the Soviet development model in the mid 1950s led to a re-appraisal of economic priorities. This was neatly summed up by Mao in his 1956 speech 'On the Ten Major Relationships'.[18] Of these ten relationships, five were of crucial importance for China's future economic development.

The first of these was the relationship between industry and agriculture and between heavy and light industry. By the mid 1950s, China faced an investment crisis. Though there had been some Soviet assistance in the form of loans, the bulk of capital investment in heavy industry came from agriculture through light industry. The future development of heavy industry, therefore, depended on raising the level of agricultural output by increasing investment in agriculture and paying much greater attention to the living standards of peasants. The second relationship was between industry in the coastal regions and in the interior. Faced with a growing disparity between the seaboard and the backward rural hinterland (a feature common to many 'developing' countries), Mao called for a great proportion of heavy industry to be located in the interior. He urged caution, however, lest the advantages of the existing coastal industries (established infrastructure, external economics, etc.) be lost. The third relationship was between economic construction and defence. Observing that the proportion of the state budget devoted to defence was excessive, Mao argued that the best way to increase military capacity was to develop the economy. The fourth relationship was between the state, the units of production and individual producers. Rejecting previous policies of excessively forced accumulation, Mao sought gradually to raise the living standards of the peasants. Finally the fifth relationship, between the centre and the regions, repudiated the centralism of the Soviet model and called for far greater latitude to be granted to local levels of administration.

Such are the main outlines of Mao Tsetung's economic strategy which provide the basis for the three chapters on the economy in this book. All three authors — Cheng, Woodward and Watson — assert the importance of this programme but suggest that its generality gave rise to serious problems of interpretation in the 1970s. At the time of its formulation, moreover, the problems of interpretation were, if anything, more acute. One might conclude, for example, that Mao's stress on the complementary nature of agriculture and industry implied that there would be a more balanced and perhaps slower pace of development. By 1958, however, whilst still maintaining the same overall strategy of simultaneous advance on all fronts, Mao was pointing to the importance of imbalance in the all out attempt to achieve results 'more, better, quicker and more economically':

> Imbalance is a universal objective law. Things forever proceed from imbalance to equilibrium and from equilibrium to imbalance in endless cycles. It will forever be like this, but each cycle reaches a higher level. Imbalance is constant and absolute; equilibrium is temporary and relative.[19]

Granted that there had developed a new notion of creative imbalance, the Great Leap forward of 1958-9 was an extreme form of the policy enunciated in 'On the Ten Major Relationships'. It featured a policy of radical decentralisation, extensive mass mobilisation and 'walking on two legs' (the simultaneous development of industry and agriculture, heavy and light industry, national and local industry, large and small enterprises and modern and indigenous methods of production). In the countryside, it gave birth to people's communes formed from the amalgamation of agricultural producers' co-operatives. These communes, subdivided into brigades and teams, were not only units of production but also units of administration responsible for education (often in the form of 'people-run' *(minban)* schools) and defence (in the form of a revitalised people's militia). As many cadres began to see these new communes as forms appropriate for the transition to a communist society, private plots of land were confiscated and plans put forward to introduce a partial free supply of food.

This 'communist wind' of 1958 was later criticised as 'commandist' and 'idealist'. It was commandist in the sense that cadres sometimes neglected the level of mass consciousness, the historically determined market structures and the overall situation in the economy, and instead sought to coerce peasants into their own view of communism.[20] This tendency was to recur in the early 1970s and forms the subject of Woodward's chapter. It was idealist in the sense that it stemmed not from a view of concrete reality but from an *a priori* view of what an unalienated existence might be like. Mao had stipulated that developmental policy should be geared to overcoming 'three major differences' (between town and country, worker and peasant, mental and manual labour). Undoubtedly this was a concern with alienation[21] but was it structural alienation, rooted in a materialist problematic, or essentialist alienation rooted in some eternal view of human nature? Doubtless some cadres believed it was the latter and unfettered human beings would spontaneously affirm the new elements of communism. The fact that most did not testifies not to some different view of the human essence, but merely to the fact that human nature is culturally determined and may not be changed overnight.

There has been much debate as to whether Mao himself took an idealist view in 1958. Some would say that what Schram calls Mao's uncertainty principle, which found its theoretical justification in his insistence on disequilibrium,[22] inevitably leads to what Schram describes as voluntarism and what Soviet commentators describe simply as idealism.[23] To be sure, remarks by some Chinese theorists would suggest such an interpretation.[24] One cannot be sure about Mao's position in 1958, however, because the Great Leap Forward, in its pristine form, did not last very long. As early as December 1958, measures were taken to restore, in part, the private plots and the basic unit of account was shifted from commune to brigade level.[25] Mao could not but affirm that excesses had taken place in the Leap and apparently went along with many of the changes. By the following year, however, he began to sense that what was under attack was not just the commandist deviations of the Leap but the very idea of the Leap itself.[26] But his attempt to revive the Great Leap in late 1959 and early 1960, was short lived. Crops were ruined by flood and drought (which went on for three years). The dispute with the Soviet Union, at first over the orientation of the International Communist Movement, escalated into a Soviet condemnation of the Great Leap and the abrupt withdrawal of Soviet assistance. Finally, disaffection within the Party itself resulted in a change of effective leadership and the adoption of policies which closed down many newly established industries as unproductive, curtailed the experiments with people-run schools, restored completely private plots of land and shifted the basic rural unit of account down to team level. Many cadres were criticised for being too enthusiastic about the Great Leap, and a whole series of measures were taken which restored a degree of petty capitalism in the countryside.[27]

As Mao and those of a more radical bent saw it, the Great Leap Forward had not been given a chance. Many of its basic policies had been modified as early as December 1958 and no policy could possibly have been able to cope with the extremely adverse weather conditions and the withdrawal of Soviet assistance. Liu Shao-ch'i and the more conservative members of the Party, on the other hand, could not but observe that utopian enthusiasm had led to the falsification of statistics, the premature reduction in the area sown in grain and the collapse of the planning machinery.[28] In Liu's view, only 30 per cent of the difficulties had been due to climatic conditions, the other 70 per cent being man-made factors.[29] These difficulties, moreover, were immense — malnutrition, a loss of peasant morale and corruption among disillusioned cadres.

Towards a Theory of 'Cultural Revolution' (1960-66)

When Mao retired as State Chairman in December 1958, it was said that he wished to spend more time on theoretical problems. Though he may have been eased out of the top leadership by those who favoured more conservative policies,[30] there can be no doubt that he did proceed to devote considerable energy to theoretical work. Indeed, in the years 1960-62, his writings reveal a search for a new approach to socialism within the Marxist-Leninist framework. It is not absolutely certain whether he found it, for the writings reveal many ambiguities. Nevertheless, some scholars have attempted to piece together what was distinctly new in his approach.

Levy, for example, points out that Mao took a fresh look at the relationship between productive forces and productive relations and between economic base and ideological superstructure.[31] Mao came to the conclusion that the process described by Marx, whereby a revolution is caused by productive forces outstripping productive relations, — i.e. when the superstructure lags behind the economic base — is valid only for advanced capitalist societies. In more backward countries, a revolution begins in the superstructure because that is the weakest link in the chain of capitalist control.[32] Thus, the productive relations may be transformed *before* the corresponding productive forces have been fully developed and the superstructure, instead of lagging behind, provides the conditions to push the productive forces forward. A *cultural* revolution, therefore, precedes a social revolution. Such an interpretation is, I believe, an accurate reflection of Mao's views. What is more contentious, both in interpretation and in substance, is Levy's suggestion that the above conclusion is seen by Mao as valid not only for major revolutions marking a seizure of power but also for qualitative leaps within the process of socialist transition. These leaps may be seen as part of a revolution which must be uninterrupted *(buduan geming)*, for the excessive consolidation of any stage in the transition process may create obstacles for the development of the next.[33] Thus, each stage must establish the preconditions for the next and these preconditions are, in the first instance, superstructural.

The above formulation is markedly different from most Soviet views of the determining role of productive forces. The official Soviet view was not a mechanistic one where changes in productive forces automatically produced changes in productive relations, or where the latter are simply a drag on the former. Indeed Stalin, in 1952, castigated the would be textbook writer Yaroshenko for absorbing the productive relations into the productive forces and reaching a mechanistic view of communism as merely rational organisation.[34] Nevertheless, Mao gave a far greater weight to the active role of the superstructure than Stalin; he even criticised Stalin on precisely that point.[35]

If the above is a correct description of Mao's view, then he had revised the orthodox view of cultural revolution. This held that changes in ideas lag behind changes in material forces and a revolutionary process is necessary to bring them back into correspondence. This had been the view which informed Mao's mid-1950s version of 'uninterrupted revolution' and it continued into the 1960s. Indeed, in the same work in which Levy suggests Mao might be arguing the reverse, one may still find paragraphs discussing cultural lag.[36] Of course superstructural push and cultural lag need not necessarily be in contradiction but one cannot use both theories to describe the same period. The study of dialectics is, after all, concerned with material and not logical contradictions. It is, however, unfair to criticise Mao too harshly for inconsistencies in a collection of annotations of a Soviet textbook on Political Economy which were not intended for publication in that form. Yet it is important to note Mao's reluctance to abandon the theory of cultural lag in favour of initial superstructural push. Such a reluctance is understandable in that

it could lead to a charge of idealism. But it need not necessarily do so.
Nowhere is it argued that the preconditions for revolution are created
in people's minds, merely that the precipitant is, in fact, located in the
superstructure and that the initial role of leadership in that sphere is
crucial. Surely, this is what Lenin's theory of the Bolshevik Party,
whereby a vanguard leads the proletariat from 'trade union consciousness' into 'revolutionary consciousness' is all about. It is not my
intention here to evaluate whether such an argument is tenable or
whether Mao's extension of Lenin's idea of the 'weakest link' is valid[37]
nor do I wish to enter the savage polemic about Mao's Marxist
credentials.[38] Suffice it to say that Mao saw himself directly in the
Marxist-Leninist tradition and, despite many and serious criticisms
of Stalin, he was under no circumstances going to allow himself to be
seen as an advocate of telescoping historical stages in the manner of
Trotsky.[39]

Another controversial point, in Levy's reading of Mao's views in the
early 1960s, is that, though each of the stages elaborated by Mao
establishes the preconditions for the next, it is discrete. Scholars
disagree as to whether these stages are really discrete or only
portrayed as such to avoid the charge of Trotskyism.[40] In my view,
though Levy presents a picture far more clear cut than the evidence
would warrant, one may only understand Mao's criticisms of Stalin in
terms of discrete stages. The first of these in modern Chinese history
constituted the bourgeois democratic revolution which ended in
1949 with the seizure of power.[41] Hence, Mao modified the earlier
view that the bourgeois democratic revolution continued through the
New Democratic stage of the 1950s. The second stage constituted the
socialist transformation which was completed by the mid 1950s, but
Mao was careful here to avoid saying that socialism had been achieved.[42]
The third stage, which began in the mid 1950s, was marked by the co-
existence of 'co-operative ownership' and 'ownership by the whole people',
but one is never absolutely sure which elements of Chinese society
belonged to which category. The fourth stage, which had yet to be
embarked upon was to be characterised by total 'ownership by the
whole people' and the fifth stage was, in fact, communism. After that,
there would be other stages which no-one at present could define.[43]
Indeed one is uncertain about how one might go about defining them.

Having elaborated these stages, Levy goes on to explicate Chinese
criticism of the Soviet Union. As Mao saw it, the Soviet leadership
applied principles valid for one stage to completely different stages.
Stalin, for example, did not see the different roles played by

commodities in different stages of socialist transition. Both Mao and Stalin agreed that labour power could no longer remain a commodity once the socialist revolution had begun. Both also agreed that commodity production was necessary so long as co-operative ownership co-existed with 'ownership by the whole people',[44] only that way could exchange between the two sectors be ensured. They differed, however, with regard to the commodity feature of the means of production. As Mao saw it, Stalin regarded the replacement by planning of the commodity feature of the means of production as a key feature of socialism.[45] Stalin, therefore, applied policies appropriate to the stage of 'ownership by the whole people' to the stage where that form of ownership still co-existed with co-operative ownership. Thus there was a prematurely excessive reliance on the planning machinery and an inefficient centralisation which dampened mass initiative. Mao's criticism was undoubtedly very apt but one might have wished for greater clarity in how to implement his theory of stages.

There is enough in Mao's theoretical writings of the early 1960s for us to conclude that his objection to the new policies pursued by the Liu Shao-ch'i leadership was that they did not establish the preconditions for the fourth stage of 'ownership by the whole people'. Some policies belonged to past stages. For example the policy of *san zi yi bao* (the extension of plots for private production, free markets, the responsibility of private enterprises for their own profits and losses and allowing each household to assume a contracted obligation towards the state for producing a fixed quantity of grain[46]) constituted a *retreat* to the second or even the first stage. The same may be said for his 'four freedoms' (to engage in usury, hire labour, sell land and run private business). Other policies revealed themselves as appropriate for the current stage in terms of the criterion of ownership but not in terms of Mao's other two criteria for the evaluation of a particular stage — relations between people at work and patterns of distribution.[47] The adoption, for example, of the Magnitogorsk Constitution for the Anshan Iron and Steel Corporation which specified a rigid staff-line pattern of authority, negated a constitution written for the corporation by Mao himself which encouraged Party leadership, mass participation in management and cadre participation in manual labour.[48] Similarly, the adoption of policies appropriate to the third stage, which stipulated the socialist principle of 'from each according to his/her ability, to each according to his/her work', in practice resulted in a revival of piecework, the negation of 'politics in command' and its replacement by 'work points in command' and 'money in command' – appropriate more to the first stage.

In my view, it is almost impossible to decide exactly how to categorise Liu Shao-ch'i's view of socialist transition. At times, he seemed to reflect the view of Stalin – the neglect of communal organisations in favour of the mechanisation of agriculture by means of state-controlled machine tractor stations[49] and the partial recentralisation of industry. At others, he adopted a contrary position in strengthening market relationships by the decentralisation of authority to units of production rather than following the Great Leap policy of regional decentralisation.[50] Perhaps, in a situation of economic confusion, he could eclectically only adopt measures which occasioned the least opposition. Perhaps he had in mind that odd mixture of policies which characterised the Soviet New Economic Policy of the early 1920s.[51] Whatever Liu's view, I doubt whether Mao's distaste for most of the above policies in the early 1960s were related to a coherent Marxist critique. They could not be, so long as a rigorous class analysis was not employed, and Mao was only just beginning to reformulate his view of classes in socialist society.

Contrary to my previous thinking on this subject,[52] I am convinced by Bettelheim that it is mistaken to evaluate socialist transition merely in terms of the relationship between market and plan.[53] After all, the strengthening of the plan at the expense of the market is characteristic of some countries where the mode of production is clearly dominated by oligopolistic or monopoly capitalism. Conversely the growth of market relationships in China, in the early 1960s, is only meaningful in terms of the transformation of classes which made such a development possible.

Throughout the early 1950s, when the orthodox Soviet view of socialism was dominant, classes were seen exclusively as residues of the past. At the time of Liberation, a complex system of class analysis was adopted in which individuals were assigned to one of several dozen categories; these categories were based on relationships to the means of production but also included groups which would not ordinarily be considered in a class context (e.g. revolutionary soldiers).[54] Throughout the 1950s individual class designations *(jieji chengfen)* remained even though changes in socio-economic structure radically altered the situation. So long as the threat of invasion from Taiwan existed and so long as old classes demonstrated their presence in opposition to movements such as land reform, there could be no change. Even in 1957, when Mao Tsetung offered a new approach to social analysis, the residual view was strong. In his 'On the Correct Handling of Contradictions among the

People' Mao differentiated between two kinds of social contradictions — those among the people (capable of peaceful solution) and those between the people and the enemy (capable only of forceful resolution).[55] Observing Mao's contention that non-antagonistic contradictions, handled inappropriately, might grow into antagonistic contradictions, one writer suggests that such is the basis of a new generative theory of classes,[56] though others argue more convincingly that the analysis of 'uninterrupted revolution' at that time is outside the framework of classes and a residual view of class is still characteristic of Mao's thought.[57]

By the early 1960s, it was evident that Mao was becoming more and more concerned that new privileged groups might provide the basis for the formation of a new bourgeoisie. He spoke of interest groups *(jide liyi jituan)*[58] stemming from the 'three major differences' which have taken on a hereditary nature.[59] In 1962 he was quite explicit:

> In our country, the system of man exploiting man has already been abolished as has the economic basis of landlords and bourgeoisie. Since the reactionary classes are now not so terrible as hitherto, we speak of them as remnants. Yet on no account must we treat these remnants lightly. We must continue to engage in struggle with them (for) they are still planning a comeback. In a socialist society (moreover) *new bourgeois elements may still be produced.* Classes and class struggle remain throughout the entire socialist stage and that struggle is protracted, complex and sometimes even violent.[60]

Thus the slogan 'never forget the class struggle',[61] which dominated the radical criticism of the early 1960s, though governed mainly by the residual view, contained the germs of a generative view of class.

The same theme is taken up once again in that seminal essay which marked a new radical shift in the series of mass movements of the 1960s — 'On Khruschev's Phoney Communism and its Historical Lessons for the World'.[62] Published in 1964, this essay warned that socialism in China might be negated in much the same way as it had been in the Soviet Union. The implications of such a position are profound though unfortunately Mao never explored them. A tentative explication of his thesis must be made, however, if we are to make sense of the events which followed. So far, two versions of 'uninterrupted revolution' have been examined. The first, articulated in the mid 1950s, was within the problematic of cultural lag. The second, put forward in the beginning of the 1960s, oscillated between cultural lag and initial superstructural push. Both of these theories are outside the framework of classes. By the mid

1960s a new theory had appeared which was eventually to be known
as 'Mao Tsetung's theory of continuous revolution' *(jixu geming).*[63] It is
suggested that so long as differences in institutional power exist, they are
capable of being transformed into class relationships (defined in relation
to the means of production). Thus, class struggle takes on a new meaning;
it is not only directed against residual classes but against newly generated
classes which may be represented in the Communist Party itself. The
constant and repeated struggles needed to reverse this generative process
must be an essential part of the negation of the capitalist mode of
production. Such, was the essence of the dictatorship of the proletariat.

The above constituted the beginnings of a theory of cultural revolution.
The generative theory of class offered a theoretical explanation of the retro-
gressive economic policies of the early 1960s and, in a developing country
pursuing an uninterrupted process of revolution, the theory of the superstructure as the weakest link explained the stress on culture. The
generative theory of class, moreover, suggested that a socialist
revolution may be negated and provided an explanation of events in the
Soviet Union and the trend of events in China in the early 1960s.

Thus, Mao's primary concern in the early 1960s was not just culture
in the narrow sense of the word. True, in the field of art, literature and
the press, there was a resurgence of pre-revolutionary themes,[64] at the
expense of socialist realism and its Great Leap Forward companion
'revolutionary romanticism', and articles and plays appeared satirising
the Great Leap and Mao himself.[65] The crux of the matter, however,
was a much wider notion of culture comprising the whole realm of
human thought *(sixiang).* The way in which human activities were
structured to produce a socialist consciousness (education in the
broadest sense) revealed serious defects. Participation in manual labour
and political movements, criticism and self-criticism and the whole
field of social intercourse were all part of a process of education and had
to be geared not only to handling current problems in Chinese society
but establishing the preconditions for the revolutionary transition to a
new stage. As for the formal education system, Mao's advocacy of
linking theory with practice, changing teaching methods and shortening
the period of schooling[66] were largely ignored. He could only admit
in 1967:

It seemed that I could not have my way in China because universities
and secondary schools had for a long time been controlled by Liu
[Shao-ch'i] , Teng [Hsiao-p'ing] and Lu [Ting-i] . We simply couldn't
get in and could do nothing.[67]

The People's Liberation Army, on the other hand, showed a contrary trend. Just prior to the revival of the Great Leap in 1959, one of the Leap's most outspoken critics – the then Minister of Defence P'eng Teh-huai had been replaced by Lin Piao.[68] Lin was entrusted with countering the 'purely military viewpoint' and turning the Army into a behavioural model for the rest of society. To this end, terms such as the 'four firsts',[69] 'five good soldier', 'four good company' and 'three eight working style' were invented. By 1964, success was such that a nation-wide movement was launched to 'learn from the Army' which, together with two other campaigns (to revolutionise art and literature and to clean up the countryside [the Socialist Education Movement]) constituted a radical attack on prevailing policies. More than that, it was an attempt to inaugurate a qualitative revolutionary leap according to the theory that revolutions begin in the superstructure.

During the movements of the early 1960s, however, the radical attack on prevailing policies was often deflected and policies were distorted. Groups with completely different views on developments in China employed the same terminology and the same slogans to completely different ends, giving rise to a confusion which the Cultural Revolution did not always dispel. Such a situation was to recur in the early 1970s and we shall return to this problem in the concluding chapter.

The Cultural Revolution and the Early 1970s – General Problems

The above suggestion that Mao tended towards a generative view of class is somewhat speculative and depends upon fragmentary evidence. In recent years, further elaborations of Mao's theory of continuous revolution have been made[70] but we lack any notable contribution from the Chairman himself. We may be sure, however, that, although it might now be possible to constitute the elements of a theory of cultural revolution, such a theory did not exist in a coherent form to provide the theoretical basis for the Great Proletarian Cultural Revolution of 1966-9. The late 1960s were not noted for great theoretical sophistication and, throughout all the polemics, a residual view of class dominated. An immediate consequence of this was not an examination of how individual cadres, as potential exploiters, contributed to the continued existence and persistent values of former exploiters but a crude denunciation of such cadres as life-long avowed capitalists.[71]

The residual view of class was most marked in the first stage of the Cultural Revolution, known as the campaign to Criticise the Four Olds (old thought, old ideas, old habits and old customs). Such, one might conclude, is inevitable if, in fact, revolutionary change is to start in the superstructure. This, as we have noted, has led Soviet critics to denounce the whole of Mao's thought as idealist. The logic of Mao's position, however, is that the task of revolutionary leadership is to make certain that it does not stay in the superstructure. Such was to be an extremely difficult task.

When the movement expanded to criticise 'top persons in authority taking the capitalist road', discussion still centred on the notion that the socialist transformation of the economic base had not been matched by a similar transformation of the ideological superstructure.[72] This was still the old pre-1960s interpretation of the term cultural revolution and fell short of Mao's thinking on superstructural push and a generative theory of class. Instead of a discussion of the objective determinants of class, attention was devoted to the role of tertiary and secondary educational establishments which were the repositories of old ideas. Student activists, privileged by having a tertiary or secondary education and the prospect of secure employment in key positions in the government, economy or cultural fields would not easily accept that they themselves might be potential exploiters. At the same time, senior members of the Party, anxious to get the heat off themselves, were only too happy to see the Red Guards focus their attention on 'feudal remnants' rather than 'those in authority taking the capitalist road'.[73] Consequently, when all tertiary and senior secondary educational institutions were closed down in mid 1966, it was anticipated that all that was required was a suspension of teaching for six months[74] so that people could get their ideas sorted out in preparation for the admission of a new batch of students and further reforms. As it turned out, the struggle for control over education became more and more complex as student-based groups came into conflict with the work teams, sent down by Liu Shao-ch'i and other senior members of the Party who aimed to ensure that the movement did not harm their own particular interests. By the time work teams were finally withdrawn in the summer of 1966, whatever theoretical clarity there was embodied in the notion of 'struggle between two lines' was not matched by any clarity in the practical world. Over the next two years, Red Guard factionalism was to become notorious.

The problem of overcoming factionalism was to dominate the latter part of the Cultural Revolution and, indeed, the early 1970s. It is a major theme of this book. In Chapter 1, Young describes the reconstruction of the Communist Party which was seen as the surest way to overcome factionalism but was itself impeded by it. In

Chapter 2, Woodward describes how factionalism prevented the early withdrawal of the Army from civilian administration and devotes considerable attention to the faction surrounding Lin Piao which in 1971 contemplated a coup. In Chapter 3, Chan deals with the problem of factionalism in education and the inability of Red Guards to overcome it. In Chapters 4 and 6, Cheng and Watson note that a major theme in the economy, in the 1970s, was the restoration of order and discipline after the factionalism of the late 1960s and, in Chapter 5, Woodward presents us with the interesting thesis that factionalism in agriculture actually postdated the Cultural Revolution.

In discussing the problem of factionalism, many of the contributors consider the problem of 'ultra-leftism'. Most would agree that it must be considered as an idealist violation of the Mass Line. Such was a frequent occurrence in the Cultural Revolution and was to recur in various sectors of society in the early 1970s. Chinese sources have never provided us with anything like an adequate definition of this 'ultra-leftism' and, since its association with an equally undefined 'ultra-rightism' in 1973, it is unlikely, in the near future, that they will. It is possible, however, to approach a definition not only by considering an idealist violation of the Mass Line but also with reference to the various stages of socialist transition outlined earlier. If each stage is characterised by different patterns of ownership, different relationships between people at work and different patterns of distribution, then a premature imposition of an advanced form of any one of these elements at the expense of the others might constitute 'ultra-leftism'. Similarly, to retard the development of two elements by concentrating on only one would help us define a rightist position and understand why the Chinese make an association between the two. This proposition will be discussed in relation to agriculture in Chapter 5. An explication of this thesis will, I suspect, offer us a tool for evaluating not only the 'ultra-leftism' of the early 1970s but also of the Cultural Revolution. One might also argue that 'ultra-leftism' might be defined in terms of an idealist disregard of resource limitations and the imperatives of technology. This is suggested by Watson in Chapter 6, though one should perhaps be wary of taking such technological imperatives as given.

The question of 'ultra-leftism' is, of course, part of the general problem of leadership. There was much experimentation in the Cultural Revolution and leadership in organisation varied from outright military control to an ambitious attempt in Shanghai and one or two other places to create a Paris Commune-type organisation with elected representatives subject to immediate recall by their constituents. At least, that was the theory. In fact, the Shanghai Commune probably did little more than institutionalise, for a short time, the balance between various factions which had emerged in the Cultural Revolution.[75] After February 1967, the stress was on the formation of revolutionary committees in which the military often played a dominant role. This has led some people to posit the view that the Army may have replaced the Party and acted like an 'alternative vanguard'[76] which to some extent kept the Mass Line alive. The Army, however, is a very different kind of organisation from the Party and, mindful of this, Mao Tsetung (contrary to revolutionaries like Guevara and Debray) has consistently held that the Army should be subordinate to the Party. Though any Leninist would affirm that Party *organisation* is important, the Party should be characterised by orientation before organisation; its cement should be ideological rather than organisational. In Schurmann's view, the Party provided the link between state and society during the period of socialist transition[77] and it was able to do this because its membership embraced both state functionaries and ordinary workers and peasants. Indeed one of the major reasons the Cultural Revolution was launched was because this link became ineffective as Party merged with State (defined in Marxist terms as a structure of class domination). The Army, on the other hand, as Woodward points out, was part of the repressive apparatus of the state. In Lin Piao's terms it was seen as a 'pillar of the dictatorship of the proletariat'. It was clear, however, that Lin meant something more by this term than a description of state structure. Since 1964, soldiers had intervened actively in the civilian sector and it is no exaggeration to say that part of the Army did act for a time as a quasi-Party.

It is possible to see the events of the 1960s not just as a radical attempt to close the gap between worker and peasant but also as an attempt to close the gap between both and the soldier. If this meant just a greater involvement of individual soldiers in productive labour and a greater degree of co-operation between regular military and militia, then such a conclusion is unobjectionable. If, however, part of the Army began to act as a quasi-Party with loyalty to Lin Piao and his network of former Fourth Field Army colleagues,[78] then the scope for factionalism was very wide. In his first contribution to this book, Woodward draws the distinction between main force units (with, on the whole, a greater loyalty to Lin Piao) and regional units. Both of these types of unit were involved in activities designed to 'support the left' and bring to an end factionalism in the Cultural Revolution, but different units acted in different ways. 'Support to the left' at various times ranged from patient persuasion to forcible suppression and the revolutionary committees, which resulted from such action, differed considerably in their composition, spirit and policies.[79] Ideally, revolutionary committees were to be based on a 'triple alliance' of revolutionary rebels and old cadres, linked by a military component which might help reconcile their differences. This|had been the prescribed form of organisation after the Liberation of 1949 where military cadres provided the link between personnel retained from the old régime and groups of activists such as Worker Picket Organisations.[80] At that time, the military personnel usually resigned their Army posts and provided the nucleus for the formation of Party branches. After the Cultural Revolution, however, military personnel often retained their Army appointments and this may have made the reconstruction of the civilian Party organisation very difficult.

The successful reconstruction of an essentially civilian Party structure, described by Young, and the return of the military to the barracks, described by Woodward, leaves us with a vital question. How will the re-affirmation of a separation of the military and civilian sectors affect the process of socialist transition? How can one prevent the Army, once again, giving priority to élitist technocratic concerns. Even more important, how can one ensure that the reconstructed Party does not develop into exactly the same kind of organisation that had been denounced in 1966? Is there a necessary contradiction between Party leadership and 'continuous revolution'? The contributors to this book may not answer these questions definitively but they will, at least, explore them more fully.

Notes

1. Often referred to as 'people's democratic dictatorship'. See Mao Tsetung, 30 June 1949, in Mao 1971, pp.371-88.
2. The separation of comprador capitalists (oriented towards an overseas economy) and national capitalists (with little or no foreign interests) is a distinctive feature of the class analysis made by contemporary pro-Chinese groups. It is strongly contested by Trotskyists and others.
3. The best account of the Yenan tradition is Selden 1971.
4. See Schurmann 1966, p.236.
5. See Brugger 1976.
6. Gray 1970, p.87.
7. Liu Shao-ch'i has been blamed for this. See PFLP 1968, p.3, *et.seq.*
8. Discussed in Rossanda 1971, p.60.
9. Stalin (22 May 1952) saw that obstacles to the development of the productive forces came not only from residual classes but also from the ageing relations of production (Stalin 1972, pp.63-4). Refuting Yaroshenko, Stalin noted that, in

a socialist society, contradictions exist between the productive forces and relations of production and suggested that, if wrong policies are pursued, these may become antagonistic (p.69). This argument was developed more fully by Mao Tsetung (27 February 1957, in Mao 1971, pp.432-79 [*SW*, Chinese edition, Vol. 5, pp. 363-402]). This is undoubtedly a move away from Stalin's earlier position but is a long way from a generative view of class.

10. Brugger 1976.
11. Schurmann 1966, p.445.
12. Ibid. pp.272-8.
13. Mao Tsetung, 31 July 1955, in Mao 1971, pp.389-420 *(SW,* Chinese edition, Vol. 5, pp.168-191.
14. See Brugger 1977, pp.121-3, 126.
15. Schurmann 1966, pp.284-93.
16. Mao Tsetung, 30 January 1962, *Mao Zhuxi Wenxuan,* p.69, (Schram 1974, p.169).
17. Mao Tsetung 1960 (or 1961-62), *Wansui* 1969, p.325 *(JPRS* 1974, p.252).
18. Mao Tsetung, 25 April 1956, in *SW,* Chinese edition, Vol. 5, pp. 267-88 (trans. *PR* 1, 1 January 1977, pp.10-25). A slightly different version in *Wansui* 1969, pp.40-59 (trans. Schram 1974, pp. 61-83).
19. Mao Tsetung, 19 February 1958, in untitled collection from Red Guard source, (sometimes included in *Wansui* collection) p.33. Another translation in *CB* 892, 21 October 1969, p.7. For an earlier formulation see Mao Tsetung, January 1957, in *JPRS* 1974, p.49 and for a later one, 20 May 1958, in ibid. p.112.
20. There did not seem to be much support for the idea that 'communism' had already arrived. See Hsü Li-ch'ün, in Bowie and Fairbank 1965, pp.479-83.
21. See Walder 1977. For a note on the Chinese use of the term 'alienation', see Munro 1974.
22. Schram 1971, p.231
23. Krivitsov and Sidikhmenov 1972, pp.49-61 *passim.*
24. E.g. Wu Chiang, *Jexue Yanjiu* 8, 1958, pp.23-9.
25. See Brugger 1977, p.186.
26. *JPRS* 1974, pp. 164-74.
27. See Brugger 1977, pp.218-22.
28. Walker 1968, pp.444-5.
29. *SCMM* 652, 28 April 1969, p.25.
30. Discussed in Solomon 1971, pp.373-5.
31. Levy (1975) elucidates what he calls Mao's 'timing theory'.
32. Ibid, pp.107-8, based on *Wansui* 1969, pp.333-4.
33. *Wansui* 1969, p.349. *(JPRS* 1974, p.272).
34. Stalin 1952, pp.60-86.
35. Mao Tsetung, November 1958 (or 1959), *Wansui* 1969, p.248 *(JPRS* 1974 p.130).
36. *Wansui* 1969, pp.359-60.
37. Levy 1975, pp.107-8.
38. See the debate between Pfeffer 1976, Schwartz 1976, Walder 1977, Wakeman 1977, and Schram 1977.
39. Mao Tsetung, 28 January 1958, *Chinese Law and Government,* Vol. 1, No.4, winter 1968-9, pp.13-14.
40. Schram (1971, p.230) basing his argument on Great Leap sources, takes a different position from Levy. When Schram's article was written, Mao's comments on the Soviet *Political Economy* textbook were unavailable.
41. *Wansui* 1969, p.325 *(JPRS* 1974, p.252).
42. *Wansui* 1969, p.345 *(JPRS* 1974, p.268). Here Mao qualifies the Soviet assertion

that China 'accomplished' the socialist revolution, preferring the term 'won decisive victory'.

43. *Wansui* 1969, pp.339, 351.
44. Mao defended Stalin against the charge that he wished to abolish *all* commodity production, *Wansui* 1969, pp.380-81 (*JPRS* 1974, p.298).
45. *Wansui* 1967 (2) p.248 (*JPRS* 1974, p.130). Discussed in Levy 1975, pp.103-4.
46. See PFLP 1968, pp.14-18. The policy may have been enunciated by Liu at the 7,000 cadres conference on 26 January 1962. See Domes 1973, pp.126-27.
47. *Wansui* 1969, p.347 (*JPRS* 1974, p.270).
48. *PR* 16, 17 April 1970, p.3. See also Mao Tsetung, March 1960, in *Wansui* 1967 (2), p.249 (*JPRS* 1974, p.230) and *PR* 14, 1 April 1977, pp.3-4.
49. See Gray 1973, pp.143-4.
50. This is what Schurmann designates as 'decentralisation I' as opposed to 'decentralisation II' (to local areas). See Schurmann 1966, pp. 175-8, 196-208. For a discussion of this policy in the early 1960s, see Brugger 1977, pp.220-22.
51. On the parallel with the Soviet NEP., see Schurmann 1964, pp.65-91.
52. Brugger 1977, p.163.
53. Bettelheim, in Sweezy and Bettelheim 1971, pp.16-19, 34-6.
54. For a survey of class categorisation, see Kraus 1977.
55. Mao Tsetung, 27 February 1957, in Mao Tsetung 1971, pp.432-79 (*SW*, Chinese edition, Vol.5, pp.363-402).
56. Starr 1971, pp.620-21.
57. This will be argued in a forthcoming monograph by Woodward and Young.
58. Mao Tsetung 1960 (or 1961-2), in *Wansui* 1969, p.351 (*JPRS* 1974, p.273).
59. Kraus 1977, pp.63-4, based on *Wansui* 1969, p.391 (*JPRS* 1974, p.306) (on the highly educated nature of people with large salaries who are also stupid) and *Wansui* 1969, p.351 (*JPRS* 1974, p.273) (on the airs put on by cadres' children).
60. Mao Tsetung, 30 January 1962, in *Mao Zhuxi Wenxuan* pp.68-9. Emphasis added. A different translation in Schram 1974, p.168.
61. Elaborated on by Mao at 10th Plenum of 8th Central Committee, 24 September 1962, *Wansui* 1969, p.431.
62. Text in PFLP 1965, pp.417-80.
63. See *PR* 46, 10 November 1967, pp.9-16; *PR* 39, 26 September 1969, pp.3-10, and Starr 1971
64. Goldman 1969, pp. 54-83.
65. See Pusey 1969; Goldman 1969 and Teng T'o 1963.
66. According to *Wansui,* Mao made no less than 18 important references to the need for educational revolution. The best known are: 18 February 1964, (*Wansui* 1969, pp.455-65; *JPRS* 1974, pp.326-38). March (or 15 July) 1964, (*Wansui* 1969, pp.465-71; Schram 1974, pp.242-50). 24 June 1964, (*Wansui* 1969, pp.526-31). 18 August 1964, (*Wansui* 1969, pp.548-61; Schram 1974, pp.212-30). 29 August 1964, (*Wansui* 1969, pp.567-77; *CB* 891, 8 October 1969, pp.46-7). 3 July 1967, (*Wansui* 1967 (1), p.30; *CB* 891, p.50). 21 December 1965, (*Wansui* 1969, pp.624-9; Schram 1974, pp.234-41). 18 February 1966, (*Wansui* 1969, pp.631-2; Schram 1974, pp.250-51). 7 May 1966, (*Wansui* 1969, pp.642-3; *CB* 891, pp.56-7).
67. Mao Tsetung, 3 February 1967, *Wansui* 1969, p.665.
68. See URI 1968.
69. The 'four firsts' were: 'man' first in the relationship between man and weapons, 'politics' first in the relationship between political and other work, 'ideology' first in the relationship between routine and ideological political education and 'living thought' first in the relationship between book learning and practice.

70. Yao Wen-yuan, *PR* 10, 7 March 1975, pp.5-10. Chang Ch'un-ch'iao, *PR* 14, 4 April 1975, pp.5-11.
71. See for example the treatment of Liu Shao-ch'i by Ch'i Pen-yu in *PR* 15, 7 April 1967, pp.5-15.
72. See the discussion in Robinson 1969.
73. Discussed in Brugger 1977, p.292.
74. *PR* 26, 24 June 1966, p.3.
75. See Esmein 1973, pp.187-90
76. The idea of 'alternative vanguards' was put forward by Rossanda (1971) but she was not thinking of the Army.
77. Schurmann 1966, p.112.
78. Whitson (1969) posits the existence of loyalty networks based on affiliation to the 5 field armies which were responsible for the administration of different parts of China after 1949. Lin commanded the 4th field army (North East and Central South).
79. Domes 1970.
80. See Brugger 1976, pp.74-5.

1 PARTY BUILDING AND THE SEARCH FOR UNITY

Graham Young

During the Cultural Revolution, the Chinese Communist Party was subjected to unprecedented criticism and attack, which effectively destroyed the role of leadership it had previously played. As it is suggested in the Introduction, events in China in the years 1969-73 must be assessed in relation to the changes brought about in the Cultural Revolution. In the period between the Ninth and Tenth Congresses, the Party resumed its leadership role. By the time of the Ninth Congress, it had become evident that the Party was to be re-established, under the general policy of 'Party building and rectification'. But although this intention was clear, there remained important questions concerning the nature and role of the Party and the way in which the process of Party building and rectification was to be effected. Because of the centrality of the Party's role in China and the trauma which the Party had suffered in the Cultural Revolution, these were questions of vital significance to the whole political system. In order to put these questions into perspective, it is worth reviewing briefly the role of the Communist Party before the Cultural Revolution and the way it had been affected by the Cultural Revolution.

The Ideological and Organisational Bases of Party Leadership

The prescribed role of the Party was best defined in terms of its direction of the process of revolutionary change.[1] This process encompassed all aspects of Chinese society, and the Party's direction related to every level of Chinese society. The central leading bodies of the Party determined the 'general line', which defined the overall orientation and nature of the revolution, from which followed 'lines' on various wide-ranging issues relating to each stage of the revolutionary movement. From these 'lines', in turn, the Party centre formulated general policies on more specific issues. The Party's directive role applied not only at the central level but extended to all levels of Chinese society. Organs of the Party at lower levels received general policy from higher levels and translated it into specific policy formulations appropriate to their own levels. The Party was distinguished from the state or government structure in that the Party was responsible for direction while the State was responsible for administration and policy enforcement. Thus, the State was supposed to

35

be subordinate to the Party in all matters of policy. Similarly, the Party guided the activities of rural communes or production brigades, of mass organisations such as the Youth League, and so on. The Army was seen as part of the State's repressive apparatus, but it also had to be under Party leadership, and this stress on 'the Party controlling the gun' has been accompanied by the encouragement of the Army's political role in civilian activities.

There were essentially two grounds on which the Party's assumption of this key role was based — one ideological, the other organisational. These were, of course, inextricably linked, but we can separate them for purposes of analysis. The ideological basis relates to the Party's identification as a Marxist-Leninist Party. In effect, this means that the Party is the authentic bearer of Marxist-Leninist theory, which is the theoretical basis of the Chinese revolution. It is this which defines the Party as a 'Communist Party' and which provides its *raison d'être*. Marxism-Leninism defines the ends of revolution, but the stress on this theory is not merely a profession of faith. It is given more far-reaching significance by the transition from theory to action. Marxism-Leninism, according to the view developed by the Chinese Communist Party, has to be used for the analysis of situations that arise within the progress of the revolution. Hence, Marxism-Leninism not only defines the ends of socialism and communism, but also guides all the actions of the revolutionary movement. It provides the 'general line' of the movement and should be used by Party organs to formulate general policies at the central level and more specific policies at lower levels. Thus, Marxism-Leninism is central to the analysis and direction of all aspects of the revolutionary movement. Because of this, only the Party, as the one organisation exclusively basing itself on and using Marxism-Leninism, can lead the revolution.

The second basis of Party leadership, the organisational, relates to the means of bringing about revolutionary change. Marxism-Leninism may be used to formulate general and specific policies, but there must be some form of organisation to put these into effect. The official documents of the Party, as well as the writings of major Party leaders, all affirm the need for a core or nucleus in the revolutionary movement. The Communist Party fulfils this core role, since it is held to be the vanguard of the proletariat and the highest form of proletarian organisation. By uniting the most advanced and conscious revolutionaries into a single organisation, the Party can give coherence and direction to the revolutionary movement. It is through this organisation and its penetration of every level of Chinese society that the Party can direct the whole process of revolutionary change. The corollary of the importance ascribed to the Party as an organisation has been the continuing emphasis on its operational procedures – on unity and discipline within the Party, and on concepts such as 'democratic centralism'. These have been considered crucial for the unity and solidarity of the Party organisation, which, in turn, is crucial for the success of the revolutionary movement.

The conception of Party leadership which pertained in China before the Cultural Revolution was, therefore, one in which Party organisations at all levels formulated policy, using Marxism-Leninism, and directed the revolutionary movement through their penetration of all other organisations and activities. There is one other crucial element in the conception of Party leadership, and this concerns the Party's relationship with those outside the Party. It is best demonstrated by the notion of Mass Line, which was articulated by Mao Tsetung in the early 1940s and has ever since been a major part of the Party canon.[2] It provides a particular interpretation of the ideological and organisational aspects of Party leadership. According to this notion, it is only through mass activities that policies can be carried out and revolutionary goals realised. But mass activity and Mass Line were by no means synonomous. In Mao's formulation and in all subsequent Party endorsement, the Mass Line is essentially a method of leadership – specifically, of Party leadership. It is seen as uniting the general with the particular and the leadership with the masses. Mao's discussion of the process of 'from the masses, to the masses', which he describes as 'the Marxist theory of knowledge', shows clearly the importance ascribed to mass participation in policy formation and execution. This is reflected also in the discussion of the ideal leadership type, the Party 'cadre', whose proper method of operation is defined by his integration with the masses, his sensitivity to mass opinion and his ability to mobilise mass activity. But this stress on the role of the masses gives only a one-sided view of the Mass Line. It is made equally clear, in Mao's discussion of uniting the general with the particular, that central Party policy could in no way be infringed, that mass activity had to be roused in accordance with the Party's concept of the nature and direction of the revolution as a whole. Hence, the other main characteristic of the ideal cadre is sensitivity to central Party policy. The dual imperatives inherent in the Mass Line are demonstrated by the discussion of the twin faults, 'tailism' and 'commandism'. 'Tailism' consists of doing only what the masses want, irrespective of Party policy. 'Commandism', on the other hand, consists of mechanically enforcing central policy, irrespective of mass desires and mass consciousness. The cadre, avoiding both these mistakes, should lead the masses according to their own desires and consciousness, but always in line with Party policy. The process of 'rectification' was designed to create and reinforce this type of work style.

Clearly these were ideals which could never be realised fully. But the main point is that the Mass Line, as first articulated and practised, concerned Party leadership. Untutored mass activity was not wanted. It had to be guided within Party policy, which was mediated through Party cadres and the Party organisation as a whole. The Mass Line gave a particular orientation to the Party's ideological and organisational leadership. Hence, if there were no guiding and integrative body like the Party, it is possible to envisage a situation in which mass activity and the Mass Line could be in opposition.[3]

The Cultural Revolution entirely shattered this previously-held view of Party leadership and demonstrated the degree of disagreement concerning the nature of socialist revolution and the Party's role in it. In the first place, the accusation of 'revisionism' at every level of the Party, the assertion that there was a 'bourgeois headquarters' within the Party, and the criticism of the whole range of Party policies, all suggested that the Party no longer fulfilled either the ideological or organisational criteria of leadership. Similarly, the criticism of Party bureaucratism and alienation from the masses suggested that the Party had abandoned the Mass Line. Even more important, however, was the decimation of the Party organisation through the attacks by mass organisations which emerged during the Cultural Revolution. This negated the Party organisation's role of ideological leadership, of guiding the relationship between theory and practice, and of providing integration and direction at every level. This was so despite the fact that the notion of Party leadership itself was not attacked, that it was maintained verbally even when the Party organisation was being destroyed. In the Cultural Revolution, the main targets were defined as 'Party persons in authority taking the capitalist road'. On the one hand, this formula was intended to indicate where the main danger to the continuation of China's socialist revolution was located. But, on the other hand, it distinguished the attack on particular incumbents of Party positions from a denial of Party leadership as such. Individuals may have become corrupted, but the Party itself was still necessary. This is also shown by the repeated assertion that the overwhelming majority of cadres were 'good' or 'comparatively good'. Similarly, Mao's response to the Shanghai Commune: 'There must be a Party somehow! There must be a nucleus no matter what we call it'[4] indicates that he maintained the necessity for an integrative organisation like the Party, of which the commune concept was an implicit denial.

Nevertheless, in the situation created by the Cultural Revolution, the concept of Party leadership could not have the same content as previously. It tended to specify leadership in only the most general sense, through general guidelines and policies expounded by Mao or the central organs of the Party. In terms of the Mass Line, the Cultural Revolution was aberrant. There was this type of general, central policy, and there certainly was a great deal of mass activity. But there was no organisation which could integrate mass activity with general policy, no way of uniting the general with the particular or the leadership with the masses. There was mass activity without the Mass Line. General policy could remain in general terms only, and there could be no authoritative interpretation and relation to concrete conditions at lower levels. Different groups could form their own interpretations, and this is the main reason for the divisions and factionalism which came to characterise the Cultural Revolution. There were other *ad hoc* means of attempting to fill the ideological and organisational void left by the decimation of the Party; calls for alliance and unity, Army intervention, workers' propaganda teams. But, as I shall suggest below, the persistence of disunity indicates that these other means were often unsuccessful. It was in this context that the moves to rebuild the Party began, and the questions concerning the role and nature of the Party became crucial for the whole political system.

The Ninth Congress

The Party's Ninth National Congress, in April 1969, was hailed as a 'Congress of unity and victory'. It consolidated the new configuration of the central Party leadership after the enormous changes wrought by the Cultural Revolution. The agenda consisted of three items: the Report delivered by Lin Piao, the revision of the Party Constitution, and the election of a new Central Committee. Most of the time of this rather lengthy Congress seems to have been spent in discussing the Report and the new Constitution in small groups.

The new Constitution differed significantly from the former Constitution adopted at the Eighth Congress in 1956.[5] Obviously, the major difference was the attempt to incorporate the Cultural Revolution into a new overall analysis of the Chinese revolution. This is reflected in the General Programme, with its emphasis on the theory of 'continuous revolution'. In general, the Constitution was far briefer and less formalistic than its predecessor. For example, the 1956 Constitution described in detail the process of application for membership, probationary period, and approval of new members by various levels. The new Constitution merely mentioned this in the briefest outline, stating that application was subjected to acceptance by the general membership meeting of the Party branch and approval by the next higher Party Committee. It did not even discuss a probationary period, but added that a Party should, in examining an applicant, 'seek the opinions of the broad masses inside and outside the Party'.[6] Hence, the new Constitution attempted to remove the organisational formalism inherent in its predecessor while reinforcing the element of the Party's relations with the masses.

The Constitution described the Party as a 'vigorous vanguard organisation leading the proletariat and the revolutionary masses in the fight against the class enemy.' It also insisted that State organs, the People's Liberation Army, and mass organisations, should all accept leadership by the Party. The Constitution itself, however, provided little specific information on the nature of Party rebuilding. It merely provided the most general outline of procedures such as admission and discipline, and of the duties of Party members and Party organisations.

The Political Report delivered by Lin Piao presented the official view of the Cultural Revolution, the interpretation of its development and a general prescription of how it should proceed. It was asserted that all of the victories of the Chinese revolution had been won under Party leadership, and this success was due, in turn, to the leadership of Mao. Similarly, all victories of the Cultural Revolution were attributed to Party leadership. Indeed, Lin claimed that 'The Great Proletarian Cultural Revolution is the broadest and most deep-going movement for Party consolidation in the history of our Party.'[7] But the chapter 'On the consolidation and building of the Party' gave no specific indication of how this consolidation and building was to proceed. Rather, it traced the history of former struggles within the Party, with emphasis on the importance of Mao's continuing correct leadership. The criticism of the Party that emerged in the Cultural Revolution was now summarised in the repudiation of what was supposed to be Liu's 'revisionist' line on Party building. This was reduced to his view of 'self-cultivation' and his 'six sinister theories': 'docile tools', 'dying out of class struggle', 'the masses are backward', 'inner-Party peace', 'joining the Party to climb up', and 'merging private and public interests'.[8] Rather than tackling the problems that the Cultural Revolution had posed for the process of re-establishing the Party, therefore, Lin's Report devoted most attention to asserting the conformity of the Cultural Revolution with Party leadership.

Nevertheless, there did emerge from the Report the general view that Party building had to be integrated with the continuation of the Cultural Revolutionary programme of 'struggle-criticism-transformation'. Lin quoted Mao on the nature of this programme:

Struggle-criticism-transformation in a factory, on the whole, goes through the following stages: Establishing a three-in-one revolutionary committee; carrying out mass criticism and repudiation; purifying the class ranks; consolidating the Party organisation; and simplifying the administrative structure, changing irrational rules and regulations and sending office workers to the workshops.[9]

The summary of the programme, however, indicated wide disparities in this process in different places.

In places where the revolutionary great alliance has not yet been sufficiently consolidated, it is necessary to help the revolutionary masses bring about the revolutionary great alliance . . . In units where the work of purifying the class ranks has not yet started or has only just started, it is imperative to grasp the work firmly and do it well in accordance with the Party's policies. In units where the purification of the class ranks is by and large completed, it is necessary to take firm hold of other tasks in keeping with Chairman Mao's instructions concerning the various stages of struggle-criticism-transformation.[10]

This passage suggests that the process in various parts of China was very uneven. In some places even the setting up of revolutionary committees had not yet been achieved, and this was the pre-requisite for all the other tasks specified. In other places the 'purification of class ranks' had not yet begun. In such cases the rebuilding of the Party could not be carried out. The implication that Party organisations at lower levels were far from resuming their former leadership role was reinforced by the attention the Report devoted to the operations of revolutionary committees. These committees were instructed to promote the study of Mao Tsetung Thought, to criticise 'revisionism' and erroneous ideas, to maintain close ties with the masses and to sweep away bureaucratism. In fact, the revolutionary committees were entrusted with the implementation of all the policies put forward by the Congress. In normal circumstances, these tasks would have been allotted to Party organisations, and the failure to mention Party organisations in this context suggests that the Party had not been rebuilt sufficiently.

Mao's speeches at the Congress put the greatest emphasis on unity. His address to the opening session shows that his description of the Congress as a 'Congress of unity' meant more precisely, a Congress for achieving unity. He compared it with the Party's Seventh Congress which 'was a congress of unity, for there were divisions in the Party then too.'[11] His speech to the First Plenum of the Ninth Central Committee discussed continuing disunity in Shantung, Shensi, Yunnan, Kweichow and Szechwan. Mao also made a point of Party building with mass participation.

> In fact the Party needs to be rebuilt. Every branch needs to be rectified among the masses. They must go through the masses; not just a few Party members but the masses outside the Party must participate in meetings and in criticism. Individuals who are no good should be persuaded to get out of the Party, to withdraw. A very small minority may have to be disciplined. Isn't this laid down in the Party Constitution? It also has to be passed by the Party branch congress and approved by the superior level. In a word we must use prudence. This must be done, it certainly has to be done, but it must be done prudently.[12]

'Open-Door' Party Building and the Problems of Disunity

The analysis of Party building and rectification in the Chinese press immediately after the Ninth Congress provides a clearer picture of what the process was supposed to involve. It indicates a continuation of building the Party from the bottom upwards according to the 'open-door' method. This policy, which had begun well before the Congress, required the greatest degree of mass participation, with the construction of new Party organisations on the basis of Party membership in revolutionary committees. The construction of new Party organisations was to proceed from the basic levels to the higher levels. In accordance with the general outline provided in Congress documents, it was emphasised that Party building should be an integral part of the programme of 'struggle-criticism-transformation'. Reflecting the two bases of Party leadership, Party building was separated into two components – ideological consolidation and building and organisational consolidation and building. It was continually stressed that ideological building should have priority, and had to be carried out before organisational building could proceed.[13] Thus, the primary task of Party building was to continue the Cultural Revolution's ideological struggles and criticism. According to the joint editorial celebrating the Party's 48th anniversary, ideological building required Communist Party members, revolutionary cadres and the masses to study Mao's theory of 'continuous revolution' and works such as 'On the Correct Handling of Contradictions among the People', and to repudiate Liu's 'revisionist' line on Party building shown by his 'self-cultivation' and 'six sinister theories'.[14]

Organisational building was to be based on the revolutionary committees. As the joint editorial put it:

> In the work of Party rectification and building, it is extremely important to do well the rectification and building of leading bodies. In the revolutionary committee at every level, according to its own specific conditions, there must be gradually formed a strong leading nucleus of the Party, which is armed with Mao Tsetung Thought, united, and maintains close ties with the masses.[15]

After the destruction of Party organisations in the Cultural Revolution, new organisations had to emerge from the only available structure – the revolutionary committee. Another factor in organisational building was the admission of new Party members and the expulsion of those considered undesirable. This was characterised by Mao's metaphor of 'eliminating the stale and taking in the fresh', the specific application to the Party of 'purifying the class ranks'. As indicated in Congress documents, there was emphasis on narrowing the target of attack and allowing Party members to rectify their mistakes, with only a few bad elements having to be expelled.[16] The view that 'none of the Party members is good' was rejected.[17] Some Party members adopted a passive attitude and merely waited to be expelled, and some of the masses wanted them to resign. Even in these cases it was maintained that expulsion was not appropriate, that they should remain in the Party and engage in study and criticism so that they could better fulfil their duties as Party members.[18] This again demonstrated the priority of ideological building: organisational sanctions were seen as appropriate for only a few Party members, while the rest were to be rehabilitated through criticism and education.

In both ideological and organisational building, there was consistent emphasis on the 'open-door' procedure and the greatest possible degree of mass participation.

> Practice proves that it is the revolutionary masses who care most about the question of Party rectification and best understand the situation of the Party organisation and members of their own units. Only by carrying out open-door Party rectification, relying on the masses, will it be possible to prevent Party rectification from 'going along the old road and returning to the old ways', better purify the Party organisation both ideologically and organisationally, and build every Party branch into a strong fighting bulwark armed with Mao Tsetung Thought. Whether or not open-door rectification is carried out by relying on the masses is certainly not a general question of work methods, but a question of basic attitude towards Chairman Mao's proletarian revolutionary line. It is the key question which determines whether or not Party rectification can be carried out successfully.[19]

Those who tried to play down mass participation and involve only a few representatives of the masses were criticised for 'opening only a small window'.[20] This again shows the intention of integrating Party building with the whole process of mass criticism. The obstacles to this included Party members' fears of mass hostility, belief that mistakes had been trivial, and the view among the masses that Party building was a matter to be handled within the Party. In refutation, it was argued that 'open-door' Party building did not damage the Party's prestige but, on the contrary, enhanced it by giving the masses more confidence in the Party.

The most detailed example of 'open-door' Party building was that of the establishment of a new Party Committee in the model Hsinhua Printing Works in Peking, and considerable press attention was devoted to this in December 1969 and January 1970.[21] Initially, there was set up a 'three-in-one leadership group for Party rectification and building', composed of Party members, outstanding workers and members of the PLA propaganda team. This group saw its first task as raising the ideological level of Party members and masses by 'launching a struggle of proletarian ideology against non-proletarian ideology',[22] thereby giving priority to ideological over organisational questions. The leading group, therefore, organised mass discussion of the nature of the Party, paying particular attention to non-Party people who thought it none of their business. Party members were required to solicit mass opinion and to listen to criticism.

The few 'proven renegades, enemy agents, absolutely unrepentant persons in power taking the capitalist road', were expelled from the Party. The leading group and the PLA propaganda team persuaded the workers to adopt a more lenient attitude to other Party members who did not fit into these categories, and not to demand that they resign from the Party. Rather, the workers were encouraged to help these members reform themselves. The leading group also encouraged mass opinion when considering the admission of new Party members. The applicants themselves were organised to study the prescribed qualities of Party members, and especially to repudiate the notion of 'joining the Party to become an official'. The principle of 'active caution' was used in admitting new members. For example, a worker who had consistently been refused admission in the past was now admitted on the basis of her active role in the Cultural Revolution. Throughout all these stages, there was constant reference to 'revolutionary mass criticism'. The next step was that the Party members elected a new 'leadership group' of the Party branch. Here the emphasis was not on the election as such, but rather on the extent of discussion and consultation on which it was based, and which involved those who were not Party members. On this basis the members finally elected the new Party Committee, after a further period of consultation both inside and outside the Party.[23]

The necessary conditions for the establishment of the new Party committee were summarised as:

1. The 'revolutionary three-in-one combination' had been consolidated
2. The class ranks had been cleared up
3. The Party branch had been established and new members admitted
4. A leadership core had been formed.

The Party committee could thus exercise 'unified leadership', on the conditions that Mao Tsetung Thought was in command, that the committee operated according to democratic centralism, that the revolutionary committee had to carry out Party committee resolutions, and that the great majority of revolutionary committee members were also members of the Party committee.

At the same time as this successful model of 'open-door' Party building was being propagated, however, there was a rapid and significant change in the orientation of Party building. The most marked aspect of the period beginning in December 1969 and continuing through 1970 was the new emphasis on the organisational basis of Party leadership, and this involved a redefinition of ideological Party building and the role of the masses. It was linked to a campaign to study the new Party Constitution. There had, of course, been discussion of the new Constitution as a major document immediately after the Ninth Congress, but after December 1969 the study and application of the Constitution assumed first priority in Party building. It was described as the basic teaching material and the criterion for all actions of Party members and organisations. Study of the Constitution was to be the main content of the Party's activities, and all other work had to be integrated with such study.[24]

Thus, the discussion of Party leadership changed, with a clear assertion of the organisational basis of such leadership. This was invariably related to Mao's theory of 'continuous revolution'. It was argued that, because classes and class struggle continue to exist in socialist society, there had to be a proletarian party, since every class is led by a political party.[25]

The Chinese proletariat required its own leading nucleus, its own 'vanguard party'. It was asserted that organisation is the proletariat's weapon in class struggle, and that the Communist Party is the highest form of proletarian organisation.

> If the proletariat does not have its own political party, then it cannot accept the teachings of Marxism, nor can it bring forward united programmes, lines, guidelines and policies. It can only be a 'class in itself', carrying out spontaneous and scattered struggles against the individual factories and enterprises of the capitalists. It cannot completely overthrow the exploiting classes and thoroughly liberate itself and the rest of the labouring people. Only if the proletariat has established its own political party . . . can it change from a 'class in itself' to a 'class for itself'. Then it can really understand the basic reason for its own exploitation and oppression, and recognise its historical mission: to overthrow exploiting classes, seize political power, build proletarian dictatorship, and ultimately realise Communism in the whole world.[26]

Thus, without organisational leadership by the Party, there could be no revolution and no dictatorship of the proletariat. Departing from or eliminating Party leadership would have the most serious consequences: 'political power may be lost from the hands of the proletariat, capitalism restored, socialist China change colour, and the people suffer misfortune'.[27]

It was also argued that the proletarian political party needs to have the proper theoretical basis to lead the proletariat to victory, namely Marxism-Leninism-Mao Tsetung Thought. There was great emphasis on Mao's personal role. He was said to have personally founded and cultivated the Party and 'with genius, creatively, in an all-round way inherited, defended and developed Marxism-Leninism, and raised it to a new higher stage'.[28] The use of Mao Tsetung Thought as its theoretical basis 'determines the proletarian vanguard nature of our Party'.[29] This ideological basis of Party leadership, however, was now closely linked to leadership by the Party organisation.

> Party leadership is the leadership of Chairman Mao, of Mao Tsetung Thought, and of Chairman Mao's proletarian revolutionary line. Party leadership is realised through Party organisations, which lead the broad revolutionary masses to carry out the line, principles and policies determined by Chairman Mao. There is complete conformity between Chairman Mao's leadership and Party leadership. Because of this, there is complete conformity between the protection of Chairman Mao's leadership and the protection of Party leadership.[30]

In this way, the view which had predominated in the Cultural Revolution and had survived into 1969, that Party leadership could be realised by mass organisations interpreting the policies and instructions of the Party centre and Mao himself, was now rejected. Party leadership had to be mediated through Party organisations, which were seen as the authentic bearers of ideological leadership.

Obviously this had a direct bearing on the relations between the Party and various mass bodies. The Party, as the highest form of proletarian organisation, was held to be superior to other organisations. It was claimed that forty-eight years' experience showed that the Party had to lead the state and the masses,[31] and that it was still necessary for every mass organisation to be subordinate to the Party. One article suggested that a mass organisation which did not accept leadership by the proletarian party, *ipso facto* accepted bourgeois leadership.[32] In particular, there was vehement rebuttal of the view that the Cultural

Revolution demonstrated that mass organisations did not need leadership by the Party. It was argued that any contributions mass organisations may have made in the Cultural Revolution should be attributed to Mao and the Party centre,[33] and that this incorrect view of the relations between mass organisations and the Party was spread by class enemies. Clearly, this argument was sophistry, since it confused the very general notion of Party leadership which applied in the Cultural Revolution with the renewed stress on Party leadership through Party organisations. It was, in fact, a means of countering people who still opposed the re-assertion of the role of Party organisations. Such people undoubtedly were correct in suggesting that mass organisations had acted in the Cultural Revolution without the leadership of Party organisations, and in fact had usually attacked Party organisations. The new emphasis on the superiority of Party organisations cannot be reconciled with the attack on them by the masses in the Cultural Revolution. If this emphasis had been promoted in 1967, it would have been entirely counter to the activities of rebelling and seizing power. The sophistry was required to disguise the inconsistency between the new policies and those of the Cultural Revolution.

The emphasis on the 'vanguard' organisational role of the Party was also reflected in the discussion of Party membership. The prescribed qualities of Party members were defined in terms of the duties specified in the Constitution — now abbreviated as the 'five musts'. These were used to indicate a clear demarcation between Party members and the 'general masses'.[34] It was claimed that, although the Party is organised out of the proletariat, not all proletarians may join. Only the advanced elements of the proletariat were suitable for Party membership, so that the Party was distinguished from a 'general mass organisation'.[35] If there were any departure from this, any lowering of the standards of Party membership, then the Party's class basis would be destroyed, and the proletarian vanguard nature of the Party would be affected. It would result in the lowering of the Party to the level of a mass organisation. Hence, there was criticism of 'the erroneous thought of mixing up the Party members with the common masses'.[36]

Such distinctions would be necessary as long as class struggle prevails:

> ... throughout the entire historical period of proletarian dictatorship there are distinctions between the proletariat and other classes, between advanced proletarian elements and the rest of the masses of the proletariat, between Party members and those who are not Party

members. These distinctions will exist until classes have been
eliminated . . . [They] serve the purpose of firmly upholding the
vanguard nature of the Party and the standards of its membership,
opposing any lowering of the Party's level and the mistaken tendency
of denying the distinction between Party members and others.[37]

This is not to suggest that the notion of ideological building was
abandoned. Indeed, the priority of ideological over organisational
building was maintained and there was criticism of people joining the
Party organisationally but not ideologically.[38] Nevertheless, the process
of ideological building was now linked more closely to the Party
organisation. Before 1970, Party building had been seen as an integral
part of the mass movement of 'struggle-criticism-transformation'.
Although this continued, the main orientation of ideological building
was now defined in terms of the study of the programmatic document
of the Party organisation, the Constitution. Thus, the most frequently
cited part of the ideological training of Party members was the
attendance at classes to study the Constitution. Among the topics of
these classes were the 'five musts', devotion to the Party and voluntary
acceptance of Party leadership, overcoming weakness in Party
discipline, and establishing the idea that 'the Party's leadership is
higher than anything else'.[39] Furthermore, Party building was now seen
not merely as a response to the situation following the Cultural
Revolution but as a continuing process. Hence, it was said that
ideological building was still needed after organisational consolidation,
and that the establishment of a new Party committee was the beginning
and not the end of Party building.[40] This may be justified in
accordance with a notion of 'continuous revolution', but it also had
the effect of separating the process of Party building from the Cultural
Revolution. By giving the central role to Party organisations, it
distinguished the current process from the former situation in which
the Party organisation had been unable to play a central role because
of the damage it had suffered in the Cultural Revolution.

The process of 'eliminating the stale and taking in the fresh'
also continued. The expulsion and admission of Party members was
still seen primarily as a part of overall ideological building. In this
there were problems from 'left' ('eliminating and taking in on a large
scale') and right ('eliminating and taking in nobody'). Especially
necessary was opposition to 'the mistaken tendency of "eliminating the
stale and taking in the fresh" on the basis of bourgeois factionalism'.[41]
There was a continuation of the policy whereby few members were

disciplined or expelled while the rest were allowed to improve through education.

The 'five musts' became the criteria for the admission of new Party members. It was considered necessary to admit 'actively and carefully' those meeting the standards of advanced proletarian elements, especially to enlarge the proportion of workers in the Party membership. Many articles demonstrated that applicants for Party membership, as well as existing members, attended special classes to study the Constitution. It was emphasised that the 'five musts' provided the only criteria for admission into the Party, and these were counterposed to several other criteria. Among these were suggestions that some people were entitled to Party membership because of their activities in rebellion in the Cultural Revolution or in accordance with positions of leadership in revolutionary committees. Another argument was that Party membership should correspond to factional divisions, with members seen as factional representatives.[42] People holding such views were accused of not understanding the nature and task of the Party or not meeting the standards of Party membership. Again, this type of statement sought to insulate the process of Party building from the types of struggles which occurred in the Cultural Revolution. It defined the conditions for entering the Party strictly in terms of the Party's own rules. It denied that those who were major actors in the Cultural Revolution had thereby earned a place in the Party, for the Party as the highest organisational form of the proletariat had to set its own, higher standards.

The stress on the vanguard role of the Party organisation and on the necessity to distinguish Party members from ordinary people inevitably had a great effect on the view of mass participation and Party-mass relations. The study of the Constitution paid considerable attention to mass participation. Indeed, it was continually emphasised that, in the Constitution itself, both the primary duties of Party members and the primary tasks of Party organisations included relying on and mobilising the masses and maintaining close ties with them. It was now made perfectly clear, however, that what was required was the Mass Line, which was again identified as a method of Party leadership. Mass participation was still necessary, but it had to be mobilised and guided by Party leadership. There was firm and consistent rejection of mass activity outside Party leadership. It was argued that the leadership of the Party and the Mass Line 'entirely coincide'.[43] In another formulation, the Mass Line was explained as the 'dialectical unity' of two aspects — the strengthening of Party leadership, and relying on the masses.[44]

Hence, while there was criticism of the view, invariably associated with Liu Shao-ch'i, that 'the masses are backward', there was also criticism of Party members and organisations 'doing only what the masses want' and 'tailism'.[45] The role of the Party organisation was that of a 'fighting bulwark' leading the masses; and the view that mass organisations should attend every Party meeting and question Party affairs was condemned. Although it was necessary for Party organisations to learn from the masses, the ideological superiority of the Party was also affirmed, since it had to use Mao Tsetung Thought to analyse and overcome their 'incomplete or incorrect opinions'.[46]

Despite the emphasis on Party members being the most advanced, it was also said that they should not feel superior to the masses or 'consider themselves higher in politics'.[47] The suggestion here was that a Party member's advanced status and his integration with the masses were identical. In fact, the maintenance of the advanced status of Party members was for 'making clear the flesh and blood *[xuerou]* relationship between Party and class, Party members and the masses'.[48] Thus, integration with the masses was emphasised as a crucial criterion of the advanced nature of Party members. While Party members had the duty to seek and heed mass opinions and put themselves 'under permanent supervision by the masses', they also had to guide them and act as models, to lead rather than merely charge to the fore.[49] Indeed, it was suggested that concern for the masses was expressed mainly in members propagating Mao Tsetung Thought, and there were frequent references to the ways in which Party members' example stimulated mass study.

The 'open-door' method of Party building was still discussed, especially the procedures of 'inviting in' some non-Party people to comment on the Party, and Party members 'going out' to seek mass opinion. Nevertheless, it was now made clear that the Party organisation itself was to mobilise and guide this mass participation. Thus, there was opposition to the 'right' view that Party building is an inner-Party affair, as well as to 'anarchist' views and those suggesting that old rebels rather than the Party organisation should take the lead.[50] While Party building was not an inner-Party matter, it certainly had to be under Party leadership.

Thus, the view of Party building which prevailed in 1970 put great stress on the organisational basis of Party leadership and asserted the dominant role of the Party organisation. Ideological leadership was linked very closely to the Party organisation and mass activity had to be under its leadership. This was far closer to the

Mass Line formulation as it had been understood before the Cultural Revolution. There was also an attempt to place Party building outside of the struggles of the Cultural Revolution, while still maintaining its consistency with the activities of 1966-8. A further indication of the stress on the Party organisation was the switch to re-establishing the higher organs of the Party. At the end of 1969, the programme of Party building from the bottom upwards was changed by shifting the focus to *xian*-level Party committees, even though it is clear from the press that the reconstruction of basic-level Party committees was far from completed. In November 1970 the focus again shifted upwards to the provincial level, even though, according to Domes, only forty-five of the 2,185 *xian* had set up new Party committees by that time.[51] By August 1971 all provincial-level Party organisations had been rebuilt. Thus, the Party organisational structure was rapidly strengthened and could better control the process of Party building and re-assert its leadership.

It seems unlikely, therefore, that this change in the process of Party building may be explained as merely the movement to the next stage of the overall strategy after the first stage had been completed. This may have been true of some places, such as the model Hsinhua Printing Works, but the very propagation of this as a model at the end of 1969 suggests that other places had not yet reached the same stage. Even a brief examination of the Chinese press in 1970 shows that Party building at basic levels has not been completed and that reassertion of the Party's organisational leadership was somewhat premature in terms of the strategy of Party building discussed at the time of the Ninth Congress. Furthermore, the strengthening of the Party organisation occurred before the consolidation in other policy areas which became evident after the Second Plenum in August 1970. Similarly, it is difficult to see this as a consequence of the struggles with Ch'en Po-ta and Lin Piao, which also become salient after the Second Plenum.

A more likely explanation of this change in emphasis is the persistence of disunity generated in the Cultural Revolution which inhibited the process of Party building. Mao's slogan at the Ninth Congress was 'unite to win still greater victories', and throughout 1969 the theme of unity dominated the press. The vehement stress on unity and the extensive discussion of manifestations of disunity testify to the persistence of these legacies of the Cultural Revolution. Lin Piao's Report had indicated that Party building was to be based on the consolidation of revolutionary committees, but much of the press discussion dealt with the continuing difficulties of these committees as unified bodies. It noted that factionalism among the masses could be reflected within a revolutionary committee, that different parts of the committee might not work together, and that the masses might not accept the legitimacy of the committee's role.

The mutual intolerance of rival mass organisations that had been formed in the Cultural Revolution proved to be a persistent problem.[52] Groups which had formed at that time and had struggled against rival groups for several years, had developed a strong organisational coherence and remained jealous of their positions and independence. These factions survived well after the Ninth Congress. Indeed, the continuing criticism of factionalism throws considerable doubt on the efficacy of the original process through which revolutionary committees were established. They were supposed to have been formed on the basis of a 'grand alliance' forged in the Cultural Revolution. It appears that this was often not the case, that revolutionary committees had been superimposed on a situation still characterised by serious factional conflict, and that this conflict therefore continued well after the establishment of the committees.

This impression is reinforced by the discussion of the harmful outbreak of factionalism in revolutionary committees. Committee members tended to be regarded as representatives of factions rather than as members of a unified body transcending factions. Hence, encouragement was given to the principle that revolutionary committees 'regard all mass organisations as equals' and that different committee members should not support different factions.[53] Similarly, committee members were instructed not to regard themselves as 'the only revolutionary' and 'the only left' and as superior to members of other mass organisations because they had acted better or more promptly in the Cultural Revolution.[54] Many of these analyses indicate that such factionalism could not be quickly or easily overcome, and the immediate problem was how to handle these factions.

As in 1967 and 1968, factionalism was condemned in the strongest possible terms, as a 'reactionary bourgeois tendency' and the principal manifestation of faults such as individualism.[55] It was argued that the fundamental interests of the proletariat could not be divided, and that the pursuit of these interests required the unity of all revolutionary forces. Those who engaged in factional disputes, therefore, would betray the fundamental interests of the proletariat and forget the general orientation of the revolution.[56] It followed that only counter-revolutionaries would benefit from factionalism, and it was hinted that those who engaged in factional activities might be defined as class enemies.[57] Although contradictions were bound to exist among the people, they were to be resolved by criticism and self-criticism, and those who had made mistakes had to be allowed to correct them.

A major related theme was that of discipline. This was manifested in a vigorous campaign against 'anarchism' and the similar concepts 'ultra-democracy' and 'the theory of many centres, that is, no centre'. These discussions suggest that many people had difficulty in abandoning the spirit of rebellion fostered in the Cultural Revolution. Hence, views that 'one who obeys the leadership lacks strong rebel spirit', and that restrictions imposed by revolutionary committees should be ignored, were rejected.[58] Another view was that the relationship between the revolutionary committees and the masses constituted a new 'principal contradiction'.[59] Clearly there were people who were dissatisfied with the view that revolutionary committees were the appropriate resolution of the struggles of the Cultural Revolution, and who sought to generate new struggles against them. To counter this it was argued that there was a great difference between rebelling against 'capitalist-roaders' in the Cultural Revolution, and opposing revolutionary committees, the new organs of power which resulted from the Cultural Revolution. Similar reasoning was used to reject a view that all rules and regulations shackle the masses and that there must be rebellion. In this case a distinction was drawn between, on the one hand, 'slavishness' and the theory of 'docile tools' (supposedly advocated by Liu Shao-ch'i), and, on the other, the requirements of conscious revolutionary discipline.[60]

Lack of discipline was also manifested in the revolutionary committees themselves. Committee members sometimes held the view that democracy is safe, centralism dangerous,[61] a reflection of the Cultural Revolution's emphasis on democracy and criticism of officials. Such cadres were also encouraged to overcome the view that reliance on mass consciousness could replace the need to exercise leadership. A further distinction was drawn between mass consciousness and spontaneity; depending on the masses did not mean that they did not need 'leadership, education, help and improvement'.[62] There were also reports of cadres disregarding the collective leadership of revolutionary committees, disobeying directions, not submitting reports, and relying too much on their own initiative. These were also condemned as sabotaging revolutionary discipline.

Another problem was resistance to the reinstatement or 'liberation'

of cadres. 'Liberation' required a process of genuine transformation of
cadres,[63] through Mao Tsetung Thought study classes, mass criticism,
and participation in manual labour. This followed from the Ninth
Congress policy that 'the scope of attack must be narrow and more
people must be helped through education'. Many people, however,
had a 'lack of confidence' in cadres, suspecting that they were likely
to make mistakes again. Another factor was the general one of
harbouring personal animosity, attitudes based on 'personal affections
or grudges and likes or dislikes' which had been enflamed in the Cultural
Revolution.[64] Moreover, there was fear that criticised cadres, once
returned to positions of authority, would retaliate against their critics.[65]
Even more serious was the suggestion that the reinstatement of cadres
would negate the achievements of the Cultural Revolution, that it was
a 'reversion to the old' and a matter of the proletariat 'losing power'.[66]
In some cases people were afraid to have any contact with cadres who
had been criticised.

The expression of all of these views, from personal animosity to
fear of political retrogression, is hardly surprising given the vigour and
bitterness of many of the previous struggles. What is surprising is the
persistence of these problems well after the supposed consolidation of
the new administrative organs, the revolutionary committees. There
were still many people dissatisfied with what they saw as a retreat from
the Cultural Revolution, concretely symbolised in the return of
people they had recently denounced. Many cadres, however, did not
want to resume positions of authority. It seems that they were so
chastened by their experiences of the preceding few years that they
wished to avoid positions where they might again be subjected to
criticism. One report of cadres' attitudes to work described several
fears. Mistakes in their work could lead to accusations of following
the bourgeois line, while attention to work could be construed as
seizing power'. Because of this, some cadres tended to retreat from
responsibility, preferring participation in manual labour which relieved
them from such dangers.[67] Thus, in order to overcome these inhibitions,
cadres were to be treated leniently.

The liberation of cadres was considered important for the 'consolidation and perfection of the revolutionary régime'. Old cadres were
valuable because of their long experience, methodical work and
understanding of central policy. What was required was that old
cadres and new cadres who had emerged in the Cultural Revolution
unite 'like the strands of a rope'. The value of new cadres was their
sensitivity to new matters, their enthusiasm and their lack of conservatism.

The aim was that the new and old cadres should complement each other, with the new cadres' faults (rashness and lack of sensitivity to policy) balancing the old cadres' faults (adherence to conventions and conservatism).[68] Despite this, there were frequent discussions of the conflict between new and old cadres. There was also conflict between military representatives and other members of revolutionary committees because of the former's arrogance, although this was by no means as significant as it was to become two years later. Such conflicts threatened the rationale of the revolutionary committee as a 'triple combination' and a source of united leadership.

The persistence of these legacies of the Cultural Revolution, which was evidenced in the Chinese press in 1969, posed serious problems for the process of gradual, 'open-door' Party building from the bottom upwards. They continued into 1970, but by then, leadership by the Party organisation was starkly counterposed to factionalism, indiscipline, and anarchism. Party leadership was consistently held to be the way to overcome these erroneous tendencies. Hence, I would argue that the change in the process of Party building was directly linked to the continuation of conflicts and divisions fostered in the Cultural Revolution. Because these conflicts often made the initial programme of Party building difficult to carry out in many places, there was new emphasis on leadership by Party organisations. The assertion of their ideological authority and the necessity for their organisational vanguard role, was intended as a means of overcoming factionalism and anarchism by restoring the integrative and directive function of the Party. Hence, 1970 was the crucial period in which the Party's role in the Chinese political system was re-established.

Operations of Party Organisations

With the reassertion of the organisational basis of Party leadership, there followed a far more extensive discussion of the operations of Party organisations. This began in 1970, but accelerated after the Second Plenum and throughout 1971. It was symptomatic of this new emphasis that Party building was now related to a continuing process based on an already established Party structure. Hence, the question of evaluating old members and admitting new members ('eliminating the stale and taking in the fresh') was no longer a major topic of discussion. The central concern now became how the Party organisation would operate, and questions such as the procedures of Party committees and the role of Party secretaries became important.

It is tempting and superficially plausible to see in this process merely a revival of the situation that pertained before the Cultural Revolution. But, although the forms of leadership by Party organisations were essentially the same, there was an attempt to ensure that the content was different. This was clearly informed by criticisms of the Party organisation that had emerged in the Cultural Revolution.

For example, one crucial factor was the organisational principle of democratic centralism, which requires adherence to majority decisions and obedience of lower level to higher level organs. Party members were instructed that adherence to this principle was just as necessary as having a correct political orientation, that it was 'definitely not (merely) a general question of methods of work.'[69] Criticism was directed against members of Party committees guilty of 'extreme democratisation', who insisted on their own views and destroyed the unified leadership of the Party committee.[70] Democratic centralism, however, was defined not only in organisational terms, which could lead to the type of rigidity and bureaucratism that had been attacked in the Cultural Revolution. It was now stressed that centralism had to be based on democracy, that is, on widespread discussion and 'ideological struggles' within Party committees. This was contrasted with the (incorrect) idea that the expression of too many views would make centralism difficult to achieve.[71] The secretary of the party committee of a textile mill made the distinction between 'uniformity in form' and 'uniformity in ideology', and drew this conclusion from a situation in which committee decisions were not properly implemented:

> This affair made me understand that the democratic centralist principle of the minority obeying the majority must be followed firmly, and this should be in no way ambiguous. But we certainly cannot be satisfied with this kind of uniformity in form; and we must also strive for uniformity in ideology. Otherwise, while there may be uniformity in form, there will not be uniformity in action, and the decisions of the Party Committee will still not be implemented.[72]

Thus, democracy was not confined to making decisions by majority vote. This was only a minimum requirement. More importantly it meant the encouragement of debate and the ability of all committee members to express opinions, on the basis of which unanimity on

the 'correct view' could be reached. The 'correct view' had to be based
on Mao Tsetung Thought, and it was argued that criticism of
incorrect views in no way inhibited democracy.[73] Though subject to
qualifications, democratic centralism was treated in a way which
indicated that it was not to be interpreted merely as a method of
enforcing hierarchical control within the Party organisation.

There were frequent analyses of the role of the secretary of the
Party committee. In particular, the secretary was required to abide by
the collective leadership of the committee and not place himself
above or outside it.[74] Yet many cases were cited in which the
secretary tended to dominate the committee — for example, where
committee members allowed the secretary to do all the talking when
discussing problems, where they waited for him to express his opinion
first when making decisions, where they always sought his approval
before carrying out any work.[75] In some cases the secretary used his
position to reverse committee decisions. The frequent repudiation of the
abuses of collective leadership suggests that, very soon after the
establishment of new Party organisations, their leading members tended
to assume a dominant position — a pattern similar to that which had
developed before the Cultural Revolution.

The attempted solution to these problems was to unite the two
elements of the authority of the secretary and the collective leadership of the committee.

> The committee members must respect and support the secretary.
> If not, the Party committee cannot become a strong and powerful
> nucleus of leadership. The most important thing, however, is that
> both the secretary and committee members respect and support
> the collective leadership of the Party committee. Without this,
> it may become leadership by the secretary alone. Therefore,
> one-sided emphasis on respect and support for the secretary without
> upholding the principle of the committee's collective leadership
> can only bring about a violation of democratic centralism and
> the weakening of the Party committee's collective leadership. It
> is necessary to unify the respect and support for the secretary
> with the preservation of the Party's collective leadership.[76]

Thus, it was the duty of the secretary to encourage and protect
democratic centralism and collective leadership, to act as a model in
observing these principles, and to ensure the thorough expression and
collection of the opinions of all committee members. Furthermore, he

was responsible for establishing a uniform viewpoint through the 'performance of ideological work' among committee members.[77] Hence, the secretary had to ensure the proper operation of the Party committee without occupying too dominant a position.

All references to the operations of the Party committee stressed that it had to be a unified leading body. It was required to deal with all major questions according to the formula 'centralisation of major power and decentralisation of minor power.'[78] All policy decisions had to be made by the Party committee while operational matters could be delegated. Methods such as developing the 'whole game of chess mentality'[79] were suggested for the integration of all work under the committee when responsibility was divided among committee members. In some cases lack of integration was given the more severe title 'departmentalism' and considered as a form of self-interest because of commitment to the interests of a small group only and not to the total situation. It was argued that the work in a particular area, for which one committee member might be responsible, could be carried out properly only if it were guided by the understanding of the overall situation, and this had to be effected through the Party committee.[80]

The problem of fostering unity among committee members was still considered important. Several sources of cleavage were identified: different geographical origin, differences of 'experience in struggle', 'level or consciousness of Marxism-Leninism-Mao Tsetung Thought,' and (most important) differences between old cadres and the new cadres who had become committee members since the Cultural Revolution.[81] More generally, it was argued that, since class struggle still existed in Chinese society, it was bound to be reflected in the Party committee. Hence, the development and resolution of contradictions within the Party were not only inevitable but also beneficial, since these led the Party and the revolutionary cause forward. Consequently, Party committees were advised not to shun or fear the manifestations of differences among members, but to resolve them through discussion and criticism, and thus achieve unity.[82] In particular, there was criticism of such people as Chang Kuo-t'ao, Wang Ming and Liu Shao-ch'i, who were accused of violating the principle of Party unity. They were said to have supported the decisions of the Party only superficially while surreptitiously undermining them, aiming to split the Party and launch a 'surprise attack'.[83] Although this was written in July 1971, it may reflect the developing Lin Piao crisis, and certainly prefigures the types of criticism directed at Lin Piao within the next year.

The principal focus of ideological building now concerned the ideological position of members of Party committees. With respect to one *xian*, for example, it was asserted that the nature of political power depended upon the line followed, and this in turn depended upon the thought of the leading men of the *xian* committee.[84] Much attention was paid, therefore, to the 'ideological revolutionisation' of Party committees and the development of 'active ideological struggle' within them.[85] There were a number of methods suggested for carrying out this ideological struggle, including work conferences, study classes and individual discussions. But by far the most common method, deriving from the principle of democratic centralism, was criticism and self-criticism within the committee itself.

Despite this increasing emphasis on the 'ideological revolutionisation' of leading members of Party organisations, there was still reference to the notion of 'open-door' Party rectification. One complaint was that, since the Cultural Revolution, general political questions had ceased to be considered as matters for mass discussion. Rather, they were considered to be the business of leading Party members only, and the job of the masses and other Party members was interpreted only as following the leadership.[86] To counter this, a combination of 'open-door' rectification and 'self-education' by leading Party members was required.[87] One *xian* committee claimed that, not remaining content with the experience already acquired, it continued to learn from the masses 'in the role of primary school students', accepting new things and studying new problems.[88] The collection of 'mass opinion' was seen as necessary for the Party's democratic centralism. Committee members were warned that they should never put on official airs or consider themselves always right, as this would lead to separation from the masses. Thus, there was approval of the activities of such Party branches as that of the Peking General Knitwear Mill.

> The leading members of this branch persist in carrying out well ideological revolutionisation among the masses. They constantly go to the masses, actively participate in labour, discuss matters with them, and are their sincere pupils . . . the relationship between cadres and the masses is extraordinarily harmonious. This has created a very lively situation in which the leadership can ask for mass criticism when it has problems, and the masses examine the shortcomings and mistakes of the leadership, daring to guide and help them.[89]

Nevertheless, all reports of mass participation made it clear that it was mobilised and guided by Party organisations. For example, the report on revolutionary mass criticism in the Changchun Automobile Works shows that the Party committee guided every stage in this process. The strategy of this committee was to identify and use the 'relatively active' elements among the workers. It then set up a group of 'policy propaganda teams' at all levels, which consisted of Party and Youth League members and leaders of work-shifts. The members of these teams attended special policy-study classes before the movement, special classes for the analysis of the situation during the movement, and evaluation classes after the movement. The intention was to enable the Party committee to keep a clear check on activities, with the committee 'leading the backbone elements and the backbone elements leading the masses.'[90]

Thus, mass participation had to be organised through the Party organisation, not outside of or in opposition to it. According to the report on the Party branch of a rural production brigade in Hopei:

> When the masses have something to say, the leading members never give it undue attention or trust and never express their attitude at random. Instead, they seek a timely exchange of views, an agreement of ideas and a concrete analysis to distinguish between right and wrong. Therefore, the leading squad can form into a single entity with energy directed to the same object.[91]

Obviously it would be very difficult to define 'undue attention or trust', or to distinguish this from separation from the masses or a situation in which committee members always considered themselves right. But the crucial point is that this quotation puts the strongest emphasis on Party leadership, and affirms the Party's role in decision making even in cases of conflict with mass opinion.

The Lin Piao Aftermath

After the downfall of Lin Piao, which Woodward discusses in detail in the next chapter, there was an acceleration of the movement to 'criticise revisionism and rectify the style of work.' This movement had begun after the Second Plenum in 1970 but was now associated with the repudiation of Lin Piao (or, as he was now called, 'a swindler like Liu Shao-ch'i'). It was closely related to the 'three do's and don'ts' issued by Mao with respect to the Lin Piao affair: 'unite, don't split;

practice Marxism, not revisionism; be open and above-board, don't intrigue and conspire.'

It is difficult to define clearly what Lin's position might have been. There is such a plethora of accusations against Lin that they cannot be fitted easily into a coherent pattern. Undoubtedly, many of the mistakes and crimes ascribed to Lin were indicative of his position and underlay the disputes which developed in the Party leadership. In other cases, however, it seems that Lin merely became the scapegoat for all deviations from the officially prescribed position. Initially, Lin was criticised for 'left' mistakes, and held to be primarily responsible for legacies of the Cultural Revolution, such as 'anarchism', which had been opposed in the preceding few years. The general argument was that, in examining the Cultural Revolution and its aftermath, it was necessary to pay attention to how 'one tendency covers up another'; that is, to be aware of the dangers of ultra-leftism while fighting against rightism. Lin exemplified these mistaken leftist tendencies that had arisen in the struggle against the rightists.

In particular, Lin was accused of undermining Party building, of sabotaging the Party's democratic centralism and collective leadership, of causing dissension among Party members and destroying Party unity.[92] He was also denounced for opposing Mao's policy of leniency in reinstating cadres by his advocacy of 'the "left" tendency of killing at a single sweep all who have committed mistakes'.[93] As in the case of Liu Shao-ch'i, this was seen as a way of 'hitting at many to protect a handful'. Lin was also blamed for fomenting conflict between new and old cadres and for the left crime of anarchism, particularly in the specific form known as 'the mountain-stronghold mentality'.

> During the great proletarian cultural revolution, swindlers of the Liu Shao-ch'i type, cunningly exploiting the dissatisfaction of the masses with the right opportunist line, vigorously encouraged an 'ultra-leftist" ' thought-trend which would have only democracy but not centralism, only freedom but not discipline. They declared that 'the word of the masses is final' and 'regulations and systems are useless', and loudly called for 'smashing everything'. Their purpose in doing so was to lead the struggle-criticism-transformation astray, utterly sabotage socialist labour discipline, wreck socialist production, and shake the economic base of the dictatorship of the proletariat at the foundations.[94]

Lin's 'anarchism' was related particularly to indiscipline in production. Thus, there was renewed stress on the distinction between the former 'irrational' rules and the new 'rational' regulations and systems set up in the Cultural Revolution.[95] Lin was accused of distorting the relationship between politics and production, by stressing politics to the detriment of production and spreading the view that 'politics can encroach upon other things' which made people ignore the needs of production.[96] At the same time, there was criticism of Lin's 'formalism' and his supposed view that 'being good in production means being good politically.'[97] Hence, although the general tendency was for Lin to be accused of left mistakes, there were, at the same time, accusations which suggested rightism.

The movement for 'criticising revisionism and rectifying the style of work' did not suggest any diminution of the stress on Party leadership. In fact, it was continually stated that the movement had to be under the leadership of Party organisations.[98] A joint editorial published soon after Lin's disappearance discussed six questions concerning Party leadership, of which the first was the need 'to strengthen the Party concept.' This was interpreted to mean that Party leadership should encompass all areas of social activity.[99] Two of the other questions, Party unity and strengthening the sense of discipline, continued the emphasis on the Party organisation evident before Lin's disappearance. Another, being 'forthright and upright', referred to Lin's attempt to stage a coup. The remaining two questions concerned education in ideology and political line, and 'practising Marxism-Leninism and not revisionism.'

As the combination of these factors suggests, 'the unity of a correct political line and a correct organisation line' was strongly affirmed.

> Whether or not the Party's unified leadership can be realised is determined by whether or not the political line is correct, and the implementation of the correct political line depends on the Party's unified leadership. Without the correct political line, the Party organisation cannot be consolidated and developed, and unified leadership cannot be realised. On the other hand, without the Party's unified leadership, the correct political line cannot be implemented.[100]

It was argued, therefore, that the mistakes in political line of all opportunists and revisionists from Ch'en Tu-hsiu to Lin Piao, were inevitably accompanied by attempts to weaken the Party's centralised leadership. Since correctness of line was said to determine everything else, criticism of revisionism had to have priority over rectification of style of work.[101]

The emphasis on the criticism of revisionism ushered in a new campaign for the *serious* reading and study of Marxist-Leninist classics — the works of Marx, Lenin and Mao. Innumerable detailed articles on the study of particular important works appeared, drawing out the implications of this study for the criticism of Lin's revisionism. Serious study was specifically contrasted with the 'study of phrases and learning by rote'.[102] This was not only a rejection of Lin Piao's promotion of the little red book of Mao's quotations, but an implicit denial of the worth of ideological campaigns during and after the Cultural Revolution. It was argued that the bourgeoisie must change its tactics to achieve its counter-revolutionary aims, and that bourgeois elements disguise themselves as Marxists. Hence, it was necessary to distinguish true and false Marxism, and this could be done only by studying Marxist-Leninist classics in detail. According to the summary of this study by one Party branch:

> Everyone came to understand that simple proletarian feeling could not replace consciousness of line struggle nor could work experience take the place of revolutionary theory, that in the sharp and complex class struggle and two-line struggle, only by laying hold of Marxism-Leninism and Mao Tsetung's thought could we recognise swindlers of the Liu Shao-ch'i type and consciously implement and defend Chairman Mao's revolutionary line.[103]

Although there were frequent references to workers studying theory in this campaign, the main focus was on study by Party members, and particularly by leading members of Party organisations. This was associated with the importance of the vanguard having a correct political line'.[104] Such an emphasis reinforced the position of the Party as the authentic bearer of Marxist-Leninist theory and as the body which would dominate the dissemination and interpretation of Marxism-Leninism.

The major theoretical criticism of Lin Piao was in terms of his 'idealism', and this had several implications for the notion of the Party's leadership, and its relations with the masses. Lin was accused of fostering the idea of '"born" to be higher than the people', which engendered an attitude of superiority to the masses and a denial of the need to obey Party discipline.[105] The criticism of idealism was also reflected in the renewed stress on basing policies on investigation and study, and continuing close contact with the masses. Hence, Lin was said to have tried to enforce his views through coercion and without proper investigation.[106] This was associated with another of Lin's idealist mistakes — that 'heroes' and not the masses make history, which also led to separation from the masses and an attitude of superiority towards them.[107] The criticism of these views led to renewed stress on the importance of the Party's integration with the masses. But Lin was also accused of the opposite mistake of 'doing what the masses want', and in this case the Party was required to guide and stimulate mass activity.

> Fully trusting and relying on the masses does not require us to worship spontaneity, nor does it require us not to deal with passivity among the masses . . . The passivity of the masses requires us to adopt correct methods, do a good job in transformation, and change passive elements into active elements. The development of the revolutionary activism of the masses must have Party leadership.[108]

In 1973, when Lin Piao began to be classified as an ultra-rightist, the emphasis was placed more firmly on his supposed attempts 'to deny the revolutionary enthusiasm of the broad masses and oppose their forward march.'[109] Now, rather than being associated with the 'left' tendencies that had emerged from the Cultural Revolution, Lin was identified as an opponent of the Cultural Revolution.

Another theme in the discussion of Party organisations was the criticism of arrogance and complacency among Party cadres.[110] This was particularly associated with Army members in civilian leading bodies. In 1971 Mao had suggested that the slogan 'learn from the PLA', should be supplemented by 'Let the PLA learn from the people of the whole country'.[111] A corollary of this was the extensive discussion of the 'three rules of discipline and eight points for attention' governing the operations of the Army.[112] The major focus of attention, however, was the reduction of the dominance of Army cadres in civilian Party organisations. Consequently, the arrogance of these cadres was denounced together with the view that they had a special privileged position.[113] The remedy was that Army cadres should abide by the collective leadership of Party committees, in the same way as other committee members, and they should respect and learn from local cadres.[114] This reduction in the role of the Army at lower levels prefigured the reduced importance of people with primarily military affiliations at the Tenth Congress in August 1973. Although there clearly was considerable concern over the Army's dominating role, this should not be linked solely with the Lin Piao affair. This had not been a case of the Army challenging the Party and had not occasioned any significant Army disloyalty to the Party centre. The phasing out of Army involvement indicates rather the renewed strength of the civilian Party structure which no longer needed any military support.

Conclusion

Because of the central role of the Party, it was inevitable that the attack on the Party in the Cultural Revolution would have many serious implications for the whole Chinese political system. In 1969, after the damage that the Party had suffered in the preceding few years, there were obviously many difficulties facing its rebuilding. Within the next two years, the Party's leadership role was re-established, but the process of Party building was not an even one. Until the end of 1969, Party building was seen as a gradual process, going from the bottom upwards, and integrated with the Cultural Revolution programme of 'struggle-criticism-transformation'. In 1970, however, Party building was greatly accelerated. There was a strong emphasis on leadership through the Party organisation and its control of Party building. I have argued that the reason for this change was the persistence of problems of disunity generated in the Cultural Revolution. In the first place, these made the prescribed process of Party building difficult to carry out. Then, in response to this, the emphasis on the leadership of the Party organisation was a way of overcoming the manifestations of disunity. Before the Cultural Revolution, the Party may have been open to challenge according to both the ideological and the organisational bases of its leadership, and may also have become alienated from the masses. Nevertheless, its role was too important to be abandoned without serious consequences. These were 'factionalism', 'anarchism' and other aspects of the mass movement criticised during and after the Cultural Revolution.

Furthermore, while the gradual process of Party building, relying on mass involvement, can be seen as a continuation of the Cultural Revolution, the discussion of Party building in 1970 was in many ways inconsistent with the Cultural Revolution. It was linked to arguments concerning the superiority of Party organisations and members, and the need for subordination to the Party organisation, which differed significantly from what had been emphasised in the

Cultural Revolution. Indeed, many of these arguments would have been strongly condemned at that time.

This was not a change in ultimate objective, since the intention to restore Party leadership both ideologically and organisationally was evident well before the Ninth Congress. The change in Party building, however, indicates more than the use of different means to achieve the same end. The rationale of the gradual, 'open-door' Party building programme had been to build a Party of fundamentally different orientation, to inhibit as much as possible the regrowth of the faults for which the Party had been criticised. This new Party was to be based on the resolution of the conflicts which had been discovered and on the formation of alliance and unity. Hence, 'ideological rectification and building' referred not only to the education of Party members, but also to a general mass movement, and this was given priority over 'organisational rectification and building'. But the very process of mass criticism outside of Party guidance had militated against this type of Party building, and it became necessary to rely on an assertion of Party organisational leadership to overcome continuing conflict. This suggests not only that the stress on the Party organisation was premature in terms of the programme of basing organisational building on ideological building, but also that Party organisational leadership was superimposed on a situation still characterised by division and disunity. Indeed, it casts considerable doubt on the efficacy of a mass movement like the Cultural Revolution for the prevention of ossification and bureaucratisation in a revolutionary Party. Such a movement may have been able to destroy the Party, but it proved unable to rebuild it.

This is not to suggest that there was necessarily a return to the situation that existed before the Cultural Revolution. All discussions of the Party, its relations with the masses, its organisational procedures, and so on, bear the marks of the criticisms raised in the Cultural Revolution. Nor should we ignore the intangible but important factor of the sensitivity of Party members to the experience of the Cultural Revolution, which would tend to prevent complacency. Nevertheless, after 1970, problems such as |alienation from the masses, which had plagued the old Party structure began to re-emerge, and were increasingly reflected in discussions of Party leadership. Of course, these can be seen as attempts to inhibit the growth of these problems, and it certainly was realised that the Cultural Revolution could not be a final solution, that problems were bound to recur. Nevertheless, it seems likely that the rapid and, in terms of the prescribed process, premature stress on the Party organisation provided the basis for the re-emergence of many of the faults of the Party that had been criticised during the Cultural Revolution.

Notes

1. The best discussion of the pre-Cultural Revolution Chinese Communist Party is that of Schurmann 1966 (especially pp.105-72). See also Lewis 1963, Townsend 1967 (especially pp.65-102) and Barnett 1967.
2. See especially Mao Tsetung, 1 June 1943, *SW,* English edition, Vol.3, pp.117-22. On the development of the Mass Line, see Selden 1971, especially pp.208-76.
3. Although, superficially, there was general agreement among different groups in the Party on the significance of these aspects of Party leadership, there were also differences in emphasis which provided the basis for significantly different overall interpretations. In the Cultural Revolution, these differences were generalised in terms of 'two-line struggle'. If we consider the different emphases of Mao and Liu Shao-ch'i, Liu was concerned mainly with the functioning of the Party organisation as a disciplined instrument of centrally-determined policy (see, e.g. Liu 1968, Vol.1, pp.369-410). He tended to see this, as well as the moral and theoretical level of the Party as 'vanguard', independently of the Party's relations with the masses, while Mao considered that the masses should have a more significantly creative role both ideologically and organisationally. An 'ultra-left' position might be characterised as one in which ideology is separated from organisation, or in which organisation is seen as inherently an enemy of ideological purity. Also suggested was a type of ideological elitism, in which 'left' policies might be enforced irrespective of mass desires and mass consciousness. All of these variations may be related to differing interpretations of the nature of socialist revolution, which lead to different conceptions of the role of the Party.
4. Mao Tsetung, 12 February 1967, *JPRS* 1974, p.453, (*Wansui* 1969, p.671).
5. The 1969 Constitution is in PFLP 1969, pp.109-26. The 1956 Constitution is in PFLP 1956, Vol.1, pp.135-68.
6. PFLP 1969, p.116.
7. Ibid., p.74.
8. Ibid. 'Docile tools' refers to Liu's supposed promotion of rigid hierarchy within the Party, which removed any initiative from lower-level Party members.
9. Quoted in ibid., pp.44-5. 'Purifying the class ranks' was the process of examining the histories, political attitudes and performance of individuals, especially those in positions of authority.
10. Ibid. pp.59-60.
11. Mao Tsetung, 1 April 1969, in Schram 1974, pp.280-81.
12. Mao Tsetung, 28 April 1969, in ibid., pp.288-9.
13. *NCNA,* Peking, 1 July 1969, in *SCMP* 4451, p.16.
14. *Hongqi 6-7,* 1969, p.7.
15. Ibid., p.8.
16. *Hongqi 3-4,* 1969, p.36.
17. *RMRB,* 7 July 1969, in *SCMP* 4458, p.5.
18. *Hongqi 3-4,* 1969, p.39.
19. *RMRB,* 12 October 1969, in *SCMP* 4522, p.3.
20. *RMRB,* 3 July 1969, in *SCMP* 4457, p.1.
21. The description here is taken from *RMRB,* 16 December 1969, in *SCMP* 4563,

pp.1-6. See also *Hongqi*,1, 1970, pp.10-15. Hsinhua Printing Works was one of the 'six factories and two universities' of Peking constantly referred to in 1969 and 1970 as models.

22. *SCMP* 4563, p.2.
23. Ibid, p.5.
24. Ho Chin-hsiu, in Yunnan Renmin Chubanshe 1970, pp.7-13. See also *GMRB*, 15 March 1970, in *SCMP* 4624, pp 85-91.
25. CCP Leading Core Group, Huai-yin Special District, in Yunnan Renmin Chubanshe 1970, p.24.
26. Hsieh Li-wen, in ibid., p.21.
27. CCP Leading Core Group, Huai-yin Special District, in ibid., p.26.
28. Study and Coaching Group of the Kwangchow Silk and Hemp Mill, in ibid., p.45.
29. Hsueh Hsiao-tsu, in ibid., p.31.
30. Study and Coaching Group of the Kwangchow Silk and Hemp Mill, in ibid., p.47.
31. *Hongqi* 1, 1970, p.78.
32. CCP Leading Core Group, Huai-yin Special District, in Yunnan Renmin Chubanshe 1970, p.26.
33. Hsieh Li-wen, in ibid, p 22.
34. *RMRB*, 28 July 1970, in *SCMP* 4718, p.195.
35. Hsueh Hsiao-tsu, in Yunnan Renmin Chubanshe 1970, p.30.
36. *GMRB*, 30 June 1970, in *SCMP* 4699, p.4.
37. *Hongqi* 1, 1970, p.77.
38. *RMRB*, 18 April 1970, *in SCMP* 4644, p.52.
39. *RMRB*, 10 March 1970, in *SCMP* 4622, p.27.
40. *RMRB*, 13 May 1970, in *SCMP* 4663, p.2.
41. *Hongqi* 1, 1970, p.67.
42. Ibid.
43. *Hongqi* 7, 1970, p.22.
44. Hua Shan-lien, in Yunnan Renmin Chubanshe 1970, p.94.
45. Yunnan Renmin Chubanshe 1970, pp. 132-36.
46. *Hongqi* 1, 1970, p.71.
47. Hua Shan-lien, in Yunnan Renmin Chubanshe 1970 pp.93-4.
48. *Hongqi* 1, 1970, p.77.
49. *RMRB*, 26 February 1970, in *SCMP* 4614, p.98.
50. *Hongqi* 1, 1970, p.62.
51. Domes 1973, p.215. *Xian* is the administrative unit below provincial level, often translated as 'county'.
52. *RMRB*, 4 June 1969, in *SCMP* 4441, pp.1-3.
53. *RMRB*, 23 July 1969, in *SCMP* 4441, pp.1-3.
54. *RMRB*, 6 November 1969, in *SCMP* 4540, p.24.
55. *Hongqi* 10, 1969, p.18.
56. *RMRB*, 4 June 1969, in *SCMP* 4441, p.2.
57. *Hongqi,* 10, 1969, p.18.
58. *RMRB*, 15 September 1969, in *SCMP* 4507, pp.1-2.
59. *Hongqi* 6-7, 1969, p.22. On the notion of principal contradiction, see Mao Tsetung, August 1937, *SW,* English edition, Vol.1, pp.331ff,
60. *RMRB*, 15 July 1969, in *SCMP* 4463, p.2.
61. *RMRB*, 29 July 1969, in *SCMP* 4470, p.3.
62. *RMRB*, 6 September 1969, in *SCMP* 4499, p.5.
63. *RMRB*, 28 March 1969, in *SCMP* 4398, p 2.
64. *RMRB*, 22 May 1969, in *SCMP* 4432, pp.1-3.
65. *GMRB*, 8 May 1969, in *SCMP* 4428, p.2.
66. *RMRB*, 29 January 1969, in *SCMP* 4364, p.2.

67. *RMRB,* 13 April 1969, in *SCMP* 4404, p.5.
68. *RMRB,* 29 May 1969, in *SCMP* 4436, p.6.
69. *Hongqi* 1, 1971, p.30.
70. *RMRB,* 8 January 1971, in *SCMP* 4824, p.110.
71. *GMRB,* 21 June 1971, in *SCMP* 4931, p.61.
72. *RMRB.* 30 June 1971, in *SCMP* 4938, p.232.
73. *GMRB,* 21 June 1971, in *SCMP* 4931, p.63.
74. *RMRB,* 27 December 1970, in *SCMP* 4816, p.9.
75. *GMRB,* 10 January 1971, in *SCMP* 4824, p.114.
76. *RMRB,* 30 June 1971, in *SCMP* 4937, p.180.
77. Ibid. p.183.
78. *GMRB,* 29 August 1970, in *SCMP* 4738, p.9.
79. *RMRB,* 8 January 1971, in *SCMP* 4824, pp.115-16.
80. *Hongqi* 7-8, 1971, p.38.
81. Ibid., p.36.
82. Ibid.
83. Ibid. p.37.
84. *RMRB,* 19 December 1970, in *SCMP* 4811, p.7.
85. *RMRB,* 15 May 1971, in *SCMP* 4909, p.70.
86. *RMRB,* 26 February 1971, in *SCMP* 4863, pp.55-6.
87. *RMRB,* 30 January 1971, in *SCMP* 4834, p.77.
88. *GMRB,* 14 January 1971, in *SCMP* 4828, p.4.
89. *Hongqi* 5, 1971, p.53.
90. *Hongqi* 7-8, 1971, p.67.
91. *RMRB,* 25 January 1971, in *SCMP* 4835, p.99.
92. See, e.g., *GMRB,* 7 July 1972, in SCMP 5177, p.85; *RMRB,* 30 June 1973, in *SCMP* 5415, p.9.
93. *RMRB,* 4 April 1972, in *SCMP* 5056, p.60.
94. *RMRB,* 14 October 1972, in *SCMP* 5241, p.58.
95. *RMRB,* 29 October 1971, in *SCMP* 5011, p.194.
96. *RMRB,* 17 May 1972, in *SCMP* 5144, p.66.
97. *RMRB,* 9 June 1972, in *SCMP* 5160 p.175.
98. *RMRB,* 30 May 1973, in *SCMP* 5393, pp.92-3.
99. *NCNA,* Peking, 30 November 1971, in *SCMP* 5032, p.23.
100. *Hongqi* 11, 1972, p.4.
101. *Hongqi* 3, 1973, p.3.
102. *Hongqi* 2, 1972, p.20.
103. *GMRB,* 1 July 1972, in *SCMP* 5175, pp.1-2.
104. *RMRB,* 14 October 1972, in *SCMP* 5241, p.61.
105. *Hongqi* 1, 1972, p.34.
106. *Hongqi* 2, 1973, p.2.
107. *Hongqi* 1, 1972, pp.11-18.
108. *Hongqi* 3, 1973, 0.13.
109. *Hongqi* 4, 1973, p.5.
110. *Hongqi* 7, 1972, p.25.
111. Schram 1974, p.297.
112. *Hongqi* 7, 1972, p.17. The three rules of discipline and eight points for attention were used to guide the actions of the Red Army before Liberation. See Mao Tsetung 10 October 1947, in *SW,* English edition, Vol.4, p.155.
113. *RMRB,* 16 October 1971, in *SCMP* 5004, p.3.
114. *RMRB,* 8 December 1971, in *SCMP* 5039, p.89.

2 POLITICAL POWER AND GUN BARRELS — THE ROLE OF THE PLA

Dennis Woodward

The Chinese People's Liberation Army (PLA) is in many respects unique. It has a long history of performing many functions which are not normally associated with a military force.[1] In pre-Liberation times, it depended on peasant support for its recruits and its continuing survival. It was closely integrated with the Chinese masses and took part in production tasks to attain a degree of self-sufficiency and to aid the peasants at the peak periods of harvesting and sowing when labour was much in demand. In an era in which China was plagued by rapacious warlords and was the victim of foreign invasion, the PLA earned a reputation as an Army of a vastly different nature. Instead of looting and pillaging, the PLA observed strict discipline, treating the peasants with courtesy and scrupulously paying for anything which it requisitioned. As a people's army, its strictly military and non-military tasks were inextricably linked. That is, it is misleading to see time spent in aiding production as being opposed to or detrimental to the Army's prime task of waging warface, since any task which served to cement the Army's relationship with the masses directly contributed to its efficacy as a fighting force.

Similarly, the relationship between the Party and the PLA was not one of mutual exclusivity. While functionally the Army was under the direction of the Party, distinct lines between military and non-military personnel were blurred by the organisational fusion of the PLA and the CCP and by the considerable interlocking of political and military leadership. The role of the Party, therefore, as the vanguard determining the direction of the revolutionary movement was vital. Its leadership over the Army was axiomatic, since without Party leadership, the Army would become directionless and degenerate to the point of becoming indistinguishable from warlord armies. Hence, to maintain Party control over the Army, there was established within the PLA itself a Party organisation which consisted of political commissars (whose tasks included directing the ideological education of the troops) and Party branches, paralleling each level of the military hierarchy. This functional distinction between the Army and an essentially civilian Party leadership was never rigidly maintained organisationally and Party members often held key posts within the Army and vice versa.

71

An illustration of this, was the number of Army personnel who, in
the immediate aftermath of Liberation, found themselves in charge
of regional administration and were maintained in that role as
civilians after the Army was phased out of administration in the early
1950s. As the Introduction notes, they simply changed from their
Army to their Party hats. Moreover, this overlapping of military and
Party personnel has continued since the early 1950s although generally to
a lesser extent. Thus, it is incorrect to view the PLA and the CCP as
totally distinct entities with necessarily conflicting interests.

Despite this background, there has continued to be disagreement
over the nature of the PLA's role in China. The primary focus of
dispute has been over the military strategy which the PLA should
adopt as appropriate for the development of a socialist country. There
have been those who argued that a strategy of defence based on people's
war led by a people's army is no longer adequate. For them, the PLA
should concentrate on developing its capacity to fight positional
warfare This would require a more 'professionalised' army, which
was highly trained and armed with the most technologically advanced
weapons possible. Opponents of this view argued that, by concentrating
on purely military concerns, there was a danger of losing sight of the goal
of building socialism. They maintained that a 'professionalised' army,
which spends most of its time in military training, ran the risk of becoming
divorced from the masses and, by not contributing to production, might
become a burden on them. They feared that such an Army might develop
into an élitist organisation with interests of its own which were in
conflict with the general orientation of building socialism. To them, a
people's army, closely integrated with the masses, was more in harmony
with the goals of the revolution and also a better guarantee of defence
against foreign invasion. Tension within the Army between those who
championed greater emphasis on political rather than military
training, and a greater involvement in political and economic matters
for the PLA (that is, those seeking a closer orientation to the
concept of a people's army) and those who advocated a more strictly
military role (that is, those advocating a more professional army) was
to become acute in the aftermath of the Cultural Revolution. Similarly,
the role of the militia (which would play an integral part in waging
people's war but was considered to be of little importance by the
proponents of a professional army) was to become an issue of
contention in this period.

The PLA during the Cultural Revolution

Much as been written on the decisive part which the PLA played throughout the Cultural Revolution.[2] It provided much of the initial logistic support for the Red Guards but otherwise took little part in the early upheavals of 1966. Later, as the Party organisation became increasingly paralysed and unable to carry out its usual administrative tasks because of Red Guard attacks on various Party members, responsibility for maintaining order, services and production fell to the Army. The Army, moreover, was explicitly called upon to actively 'support the left' in the seizing of power from the old Party committees. But, many military commanders had difficulty in reconciling the contradiction inherent in maintaining order yet simultaneously supporting the revolutionary rebels in seizing power. Indeed, military commanders were no better qualified to discern which of various factional groups represented the 'true left' than the general populace who often found themselves confused by the claims of competing mass organisations. Faced with such seemingly unsolvable problems, the response of Army commanders varied. In some instances, the PLA supported radical factions in their power seizures (notably in Heilungkiang province which become the model for power seizures), while in other cases they favoured the status quo and attempted to suppress radical Red Guard factions.

The dangers of involving the Army in policy determination without giving it any clear policy guidelines, soon became apparent. Not only did Army units clash with Red Guards but in some instances there was fighting between various branches of the PLA – notably in Wuhan.[3] While some Red Guard groups saw this as symptomatic of conservatism and called for the 'dragging out of the handful in the Army', the Cultural Revolution Group as a whole was not prepared to countenance a full scale mass attack on the Army and so allowed the military to conduct its own Cultural Revolution within its own ranks. The Army, furthermore, was allowed to use force if necessary to defend itself from attack by hostile factions. With this authoritative backing, the PLA was able to restore order in most regions and to enable the formation of revolutionary committees, although in some cases the process took considerable time. Military figures tended to dominate the newly formed provincial revolutionary committees as is witnessed by the fact that nearly all their chairmen were PLA men.[4]

The Post-Cultural Revolution Period: Introduction

At the close of the Cultural Revolution, the Army was in a pre-eminent position as virtually the sole organised political and administrative force.[5] The Party structure was in considerable disarray so that, even though its lower levels (for example, commune Party committees) had survived largely intact, they found themselves unable to perform the functions of leadership since higher levels of the Party were not operating. It was only in the Army that Party committees remained unimpaired at all levels, with an unbroken hierarchy which extended through military district (province) and military region right up to the national level. The prominence of military commanders on provincial revolutionary committees was reflected in the composition of the Central Committee elected at the Ninth Congress of the CCP. Nearly half the seats on the Central Committee and 55 per cent of the members of the Politburo were identified as military personnel.[6] This military dominance, moreover, was 'dramatically underscored' by the fact that Lin Piao (then Minister of Defence) gave the main address to the Ninth Congress and was named as 'Mao's successor' in the new Party Constitution.[7]

Confronted by this highly visible increase in military men in the higher organs of power, some commentators predicted that the Army might displace the Party as the ruling élite in China,[8] and that China was experiencing military rule similar to that of many Third World countries.[9] These analysts, however, were mistaken. They failed to discern the strength of the ultimate desire to rebuild the Party as the 'vanguard', which was evident throughout the Cultural Revolution, and particularly in the Report to the Ninth Congress, as Young has already indicated.[10] Furthermore, by talking as though the Party and the Army were discrete entities, these commentators saw the holding of leadership positions in China in terms of a zero sum game. To them, an increase in the percentage of people who were most noted for their military background in the central Party organs was *ipso facto* proof of a military takeover. This view ignored the fact that the 'military' men who held key positions at the end of the Cultural Revolution, did so not simply by virtue of their positions in the Army, but also by virtue of their positions within the *Party* itself. That is, with the civilian Party structure seriously impaired as a result of attacks on certain of its personnel during the Cultural Revolution, Party rebuilding and general administration (especially at the provincial level) was taken over by the intact Party organisation within the PLA – 'party-soldiers' as Powell has called them.[11] Powell argued that, 'a reorganised Party still controls the gun, but only because the generals control the Party',[12] but the distinction between this situation and one of a military takeover needs to be made. The principle of Party leadership over the Army did not appear to have been seriously questioned, although functional leadership appeared to be little more than nominal while the civilian Party organisation was being rebuilt. The organisational fusion of leading Army and Party personnel makes it virtually impossible to define such people as primarily Army or Party representatives. Thus, to depict this situation as a military takeover, rather confuses our understanding of what took place and ignores both the signs that the civilian Party apparatus was to be rebuilt, and the similarities between the situation at the close of the Cultural Revolution and that of the early 1950s.

The period after the Cultural Revolution was to witness the eventual rebuilding of the Party apparatus and the general disengagement of the Army from most of its political and economic tasks. Unlike the early 1950s, however, the transition from 'military' administration to that of civilians was effected not by the maintenance of the same personnel in non-military guise, but by their replacement while the Army returned to its barracks. Moreover, if the increased political role of the PLA was highlighted by the elevated position which Lin Piao attained at the Ninth Congress, then the playing down of this role was to be symbolised by his disappearance.

The Tasks Undertaken by the PLA

When Lin Piao described the PLA as the 'unbending pillar' (*jianqiang zhizhu*) 'of the dictatorship of the proletariat' in his Report to the Ninth Congress of the CCP on 1 April 1969,[13] he was indeed accurately describing the prominent position which the PLA then held. Its work of 'three supports and two militaries' (that is supporting the broad masses of the left ['and not any particular faction'], supporting industry, supporting agriculture, and maintaining military control and military/political training) was continuing apace. This encompassed many diverse tasks. The PLA was reported to have supported spring farming,[14] to have helped to 'purify the class ranks' and to have supported the revolutionary committees.[15] In many instances, it had undertaken the unenviable task of attempting to resolve ideological differences between old and new cadres on the revolutionary committees and, we are told, had often succeeded in doing so.[16] So long as the Party was unable to carry out its organisational tasks, these were largely in the hands of PLA members. In a similar manner, the PLA performed some of the ideological tasks which were normally the preserve of the Party. For example, PLA Mao Tsetung Thought

propaganda teams were ubiquitous and the Army also held numerous
congresses of activists in the study of Mao Tsetung Thought.[17] The PLA
had also to maintain its military vigilance as there had been several
border clashes with Soviet troops — the most publicised of which had
occurred at Chenpao Island where, according to Chinese reports, the
PLA, using the 'magic weapon' of Mao Tsetung Thought, had
defeated the Soviet troops.[18]

The effusive praise for the PLA in the media mirrored the crucial and
all embracing role which its members were playing. Throughout 1969
statements such as the following were commonplace:

> the practice of struggle in the past year tells us that, for the
> proletariat to hold power, it must have the PLA as its powerful
> backing. In essence, the State is the Army. Of all the factors in the
> régime, the Army is the most important factor, *the centre of centres
> and the key of keys.*[19]

It should be noted, however, that such statements, which stressed the
Army's central role in the context of the state structure, in no way
claimed that it was more important that the Party, or that the Army
should replace the Party as the 'vanguard' leading the Chinese
revolution.

Throughout 1969, the PLA apparently had continual difficulty in
its attempts to reconcile and unite opposing mass factions. The genie
of rebellion once unleashed was not easily returned to its former
abode, and there is evidence which suggests that the Army was
bearing the brunt of hostility from rebels who were not prepared to
unite with their enemies of the recent past. Exhortations which stated,

> One's attitude to the PLA represents one's attitude to the
> dictatorship of the proletariat. *Our Revolutionary comrades*
> must at all times and in all circumstances trust and rely on the
> PLA and support and uphold the PLA. They must cherish the PLA,
> the steel great wall, as they cherish their own eyes.[20]

revealed that some 'revolutionary comrades', at least, were opposing
the actions of the Army. The Chinese press regularly featured
examples (held up as models) of the PLA representatives on
revolutionary committees promoting unity by means of lengthy and
patient discussion.[21] Recalcitrant members were condemned for not
having freed themselves from 'bourgeois factionalism',[22] yet such

factionalism was not readily dispelled as Young has shown.[23]

The acute problems which the PLA must have encountered in the task of reconciling opposing mass organisations, is illustrated by a CCP Central Committee directive issued on 23 July 1969 to curb the armed struggle in the Shansi area.[24] It noted the 'extremely good situation' in Shansi as in the rest of the country, but went on to state,

> . . .However, in some areas in the city of Taiyuan and in central and southern Shensi [sic] , a handful of class enemies and evil chieftains mixed up in the *various factions of mass organisations* have taken advantage of the factionalism of the bourgeoisie to hoodwink a portion of the masses.[25]

These factions had perpetrated a number of 'serious counter-revolutionary crimes', which included organising teams for armed struggle 'to engage in beatings, smashing, robbing and unwarranted arrest.' They were also said to have refused to join in a 'great revolutionary alliance', and to have attacked PLA organs and troops, 'seizing the PLA's weapons and equipment and beating up, kidnapping and killing PLA commanders and fighters'.[26] While such extremes appear to have been the exception rather than the rule throughout 1969, this example does highlight one pole of the spectrum of relations between the PLA and mass organisations.

Even if the opposition to the Army from various factions was more verbal than physical, it seems that, in some cases, the PLA reacted against such opposition and restored unity in a rather heavy-handed way. In such cases, it was often at the expense of the extreme radicals whose organisations were forcibly suppressed. In other cases, all mass organisations suffered the same fate. One broadcast about a PLA study class, admitting that its errors were due to a lack of faith in the masses, revealed,

> At the study class, the fighters pointed out that, from the outset, some of them had expressed their dislike of the revolutionary behaviour of the young Red Guard fighters.[27]

If this dislike was mutual, as appears likely, there is little wonder that the Army did not find its tasks of political reconstruction particularly simple.

Indeed, the difficulty of achieving unity amidst such factionalism which hampered Party reconstruction, necessitated the constant involvement of the PLA during 1969. As already mentioned, 'three support and two military' work figured prominently in the Chinese media. Similarly, there were numerous references to provincial meetings of Party members being convened by the Party committee of the PLA units in the provincial capitals in conjunction with the provincial revolutionary committees.[28] Rather than carrying out a military takeover, the 'party-soldiers' were endeavouring to accelerate the rebuilding of the Party. It appears, however, that within the Army itself differences of opinion were emerging on the related issues of sustaining such a high level of political and economic involvement and of striking the correct balance between political and military training.

On the one hand, there was the view that the Army should maintain its highly politicised character and continue to play an active role in political, administrative and economic work. This position, which, as the Introduction has noted, can be most closely associated with Lin Piao's leadership of the Army since 1959, was given expression in the 'four good' and 'five good' movements, and in the 'three-supports and two military' movement. The 'four good' movement stressed that a soldier needed to be 'good in political and ideological work, good in the "three-eight" work style, good in military training, and good in management of Army livelihood'. The 'five good' movement was almost identical.[29] Such movements continued to be widely promoted within the PLA and even within the civilian population.[30] These campaigns, moreover, were a constant feature of the Chinese media throughout most of 1970,[31] although they tended to fade from prominence after the eclipse of Lin Piao.

On the other hand, it appears that this 'Linist' position was being successively restated to counter an opposed view, which could best be characterised as the 'professional military view' in a revived professional versus people's army debate. For example, a Wuhan broadcast in May 1969 mentioned a PLA unit which had 'got [ten] rid of the erroneous idea that the "work had been completed successfully, so we can withdraw the troops and return to the barracks" '.[32] Similarly, a *People's Daily* article in August 1969, stated that 'three-support and two-military' work was essential for 'keeping our socialist fatherland red forever.' It was argued that such work enabled the people's interests to be safeguarded and also increased the combat power of the Army. 'Three-support' work, moreover, was said to be *the best form of Army building and war preparedness.*[33] This revealed that there were obviously some military commanders who were concerned at the possibility of war with the Soviet Union and sought to increase war preparedness by concentrating more on strictly military duties. Perhaps the difficulties which certain PLA units had encountered in carrying out their 'three-support' tasks, contributed to a desire to relinquish such work as soon as possible and return to military training which was less contentious. Certainly, some members of the PLA continued to opt for a lessening of civil involvement and a strengthening of military training, as reports criticising such an attitude testify. For example, a Nanchang broadcast attacked those who argued that,

> Since the start of the Cultural Revolution we have engaged in political studies or carried out 'three-support and two-military' tasks. Now that we are talking about strengthening our preparedness against war, *we ought to carefully grasp military training.*[34]

This view of increasing attention to military tasks (and by implication withdrawing from non-military tasks) was seen as being opposed to the concept of a people's army, and was roundly denounced as a 'bourgeois' expression of the 'purely military viewpoint'.[35] It was felt that, by concentrating solely on military affairs, the Army would not be paying attention to the needs of the people nor to the direction of the revolution, and as a result the goal of building socialism would suffer.

Thus, while there is evidence to indicate some opposition within the PLA to its maintaining multitudinous non-military functions, this opposition was in eclipse until after the Second Plenum and probably until Party committees had been re-established at the provincial level in August 1971. There were, however, indications of a partial shift in emphasis towards greater attention to military training as early as December 1969. This is well illustrated by an article from the editorial department of *Liberation Army Daily* which advised: 'Nevertheless, we should not think that by putting politics in command, military affairs can be neglected.'[36] Similarly, February 1970 witnessed the start of a new campaign to stress the task of building the militia.[37] This campaign, however, was consistent with a people's army orientation and should be seen as the response to the need for war preparation by those who favoured people's war rather than a professional army in the ongoing debate. Re-emphasis on the militia (which was apparently neglected during the Cultural Revolution) was a feature of the entire post-Cultural Revolution period and has been linked with the fall of Lin Piao. Ironically, Lin, under whose aegis the militia was revived in the early 1960s, was to be accused (after his demise) of playing down the significance of the militia and allowing its organisation to lapse.

The Outcome of the Second Plenum

Much has been written on the fall of Lin Piao.[38] Nearly all accounts see the Second Plenum of the Ninth Congress of the CCP, which was held at Lushan in late August and early September 1970, as marking a crucial turning point in his political fortunes. It was at this plenum, we are told, that Lin through his supporters, attempted to re-appoint Mao to the position of Chairman of the People's Republic – a position which had remained vacant (or rather non-existent) since Liu Shao-ch'i was removed from it during the Cultural Revolution. Lin's supporters, led by Ch'en Po-ta, knowing that Mao would decline the position, hoped that, by this tactic, Lin would be appointed to the revived post and thus cement his position as Mao's eventual successor.[39] The gambit failed because of Mao's opposition to restoring the office of Chairman and, as a result, probably dashed Lin's chances of succeeding Mao. Lin's supporters had overplayed their hand, and by doing so, had convinced Mao that Lin was an unworthy heir apparent.

In the months following the plenum, moves were taken to undermine Lin Piao's base of support as a prelude to his eventual demotion or dismissal. These moves, described by Mao as 'casting stones, digging up the cornerstone, and blending with sand', embraced the launching of a campaign to criticise Ch'en Po-ta and to oppose arrogance and conceit within the PLA, the reorganisation of the Peking Military Region, and the addition of more members to the Military Affairs Committee.[40] The campaign to criticise Ch'en Po-ta and to 'oppose idealism and metaphysics' followed immediately after the end of the plenum, and, as Young has narrated, was coupled with an ideological drive to study Marxism 'seriously' by reading the classics of Marxism-Leninism as well as the works of Mao.

The seven 'big fighters' (Huang Yung-sheng, Wu Fa-hsien, Yeh Ch'un, Li Tso-p'eng, Ch'iu Hui-tso, Li Hsüeh-feng and Cheng Wei-shan), who were Lin's closest supporters and who had championed his cause at the Second Plenum, were criticised in December at an Enlarged Politburo Conference at Peitaiho.[41] In January 1971, the Peking Military Region was thoroughly reorganised. The 38th army (reputedly loyal to Lin) was transferred from the region and the commander and second political commissar were both replaced.[42] Simultaneously, other members were added to the Military Affairs Committee of the CCP in an attempt to lessen the dominance which Lin Piao and his small group of followers had exercised over the centralised control of the PLA.[43]

If the Second Plenum marked the beginning of the end for Lin Piao, it does not appear to have been such a watershed for the Army as a whole. Indeed, sudden changes in the orientation of the PLA were not readily observable in the wake of the plenum, although references to the Army's 'three-support and two-military' work were perhaps not as evident as they had been before. Certainly, criticisms of 'support-the-left' personnel who thought that their job was almost done and wanted to return to their barracks,[44] largely disappeared from the Chinese press. But, these gradual shifts in emphasis can be readily explained by the Army relinquishing some of its tasks as the Party organisation was being rebuilt. They do not appear to be linked to the outcome of the Second Plenum nor to reflect the status of Lin Piao save in the most tenuous manner.

While the Second Plenum seemingly had little bearing on the general orientation of the PLA, it was crucial in initiating a campaign to raise the ideological level of Army personnel. This campaign, which was principally aimed at cadres at regimental (brigade) level and above, was part of the wider campaign to study Marxism and to oppose 'idealism and metaphysics' (mentioned above). This was made most explicit in a Tsingtao broadcast which stated:

> Recently, *inspired by the communiqué of the Second Plenum* of the Ninth CCP Central Committee, the PLA units stationed in Tsingtao held a Mao Tsetung Thought study class *for cadres above regimental level.*[45]

Military commanders were warned that complacency and pride in past achievements were a sign of arrogance.[46] They were admonished for thinking that their past experience in fighting battles, in Army building and in 'supporting-the-left' meant that they did not have to study philosophy.[47] There was a touch of irony in many of the articles which criticised leading cadres who had been guiding other people in the study of Mao Tsetung Thought but had done little study of their own.[48]

This campaign, moreover, was not restricted to matters of a purely ideological nature, but was also broadened to rectify methods of work.

In particular, Army personnel, who had become divorced from the
masses and were consequently prone to issue orders without
adequately employing collective leadership, found themselves
subjected to criticism. As one broadcast noted:

> Some comrades who had been supporting the left for a long
> time, feeling that they had been in the same units for a long
> time and were familiar with the situation there, did little
> investigation and study but relied on jumping to conclusions to
> solve problems.[49]

This 'commandist' work-style was seen as being symptomatic of
arrogance within the upper echelons of the PLA and complaints
that 'some comrades' had 'placed themselves above the masses and
regarded themselves as in a special category'[50] were commonplace.
Similar campaigns attacking arrogance within the PLA were
prominent in the period after Lin Piao's disappearance.

Closely paralleling the movement for commanders to remould
their world outlook, was a renewed drive to develop the militia. This
was particularly salient in the Chinese media during the latter half of
September 1970 and continued during October. It was argued that
militia work had been neglected, as a result of the Army being
preoccupied with 'support-the-left' work, and that the PLA should
ensure that sufficient attention was paid to both tasks.[51] Similarly,
a conference on militia work in Hunan which was held in September
urged the promotion of militia work and the strengthening of the
Party's leadership over militia work.[52] Evidence of conferences on
militia work in other provinces,[53] and of widespread calls for militia
building,[54] strongly indicate a general campaign which was to be
renewed and intensified after Lin Piao's death.

The Fall of Lin Piao and its Aftermath

The disappearance of Lin Piao in early September 1971, marked an
important turning point in the orientation and role of the PLA. He is
said to have attempted a coup which failed, and to have been killed
in a plane crash while attempting to flee to the Soviet Union.[55]
Those military men who had close ties with Lin (especially the
'big fighters') were also removed from their posts shortly after Lin
vanished. Nevertheless, most regional commanders of the PLA
retained their positions (at least initially) in what Joffe has argued was
a selected purge on the 'Linist' faction rather than a general assault on

the Army as a whole.[56] Yet there do seem to have been substantial
changes of a general nature throughout the entire Army in the
aftermath of the Lin Piao affair which foreshadowed diminished PLA
influence.

The most obvious of the changes was the campaign which began
in January 1972 adding to the previous slogan of learning from the
PLA by urging the PLA to 'learn from the people'. At least one
commentator saw this as part of a general campaign to play down
the role of the Army.[57] In the same manner as the campaigns to
combat arrogance within the Army which had taken place in late
1970, this campaign was aimed at rectifying the work style of Army
commanders. No longer were members of the PLA to display pride,
but were to humbly learn from the local cadres and the people.[58]
'Taking factories and rural areas as class-rooms' and learning humbly
from the masses, moreover, was stressed as part of Army building.[59]
This campaign, which permeated the Chinese media during 1972, can
be seen as a direct consequence of the Lin Piao affair. Its origin was
a statement of Mao:

> Learn from Taching in industry and from Tachai in agriculture
> and the whole country should learn from the People's
> Liberation Army. This is not perfect. It is necessary to add one
> item, the Liberation Army must learn from the people of the whole
> country.[60]

This was an implicit assertion that the Army had become divorced
from the masses and needed to return to a style more in keeping with
its origins as a people's army.

Similarly, the 'four-good' and 'five-good' movements, which were
associated with Lin Piao, totally disappeared and were replaced by
renewed emphasis on the 'three main rules of discipline and eight
points for attention'. These rules (1. obey orders in all actions,
2. do not take even a needle or a thread from the masses, 3. turn in
everything which is captured) and points (1. speak politely, 2. pay
fairly for what you buy, 3. return everything you borrow, 4. pay for
anything which you damage, 5. do not hit or swear at people,
6. do not damage crops, 7. do not take liberties with women, 8. do
not ill-treat captives)[61] were the basis of the PLA's code of
conduct from its inception and their revival symbolised the intention
of the Army to return to its original orientation as a people's army.
Again, this campaign derived from criticisms which Mao made during

his southern inspection tour prior to Lin Piao's disappearance.[62] Mao's call was duly taken up in the Chinese press.[63]

At the same time as these campaigns, which suggested a return to a closer integration with the masses (and hence to a people's army), were taking place, there was also a drive to re-assert the importance of military training which was more in keeping with the professional side of the people's versus professional army debate. While it was still conceded that politics was in command of military affairs, it was argued that 'it cannot replace military affairs'.[64] An important corollary of this renewed stress on military training was a sharp reduction in the Army's non-military activities. If military affairs had been somewhat neglected since the inception of the Cultural Revolution because of the Army's increased involvement in administrative tasks, it is evident that, with the Party organisation now largely rebuilt, the time had come for the Army to be phased out of these tasks in favour of more strictly military work. That Mao held this view is evidenced by his remarks in the Central Committee document which was used as study material in the campaign to criticise Lin Piao. Thus Mao said,

> In the past we have had the course of basic drilling for our military training. It took about five to six months to proceed from individual training to the training of a battalion. Now we only engage in civil (*wen*) training, and not military training. *Our army has become a cultural (wenhua) army.*[65]

This imbalance was now to be rectified. The previous stress on 'three support' work as essential to consolidate the dictatorship of the proletariat was reversed. It was now argued that *grasping military training* was appropriate for the consolidation of the proletarian dictatorship.[66] A feature of this renewed emphasis on military training was a stress on combat exercises. Such exercises often took the form of forced marches over long distances and camping in adverse weather.[67] It was again a case of getting back to basics for the PLA.

The movement to intensify military training can be seen as directly linked to the fall of Lin Piao. It coincided with the campaign to criticise him, and Lin was explicitly blamed for the neglect of military training. As one article revealed:

> Strenuously opposing Chairman Mao's Army-building line, *Liu*

Shao-ch'i and swindlers like him said such absurd things as
military training did not matter very much, it was not necessary
to study specialised techniques, since they could be very
quickly mastered when they are needed; and so on.[68]

We have noted time and again that the formula 'Liu Shao-ch'i and
swindlers like him' was used to denote Lin, and there is little doubt
who was being held responsible for the decline in military proficiency.
Nevertheless, the change in orientation from its varied tasks to
martial ones was not a straightforward one for the Army as a whole.
It appears that initially there was some reluctance to embrace
wholeheartedly this alteration in policy; after all, it smacked of the
'purely military viewpoint' which had been so consistently
denounced during the previous ten years. Many units had to have
explained to them the 'clear demarcation line' which existed
between their assiduously learning military skills for the purpose of
consolidating the dictatorship of the proletariat, and the 'purely
military viewpoint' which encouraged concentrating on military
training as an end in itself.[69] The former was good and to be
encouraged, while the latter was bad and to be guarded against. In
this way, an apparent reversal of policy or at least a substantial shift
in emphasis, was engineered with minimal disruption. By the latter
part of 1972, the military training programme was proceeding
smoothly.[70]

Commensurate with the diminution of the Army's political role,
was the gradual resumption by the reconstructed Party of its
primary position of ideological and organisational leadership. As
already noted, the intention to rebuild the Party as the organised
'vanguard' of the Chinese revolution had been consistent. Yet this
process proved to be extremely difficult because of the legacy of
factionalism left by the Cultural Revolution.[71] But, once the Party
had been basically rebuilt, its leadership over all other organisations
was vigorously asserted. This leadership was no less applicable to the
Army. As one article stressed:

It is only under the absolute leadership of the Party that our
Army can retain the character of being the people's army. If
we depart from the Party's leadership, Army building will slip on to
the evil road.[72]

Clearly, the Party was to regain control of the 'gun'. Or to be more

precise, the revamped civilian Party apparatus was to resume control of
the Army which had (in its absence) been exercised by Party personnel
within the Army.

Many analysts have argued that the fall of Lin Piao was due to his
opposing the subordination of the Army to the Party.[73] Evidence to
support this view is not hard to find. For example, according to
diplomatic sources in Peking, Mao, himself, told Mrs Bandaranaike and
Maurice Schumann (then Foreign Minister of France) that Lin had
opposed the rebuilding of the Party apparatus after the Cultural
Revolution.[74] There is also the circumstantial evidence that the delays
in rebuilding the Party closely corresponded with the period of Lin's
apparent dominance. That is, given that the Party was to be
reconstructed, there was a considerable time lag between the
launching of Party rebuilding before the Ninth Congress and the
formation of Party committees in all provinces in August 1971. Since
the Army was in control of administrative work during this period,
and since Lin Piao commanded the Army, it is not an unreasonable
hypothesis to assume that the apparent obstruction which Party
building encountered can be traced to Lin. The accusations levelled at
Lin that he was a 'bourgeois careerist', further bolster this view that
Lin wanted to maintain power based upon his leadership of the PLA and
the leading position of PLA in China, by opposing the re-establishment
of the Party.

Similarly, the numerous articles which stressed Party leadership
after the disappearance of Lin Piao,[75] imply that Lin had not
sufficiently observed such leadership. This accusation was made most
explicit in an article some twelve months after Lin's demise. It
criticised:

> . . . the crime of *swindlers of the Liu Shao-ch'i type* of making a
> vain attempt to alter the Party's line, *abolish Party leadership*
> and interfere with and sabotage our army's political work from the
> left and the right.[76]

Thus, there is both circumstantial evidence and direct charges aimed at
Lin which appear to form a compelling case for believing that his fall
was a direct result of his attempt to undermine the leadership of the
Party.

Close examination of the evidence, however, casts substantial
doubt upon this popular interpretation and provides equally plausible
alternative hypotheses as to the reasons for Lin Piao's fall. There is

simply no evidence to support the view that delays and difficulties in Party reconstruction were a result of the Army (deliberately or otherwise) sabotaging such work in order to maintain its pre-eminent position. On the contrary, all indications show that the Army was the major force in carrying out the tasks associated with rebuilding the Party and, as Young argues most forcefully, the delays and hindrances which bedevilled Party reconstruction were caused by factionalism. Rather than seeking to maintain its responsibility for administration and production, there are ample instances which show that the PLA (or at least substantial sections of it) had to be cajoled into continuing its 'three support' work.

To see Lin Piao's fall in terms of a Party versus Army debate in which Lin loses, moreover, is to make the mistake (outlined earlier) of seeing the Army and the Party as completely discrete entities. It must be remembered that Lin was not only a military figure, but also Vice-Chairman of the CCP. From this perspective, the accusation that Lin was a 'bourgeois careerist', need not imply that his 'careerism' took the form of wanting to maintain the Army as the leading ideological and organisational force and that he, therefore, opposed the rebuilding of the Party. On the contrary, it seems more probable that Lin's personal ambition took the form of ensuring that he maintained his leading position within the reconstructed Party, that he reinforced his control over the centralised leadership of the PLA, and that he attempted to buttress his claims as Mao's successor by becoming State Chairman. One searches in vain for any speech in which Lin proposed that the Army should replace the Party as the 'vanguard' of the Chinese revolution.

Likewise, articles stressing the need for Party leadership were evident both before and after Lin's disappearance, and can be seen as a result of Party rebuilding rather than being necessarily connected with Lin Piao. Their intensification after Lin's fall can be readily explained as the natural reassertion of Party leadership once Party committees had been re-established — a process which had been completed the month before Lin is alleged to have made his coup attempt. If Lin opposed the rebuilding of the Party apparatus, he showed a remarkably poor sense of timing by waiting until the Party organisation was already reconstructed to launch his coup attempt rather than acting a few years earlier when the process of rebuilding was just beginning.

The accusations in the Chinese media that Lin had attempted to 'abolish Party leadership' should also be regarded with a certain amount of caution. The charge is nowhere supported with any

evidence and can be seen in the same light as the charge of being
'anti-Party'. That is, it tends to be a blanket condemnation which covers
a multitude of (often unspecified) sins. It is a common practice in
China to heap criticisms on somebody who has been dismissed, which
are really directed at persons or tendencies which are currently being
opposed, and which may well be totally unrelated to the reasons for
the original dismissal. It seems probable that this was the case with
Lin Piao, and that criticisms claiming that he opposed Party leadership
were in fact directed at those mass factions ('ultra-leftists') which
were refusing to accept the leadership of a rebuilt Party which
included many rehabilitated cadres. Bearing in mind the numerous
(and often contradictory) charges which have been directed at Lin
since he disappeared, it is difficult to seize on any one of them as the
cause or the main cause of Lin's fall. For example, as well as the
accusation that Lin attempted to 'abolish Party leadership', he has
at various times been criticised for 'ultra-leftism', 'ultra-rightism',
opposing the new foreign policy line, having illicit relations with
foreign countries, being a follower of Confucius, sabotaging the militia,
opposing Chairman Mao's military line, regarding himself as being
above the masses, being a careerist and a conspirator, and opposing
the policy of sending educated youths to the countryside. Observers
have also attributed Lin's fall to his losing debates on matters of
economic policy,[77] to the possibility that he unsuccessfuly championed
the cause of developing intercontinental ballistic missiles rather than
intermediate range ballistic missiles which was related to a 'steel
versus electronics' debate,[78] to the possible impact which factions
within the Army may have played,[79] or to Lin losing in a power struggle
with Chou En-lai over the succession.[80] Without delving into this
plethora of charges and explanations, suffice it to say that there are
ample plausible hypotheses apart from the rather simplistic postulate
that Lin Piao's fall resulted from his opposing the rebuilding of the
Party in a Party versus Army debate.

The Return to Party Leadership and Reorganisation of the PLA

By 1972, the process of phasing out the Army from administration
and replacing it with the newly reconstructed Party was gaining
momentum, especially at the lower levels. Nevertheless, a number of
commentators continued to see China as under military domination
and argued that a reduction in the political role of the PLA was
unlikely.[81]

Chang, in particular, argued that the provinces were 'dominated by military personnel' who had acquired a 'substantial degree of political and economic autonomy vis-a-vis the central leadership.[82] This view was coupled with the assumption that 'strong regionalist overtones' would emerge[83] to suggest that something akin to a new warlord era was emerging in China. Such a view was founded on a number of misconceptions and represented a misreading of the events which had and were taking place in China. As has already been argued, Chang and Domes made the fundamental error of regarding the Party and the Army as totally separate entities and, therefore, saw an increase in military personnel in positions of leadership as proof of the eclipse of the Party and the rise of military rule. To reiterate, those military commanders who held positions of leadership were also Party members and their authority was based equally on their *Party* and their Army ties. Once the civilian Party organisation had been rebuilt, they stepped down and allowed it to resume its pre-Cultural Revolution role of leadership.

Since such analysts focused their attention on the composition of the élite in this way, they saw an increase in military dominance at the very time when the Army's political role was diminishing. Thus they found support for their view in statistics which showed that the percentage of PLA representation *increased* in the new Party committees (at provincial level) over the level of representation on the revolutionary committees.[84] At lower levels, however, the civilian Party apparatus was resuming leadership and this trend was to be reflected in the composition of the Chinese leadership at the Tenth Congress of the CCP. The Central Committee which was elected at this Congress (August 1973) had a significantly reduced 'military' component. In percentage terms, those identified as primarily military men dropped from 44 per cent to 32 per cent.[85] That is, the ratio between civilian and military members of the Party Central Committee was restored to approximately the same level as had existed prior to the Cultural Revolution.

The belief that renewed regionalism was a major outcome of the Cultural Revolution and that provinces had gained considerable autonomy from the central leadership, was likewise an incorrect interpretation of events. Regional military commanders were far from being able to assert their independence from the central leadership and rule in a warlord style. It is important to bear in mind the fact that there are substantial differences between military units. In particular, there is a significant difference between main force units, which are centrally controlled and can be deployed anywhere,

and regional forces which are garrisoned in a fixed region and initially
subject to regional commanders.[86] (The Wuhan incident during the
Cultural Revolution amply demonstrated how main force units could
be deployed to bring any recalcitrant regional commander to heel.)
Rather than evidencing a strengthening of regionalist tendencies,
the reorganisation of military personnel during the Cultural
Revolution demonstrated the power of central control. For example,
between 1966 and October 1970 out of twenty-nine provincial,
municipal and garrison commands, twenty-one of the commanders
were transferred.[87]

Given this, Bennett has correctly noted that a large proportion of
the new secretaries and deputy secretaries of provincial Party
committees, formed after the Cultural Revolution, were recruited from
outside that province.[88] This flatly contradicts the view that
provincial localism emerged with a vengeance as a result of the
Cultural Revolution. Moreover, the only regional unit which was
basically unaffected by central intervention during the Cultural
Revolution (Kwangchow) was greatly reorganised late in 1971.[89] (This
was, of course, due to the removal of close associates of Lin Piao.)
Bennett's conclusions which contradict the thesis that central
authority was weakening, were to be spectacularly reinforced by
events.

A news dispatch on New Year's day 1974 revealed the most extensive
military reorganisation in China since 1954. Except for the three
military regions of Chengtu, Kunming and Sinkiang, the commanders
of all the military regions[90] were reshuffled.[91] This transfer of
military commanders can be seen as a move designed to remove them
from possible bases of support, and to ensure that new power bases
were not formed. As such, it was a clear demonstration of central
Party control over the PLA and in particular of control over those
key commanders whom some commentators had seen as the 'new
warlords'. This major reorganisation of prominent PLA members,
furthermore, has seriously undercut Whitson's 'field army thesis'
which argued that the PLA was composed of loyalty networks based
on the five field armies of 1949 which had evolved a separate identity
maintained through their stable deployment since the Korean War.[92]
For Whitson, the central leadership generally attempted to maintain
a balance between former members of these field armies, and
conflicts among the leading military commanders could be explained
in terms of conflict between different loyalty-groups. Using this
framework, it is possible to see Lin Piao as having attempted to cement

his personal control over the central military command by appointing
people from his Fourth Field Army Group to the central Military
Affairs Committee. Despite its apparent usefulness as an explanatory
device, Whitson's 'field army thesis' has already been seriously
challenged by Parish.[93] If Whitson's thesis did once have considerable
validity, the transfer of military commanders from the regions in
which their field army had been stationed has reduced (or perhaps
destroyed) any impact which former field army connections may have
had.

Conclusion

The Chinese People's Liberation Army has always been more than
simply a fighting force. Almost from its inception, it has combined
its military functions with participation in economic tasks. Similarly,
it has been a highly politicised army and has played an active role in
political affairs at various times throughout its history. Moreover,
clear-cut deliniations between Army and Party members have
never been maintained as there have always been organisational
connections between the two. To talk blandly of a military takeover
in China as a product of the Cultural Revolution, as some analysts did,
simply ignored this tradition and the similarities with the situation
immediately after 1949. Nevertheless, during the Cultural Revolution,
the PLA did dramatically increase its involvement in political and
economic affairs to a level not seen since the early 1950s. Since this
level of involvement was sustained for a considerable period after
the Ninth Congress, some people were led to assume that such a level
would be a permanent feature of Chinese politics. As noted in the
Introduction to this book, there was even some speculation that the
Army might replace the Party as the 'vanguard' of the Chinese
revolution. Such views were mistaken. They were based on an
underestimation of the determination to rebuild the CCP so that it
could resume its leading role. There is no evidence to suggest that
this determination wavered at any time in the post-Cultural Revolution
period, but rather, that delays sustained in the process of re-establishing
the Party resulted from problems of overcoming factionalism.

   The role of the Army in the period between the Ninth and Tenth
Party Congresses indeed reflected such a sitution. There was a
gradual lessening in the involvement of the PLA in its administrative
tasks as it was replaced by the newly reformed Party committees. At
approximately the same time, there was a renewed emphasis on military
affairs and military training which also included greater attention to

militia work. The composition of the Central Committee elected at the
Tenth Congress mirrored the decline in 'military' representation in the
Chinese leadership towards the pre-Cultural Revolution levels.
Furthermore, if there were still any lingering doubts as to the Party
controlling the 'gun', the massive reorganisation of the PLA high
command at the end of 1973 dispelled them.

The most perplexing event of this period remains the disappearance
of Lin Piao. While he has been blamed for any failings in the
orientation and performance of the PLA, it is difficult to determine
which of the many criticisms may be concretely substantiated. It
seems most likely that he has been used to symbolise those policies
and tendencies which the Party leadership was attempting to correct.
Suffice it to say that the most common interpretation of Lin's fall (in
terms of his opposition to rebuilding the Party), is based on particularly
thin circumstantial evidence and needs to be seriously questioned. Yet,
if questions on the role of individual personalities remain hard to
fathom, policy orientations which are far more significant can more
easily be discovered. In this regard, the overall trend in this period
for the Army to withdraw from its 'three-support' work and to
concentrate on military training as its predominant concern, was
unmistakable.

Notes

1. See Gittings 1967, pp. 176-201.
2. E.g. Wilson 1971; Nelsen 1972; Nelsen 1974; Domes 1970.
3. See Robinson (in *CQ*), 1971.
4. See Klein and Hager 1971, p.53 and Domes (in Wilson) 1973, p.9.
5. Sims 1969, p.26.
6. Klein and Hager 1971, p.52; Domes (in Wilson) 1973, p.9; Chu 1971,
   p.865 *et. seq.*
7. Sims 1969, p.26; *PR* 18, 30 April 1969, p.36.
8. Ibid., p.31.
9. Domes (in Wilson) 1973, p.18 *et.seq.*
10. See pp.40-42.
11. Powell 1970, p.444.
12. Ibid., p.471.
13. Lin Piao, *Hongqi* 5, 1969, p.19, (*PR* 18, 30 April 1969, p.25)
14. *SWB,* FE/3048.
15. *SWB*, FE/3041/B1/1.
16. *SWB*, FE/3041/B1/14.
17. *SWB*, FE/3041/B/2.
18. *RMRB*, 24 May 1969, in *SCMP* 4429, p.1 *et.seq.*
19. *SWB*, FE/3045/B1/3 (emphasis added).
20. Ibid. (emphasis added).
21. E.g. *RMRB,* 13 June 1969, in *SCMP* 4446, p.3.

22. Ibid.
23. See pp.52-56.
24. CCP CC, 23 July 1969, in *Issues and Studies,* Vol.6, No.1, October 1969, pp.97-100.
25. Ibid (emphasis added).
26. Ibid.
27. *SWB* FE/3044/B1/2.
28. *SWB* FE/3091.
29. I.e. 'good in political ideology', 'good in military technique', 'good in the three-eight working style', 'good in carrying out assigned tasks' and 'good in physical training'.
30. E.g. *SWB*, FE/3470/B11/13.
31. For a typical example see *SWB*, FE/3474/B11/5.
32. *SWB*, FE/3079/B11/3.
33. *RMRB*, 2 August 1969, in *SCMP* 4478, p.5 (emphasis added).
34. *SWB*, FE/3175, (emphasis added).
35. Ibid.
36. *PR* 51-2, 26 December 1969, p.8.
37. *PR* 6, 6 February 1970, pp.7-9.
38. See e.g. Van Ginnekan 1976; Kau and Perolle 1974; Burchett 1973; Birdgham 1973; O'Leary 1974.
39. *Zhongfa* 1972/12, in *Issues and Studies,* Vol.8, No.12 (September 1972) p.67.
40. Ibid.
41. *Issues and Studies,* Vol.8, No.8 (May 1972).p.78.
42. Kau and Perolle, 1974, p.561.
43. Parish 1973, pp.691-2.
44. *GMRB*, 8 August 1970, in *SCMP* 4720, p.32.
45. *SWB*, FE/3505/B/5.
46. Ibid.
47. *RMRB*, 9 October 1970, in *SCMP* 4760, pp.1-6.
48. *SWB*, FE/3526/B11/3.
49. *SWB*, FE/3513/B11/7.
50. *SWB*, FE/3526/B11/3.
51. *SWB*, FE/3489/B11/15.
52. *SWB*, FE/3495/B11/11.
53. Ibid.
54. E.g. *SWB*, FE/3498/B11/3; *SWB*, FE/3498/B11/5
55. See Burchett 1973, p.22; Chou En-lai, in PFLP 1973, p.6.
56. Joffe 1973, p.477.
57. *Current Scene,* Vol.10, No.3, pp.17-18.
58. *RMRB*, 2 January 1972, in *SCMP* 5054, p.201.
59. *GMRB*, 7 January 1972, in *SCMP* 5060, p.1.
60. *Zhongfa* 1972/12, in *Issues and Studies,* Vol.8, No.12, September 1972 p.70.
61. Mao Tsetung, *SW* English edition, Vol.4, p.155.
62. Ibid.
63. See e.g. *RMRB*, 29 July 1972, in *SCMP* 5192, pp.92-5.
64. *Hongqi* 5, 1972, p.32, trans. in *Chinese Law and Government,* Vol.5, No.3-4.
65. *Zhongfa* 1972/12, in *Chinese Law and Government,* Vol.5, No.3-4. (This translation is slightly different from that in *Issues and Studies,* Vol.8, No.12).
66. *Hongqi* 5, 1972, p.34.
67. See *SCMP* 5107, p.100.
68. *Hongqi* 5, 1972, p.32.
69. *RMRB*, 19 July 1972, in *SCMP* 5187, p.97.
70. *RMRB*, 3 August 1972, in *SCMP* 5194, p.9.

71. See pp.52-56.
72. *GMRB,* 15 July 1972, in *SCMP* 5183, p.120.
73. E.g. Bridgham 1973, p.428; Powell 1972, p.102.
74. *CQ* 52, 1972, p.768.
75. E.g. *RMRB,* 1 December 1971, trans. *PR* 50, 10 December 1971, pp.4-5.
76. *GMRB,* 8 October 1972, in *SCMP* 5240, p.6 (emphasis added).
77. Goodstadt, *FEER* 48, 27 November 1971, *passim.*
78. Goodstadt, *FEER* 40, 2 October 1971, *passim.*
79. Parish 1973, *passim.*
80. Hinton 1973, p.201.
81. Notably Chang 1972, pp.1012-3.
82. Ibid., p.1007.
83. Domes (in Wilson) 1973, p.20.
84. Ibid. p.11; Joffe 1973, p.466.
85. Robinson 1974, p.3.
86. Nelsen (in *CQ*) 1972, p.444 *et.seq.*
87. Chu 1971.
88. Bennett 1973, p.294.
89. Ibid.
90. The military regions are outlined in Waller 1970, pp.116-17.
91. For a full list of the changes, see Hsu 1974
92. Whitson 1969.
93. Parish 1973, p.695 *et.seq.*

3 REVOLUTION IN HIGHER EDUCATION

Sylvia Chan

For Mao Tsetung, man was the determining factor in the development of history;[1] consequently, culture and education were of crucial importance. The Introduction to this book dwelt upon the political significance of cultural developments. It suggested that Mao emphasised the active role of culture and rejected the view that it was a mere reflection of productive forces.[2] The active dimension of culture is, of course, education. Thus, if we take culture in the widest sense to include the whole realm of human thought, then education consists of every activity which establishes the ideological preconditions for socialist transition. Although the focus in this chapter is confined to revolution in the sphere of formal higher education, it will make sense only in the above context.

The Roots of Factionalism

Earlier discussions in this book suggested why the Cultural Revolution started in the field of higher education and we may easily understand the symbolic importance of the early struggles at Peking University[3] — the humanities departments of which enjoyed considerable prestige throughout China. We saw also that the sheer complexity of the struggles in the field of education made it extremely difficult to fit the innumerable currents and counter-currents neatly into the pattern of 'struggle between two lines'.[4]

No generalisation of such a complex picture may be wholly satisfactory. It is clear, however, that factions in universities and colleges were closely associated with divisions in the Party centre and in the Army.[5] Recognising their importance, both Mao's supporters and enemies vied for the support of university students and staff. But such was not the main cause of the splits within the student movement, for once someone was officially denounced as an opponent of Mao, even student organisations disposed to be sympathetic to him promptly changed sides and joined in the denunciation. In fact, over major issues which clearly involved 'the struggle between two lines' (such as the denunciation of T'an Chen-lin and the 'February Adverse Current',[6] the downfall of Ch'i Pen-Yu[7] and the condemnation of Yang Ch'eng-wu[8]), nearly all Red Guard organisations acted in perfect accord. What then were the main causes of the splits?

It must be remembered that the 'rebels' were themselves products of the old education system, now known as the educational 'black line'. As such, they displayed all the inherent weaknesses of the old intellegentsia which the former system had inculcated within them or at least failed to obliterate. Egotism, personal careerism, discrepancies between word and deed — in fact all those faults which they denounced in others as anti-social and counter-revolutionary and for which they professed the utmost contempt — were all part of their own intellectual make-up. This cultural heritage, which they could not shake off even in a battle supposedly waged against that heritage, finally bogged them down in the quagmire of unprincipled fighting for self-interest and rendered them totally unequal to the task of leading that battle. In their tragic failure, one finds a most eloquent indictment of the old education system — that it had hopelessly fallen short of bringing up a generation of new socialist people.

Perhaps no-one was more disappointed at such an outcome than Mao himself. He had evidently been confident that the rebel students could 'educate themselves' and carry out the Cultural Revolution in universities and colleges without outside interference.[9] In March 1967, however, when the factional war among students had already reduced higher educational institutions to chaos, he decided to move in the PLA to help reopen the schools, re-adjust school organisation, set up leadership bodies according to the 'three in one' alliance and carry out 'struggle, criticism and transformation'.[10] In May of that same year, a disillusioned Mao confided to an Albanian military delegation: 'Originally I intended to foster [the development of] some successors [to the revolution] from among the intellectuals, but now it seems [the results] are far from ideal'.[11] He then concluded: 'The broad masses of workers, peasants and soldiers who are the masters of our age, have to be relied on as the main force to carry out a thorough revolution . . .'[12]

Fifteen months later, when an increasing number of casualties had resulted from the faction fighting, the first workers' and PLA Mao Tsetung Thought propaganda team moved into Tsinghua University.[13] In a matter of days, such teams took control of most universities and colleges throughout the country.

Working Class Leadership

The entry of propaganda teams into universities and colleges marked the end of more than two years of chaos and the beginning of serious efforts to make a lasting revolution in higher education. Mao's action should not be seen merely as an expedient to restore order but as a long term strategy to establish working class leadership over higher education and eventually over what (in Marxist terms) was viewed as the whole ideological superstructure. Its aim was no less than the termination of 'bourgeois' domination over education, be it that of 'persons in authority taking the capitalist road' or Red Guard recalcitrants.

> In carrying out the proletarian revolution in education, it is essential to have working class leadership . . . The workers' propaganda teams should stay permanently in the schools and take part in fulfilling all the tasks of struggle-criticism-transformation within them: they will [moreover] always lead the schools.[14]

Nevertheless, the initial propaganda teams were to some extent inadequate. They lacked experience in university administration and could not replace the teachers as transmitters of knowledge. Thus, their effectiveness hinged on how successfully they won the voluntary acceptance and co-operation of the former administrators and academic personnel. Most of these latter had been pushed aside as 'capitalist roaders', or 'reactionary academic authorities' and were passively awaiting dismissal. An immediate task of the propaganda teams, therefore, after forging the student factions into 'big alliances', was to rehabilitate suitable cadres and teachers. This was the process known as 'purifying the class ranks' which has been discussed in Young's article above.[15] It required that teams sort people out into four categories:[16]
1. the 'good'
2. the 'comparatively good'
3. those who had made serious mistakes but had not degenerated into the fourth category
4. 'anti-Party anti-socialist rightists.'
Of these four categories, the first three might be re-employed after suitable re-education. To facilitate this programme of 'purifying the class ranks' and re-education, personal files and work records of many of the cadres and teachers were subjected to close investigation. Such people often underwent 'mass struggle and criticism sessions' (organised under the aegis of Mao Tsetung Thought study classes). They were also required to 'contrast the bitterness of the past with present day happiness' and 'recall revolutionary

traditions', the most important of which was participation in productive manual labour. Thus, the year 1969 witnessed a large scale exodus of university students and staff to factories and rural areas to be 're-educated by the workers, peasants and soldiers'. It saw also a mushrooming of university-run 'May Seventh Cadre Schools' all over China.

'Struggle-Criticism-Transformation' (1968-71)

Although most universities and colleges did not undertake full-scale admission of new students until the autumn of 1970,[17] many of them had admitted small numbers of students on a trial basis since late 1967.[18] It was these students, under the leadership of workers' and PLA propaganda teams who, together with university staff, brought the educational revolution to a 'high tide' in the years 1969-71. This 'high-tide', which surpassed in scope the earlier 'high tide' of 1958, saw bold innovations and experiments in the system of admission, curricula, methods of teaching and assessment and, most important of all, in fostering attitudinal change on the part of students and staff themselves. Throughout this period of experimentation, there seemed to be an absence of any concrete instructions from above which might act as a curb on the creativity of the masses. They seemed to be guided by nothing more than Mao Tsetung's ideas on educational revolution, neatly summed up in point ten of the sixteen point 'Decision of the Central Committee of the CCP Concerning the Great Proletarian Cultural Revolution'.

1. Admissions Policy

The sixteen point 'Decision' stipulated that the primary task of the educational revolution was to end the 'bourgeois domination over schools'. As has been noted, this was partly achieved by stationing workers and PLA propaganda teams in universities and colleges, by the movement to 'purify the class ranks' and by the subsequent establishment of new leading bodies composed of a triple combination of workers, former cadres and staff-student representatives. Since the majority of people who made up a university were students, however, the nature of leadership depended directly upon the composition of the student body. One article in the CCP Central Committee journal *Red Flag* went so far as to declare: 'The focal point of the struggle between the two classes and the two lines in schools manifests itself first of all in the system of enrolment'.[19] It was, after all, the question of enrolment which provided the first focus of attack on the old education system back in 1966. At that time, a group of students at Peking No.1 Girls Secondary School maintained that the system of admission to higher educational institutions was 'a tool for cultivating new bourgeois elements and revisionists'. It 'shut out large numbers of outstanding children of workers, peasants and revolutionary cadres' by laying undue stress on book learning and judging a student only by the marks he or she scored in the entrance examination.[20] This was to be one of the recurrent themes of criticism in the subsequent Cultural Revolution and statistics show how well grounded the complaints were. During the 1958 'high tide', when universities and colleges were supposed to throw open their doors to workers and peasants, the proportion of students from worker-peasant backgrounds was only some 48 per cent [21] This rose slightly to 54 per cent in 1963[22] but, since workers and peasants constituted some 80 per cent of the total population and since it was they who shouldered the bulk of expenditure on education, the injustice was all too apparent. In 1969, this injustice was dramatised by a group of disgruntled poor and lower-middle peasants, who wrote:

> Our Tungsheng People's Commune is located in the western suburbs of Peking. Within the confines of our commune there are fourteen universities and colleges. In the past ten or more years, we set aside close to 1,000 *mu* (67 ha.) of fertile land for the construction of these schools . . . Our great saviour Chairman Mao wanted to send the sons and daughters of us poor and lower middle peasants to universities for training. We were filled with joy as we saw one university built after another. Since liberation, however, ten of the sons and daughters of the poor and lower middle peasants have sat for and passed the university entrance examination, but under the persecution of the counter-revolutionary revisionist line in education, they were forced to leave school one after another.[23]

Another article complained that, in one village, three of the four university students were children of landlords and none was from a poor or lower middle peasant family.[24]

The new post-Cultural Revolution admissions policy reversed the previous situation by giving priority to workers, peasants and soldiers, in line with Mao's instruction that 'students should be selected from among workers and peasants with practical experience'.[25] In theory, each applicant was to have graduated from junior secondary school and was not to be above the age of twenty. But, in practice, a new requirement that no student was to go directly from secondary school to university until he or she had taken part in productive labour for about three years, meant that the application of pre-requisites was flexible — the more so when veteran workers and peasants were considered.[26]

The actual process of recruitment now involved four procedures:
1. application by the worker, peasant or soldier
2. 'recommendation by the masses': (these were in fact the applicant's workmates who were required to make an assessment of his or her socio-political attitude as shown in productive labour, political study and life style)
3. approval of the 'leadership' (of the applicant's commune, factory or military unit)
4. approval of the university or college

This new policy of recruitment was adopted not only out of consideration for distributive justice but aimed to recruit politically reliable students whose duty was not just to study but to assist in the 'management and transformation' of the institutions themselves.[27]

The numerical superiority of workers, peasants and soldiers in the student body did not in itself guarantee the predominance of proletarian values. There was always the danger that such values might become corroded where the gap in living standards between town and country and between mental and manual labour remained wide; the more so in a country where, for two thousand years since the days of Confucius, education had been associated with élitism.[28] Perhaps the danger was most acute amongst those students who assumed that their worker, peasant or soldier origin was a sure guarantee of political soundness and saw no further need for ideological remoulding. Such was the theme of many articles which appeared in the press after the Cultural Revolution, pointing out that higher education was still a hotbed of bourgeois intellectual fallacies such as 'priority should be given to professional learning', 'the purpose of study is to become officials' and 'mental labour is superior to manual labour'. Negative examples were cited of worker-peasant-soldier students who had fallen prey to such views and who were ashamed of the consequences of their origin. One report, for example, told of a peasant student in Amoy University who had been presented with a pair of straw sandals by his fellow labourers as a memento of his class origin. Once at the university, however, he discarded them so as to avoid giving the appearance of a rustic.[29] Another report described how a group of students of foreign languages in Liaoning University succumbed to the notion of the superiority of professional learning and were struck with awe at the erudition of a teacher who uncritically taught 'bourgeois' material.[30] In such situations, the political education of worker-peasant-soldier students was seen as imperative.

2. The Examination System

It is not at all clear whether entrance examinations played a part in the full-scale enrolment of students in 1970, though we can be sure that veteran workers and peasants who had never been to secondary school (or who had attended in the distant past) were not usually required to sit an examination. There is, moreover, no evidence that a candidate 'recommended by the masses' and approved by the leadership of his work place was ever refused entry to a university solely on the grounds that he or she had failed the entrance examination.

It was evident by 1970, therefore, that whatever new examinations might be introduced, great care was to be exercised to see that they did not undermine the new class-based criteria for university enrolment. As for the examinations themselves, people were undoubtedly mindful of Mao's 1964 indictment of current procedures:

> Our present method of conducting examinations is a method for dealing with the enemy, not a method of dealing with the people: It is a method of surprise attack, asking oblique or strange questions. This is still the same method as the old eight-legged essays. I do not approve of this.[31]

Mao's remedy was quite original:

> I am in favour of publishing the questions in advance and letting the students study them and answer them with the aid of books. For instance, if one sets twenty questions on *The Dream of the Red Chamber*[32] and some students answer half of them and answer them well, and some of the answers are very good and contain creative ideas, then one can give them 100%. If some other students answer all twenty questions correctly, but answer them simply by reciting from their textbooks and lectures, without any creative ideas, they should be given 50% and 60%. At examinations, whispering into each others ears and taking other people's places ought to be allowed. If your answer is good and I copy it, then mine should be counted as good. Whispering in other people's ears and taking examinations in other people's names used to be done secretly. Let it now be done openly.[33]

It is interesting to see how this suggestion was implemented. The Educational Revolution Group of the South China Normal (Teachers') College, for example, held an examination in electrical science. It consisted of four questions on the most basic knowledge which were communicated to the students in advance. The papers were collected and then marked in the presence of students who usually performed inadequately. As marking proceded, the students were told of their mistakes and allowed to correct them.[34] We do not know whether they were allowed to consult books during the examination or to discuss and copy each others' answers but, at least, we may conclude that the South China example was an attempt to combine teaching and assessment and was a considerable advance on the old method of screening.

Examinations were, wherever possible, to test not only knowledge but initiative and creativity. The Welding Specialty of Tsinghua University, for example, developed a new form of examination whereby groups of six or seven students were sent into a factory to work on a particular product. Instead of conducting the examination indoors with modern equipment, the leadership and some skilled workers from the factory (the examiners) asked each group of students to assemble and weld two of the factory's normal products in the open air without modern equipment. At the end of the two-day examination, it was said that all the students' products met the factory specifications.[35]

3. Curriculum and Teaching Materials

We have noted already the continued importance of the CCP Central Committee's sixteen point 'Decision' of 1966 in the educational reforms which followed the Cultural Revolution. The document specified that:

> The period of schooling should be shortened. Courses should be fewer and better. The teaching material should be thoroughly transformed, in some cases beginning with simplifying complicated material. While their main task is to study, students should also learn other things. That is to say, in addition to their studies they should also learn industrial work, farming and military affairs, and take part in the struggles of the Cultural Revolution, to criticise the bourgeoisie as these struggles occur.[36]

There can be no doubt that shortening the period of schooling served the purpose of economising on national resources — so necessary in any developing country.[37] Such, however, should not be seen as the sole or even primary purpose. Mao, who always expressed contempt for intellectuals divorced from production,[38] could not but acknowledge that formal education, however reformed, requires a certain detachment from at least the first two of the three major activities necessary 'to guarantee that communists will be free from bureaucratism and immune against revisionism and dogmatism and will for ever remain invincible.'[39] These three activities were class struggle, the struggle for production and scientific experiment. In Mao's view, a long period of schooling, in cutting the student off from the above two major struggles, can only advance the process of bureaucratism and make the student susceptible to the virus of 'revisionism and dogmatism'.

Shortening the period of schooling naturally entailed a criticism of existing curricula and teaching materials and their simplification. Many believed that old curricula comprising some twenty to thirty courses and old teaching materials running to several hundred pages had served merely to flaunt the knowledge of 'bourgeois intellectuals' and to intimidate the less educated workers and peasants. Curricula and teaching materials, it was felt, should not exist to maintain the monopoly of such intellectuals. A much approved professorial self-criticism succinctly noted:

> I write (textbooks) not to serve the people but to display my talents and demonstrate my learning. I used all those formulas and those foreign quotes to inspire admiration, to show how able I was. Simple problems that could be explained with a few well chosen sentences, I made complex. An able worker who had made a number of inventions lost confidence in himself after he heard me explain Ohm's Law. He felt he could never understand electricity.[40]

In the above spirit, the simplification of courses and teaching materials after 1969 sometimes achieved outstanding results. One college of agriculture was reported to have reduced its former twenty-nine courses to six[41] and a college of engineering its thirty to seven.[42] Another report told of a 370,000 word textbook reduced to one ninth its original length.[43]

4. Theory Linked with Practice: Education Combined with Productive Labour

The policy of linking theory with practice and education with

productive labour had been one of the basic policies of the CCP
since Yenan days[44] but, after the nation-wide victory of the Party
in 1949, it had been perhaps more honoured in the breach
than in the observance. After a brief re-affirmation during the
educational revolution of 1958,[45] it was not until 1969 that the
policy was implemented in anything like a thorough-going
way.

The concept 'open door' was applied to many fields in the period
after 1969. In an earlier chapter, Young described the application of the
concept to Party building. In this chapter we have seen how it applied
to university admissions policy. The same principle applied also to the
process of learning itself.

Teaching and learning were no longer to be confined to the class-
room but were to be integrated with agricultural and industrial
production. Thus, colleges of science and engineering set up factories
and agricultural colleges ran farms. At the same time, universities might
make permanent arrangements for teachers and students to teach
and labour in the regular factories and agricultural production brigades
and for technicians and veteran workers and peasants to lecture in
the universities.

Perhaps the most remarkable example of such integration was that of
T'ungchi University, one of Shanghai's most famous universities
which specialised in civil engineering. In October 1967, this university
in collaboration with the Shanghai Civil Engineering Bureau and the
municipal Civil Engineering Design Board, established a 'May Seventh
Commune'. Here, the teaching programme was integrated with the
participation of students and staff in regular design and construction
work, with workers and design technicians supplementing the role
of university teachers. The challenge of actual concrete production
tasks, it was felt, acted as a powerful motivating force for students to
study technology.[46]

The importance of the T'ungchi example is, of course, much wider
than the area of motivation. It is a basic principle of pedagogy in any
society (of whatever political persuasion) that theories become more
readily understood once they are made concrete and tangible. This is
particularly the case when students come from worker, peasant or
soldier backgrounds with experience which is more practical than
theoretical. Thus, for example, it was no longer sufficient to demonstrate
the liquid pressure in the oil groove of a shaping machine solely by
a bewildering display of multi-coloured lines; students had to be
confronted with the machine itself in the factory.[47] Neither was it

sufficient to discuss the diagnosis and treatment of diseases solely with reference to diagrams; students had to examine patients.

The integration of theory and practice in the field of medicine meant much more than early confrontation of students and patients. Even before 1958, medical colleges (especially the larger ones) frequently ran out-patient clinics and, in the cities, there was a long tradition of community service. What is significant about the post-Cultural Revolution reforms in this area lay not in the extension of this system (for the urban medical network remained as before), but in the creation of a new *rural-oriented* network. In increasing numbers, students and staff of medical colleges were sent to the countryside to staff local hospitals and to join permanent or itinerant medical teams in the villages.[48]

The extension of the medical network into the villages was accompanied by a rediscovery of the values of traditional Chinese medicine. Medical colleges began to combine Western medicine with the traditional Chinese concern for acupuncture and herbalist remedies.[49] This was part of a much wider process which began with the repudiation of teaching materials containing much that was copied mechanically from foreign countries without reference to either the Chinese tradition or particular Chinese conditions. At best, the foreign material was too narrow (as in the case of medicine). At worst it was inapplicable. Textbooks from the Rail Transport Department of the Tangshan Railway College before the Cultural Revolution, for example, were said to be all geared to a system where rail traffic runs to the right whereas in China rail traffic runs to the left.[50]

What was objected to was not just the narrowness or inapplicability of foreign models but the mood they instilled in students. An aversion to things Chinese and a blind faith in foreign technique killed that initiative and independence of mind which Mao considered to be one of the most valuable assets of a revolutionary.[51] Such independence, was in fact the key to his own success in leading the Chinese revolution[52] and it is not surprising, therefore, that a recurrent theme of the educational revolution was a repudiation of the 'mentality of a foreign slave'[53] and the demand that the content of teaching be specifically adapted to Chinese conditions. The basic assumption was that Chinese methods were often better in solving Chinese problems than those derived from abroad, and that the collective wisdom of a long and continuous civilisation must be tapped. Such was the basis of the new approach to medicine, but it applied to all fields of endeavour. Agricultural colleges, for example, incorporated indigenous farming traditions. In feeding pigs, the new teaching material recognised the time-honoured practice of using native yeasts to promote growth[54] and peasant experiments with plant hybridisation were given an honoured place.[55] Even in advanced fields of technology, some Western theories were rejected in the light of new experience. In Shanghai, for example, the Synthetic Board Works disproved the theory that single-phase, half-wave rectifiers could not be used in engineering work because of their great wave motion by successfully building an automatic feeding machine which did, in fact, utilise the great-wave motion of such rectifiers.[56] Proudly, such discoveries were incorporated into the new teaching materials.

The pedagogical and economic value of combining theory with practice and education with productive labour will be quite apparent. But no discussion of this policy can rest with a consideration of immediate utility. As Marx saw it, education in communist society is 'an education that will, in the case of every child over a given age, combine productive labour with instruction and gymnastics, not only as one of the methods of adding to the efficiency of production but as the only method of producing fully developed human beings'.[57] For Mao, the fully developed human being is the 'cultured socialist-minded labourer'[58] well trained certainly, but above all loyal to the socialist cause and labouring people.

Disdain for manual labour and contempt for the labouring people has been a general feature among intellectuals everywhere. In Confucian China this probably reached an extreme and even the young Mao was affected.[59] If China is to preserve its socialist identity, therefore, no effort must be spared to create a new generation dedicated to serving the workers and peasants – the main prop of state power. Furthermore, as the contributors to this book have remarked time and again, that generation must also be dedicated to the eradication of the 'three major differences' which contradict socialist egalitarian ideals – the differences between worker and peasant, between town and country and between mental and manual labour.

Mao, we have observed, held that it is precisely by participation in collective productive labour that cadres might 'overcome bureaucratism and prevent revisionism and dogmatism' – the current vices of the Soviet|leadership.[60] Social productive labour, of necessity collective in a socialist country, served to check the individualist tendency inherent in mental work. Moreover, by working closely with the labouring masses, the intellectual would be sensitive to their needs, problems, thoughts and feelings. 'Serving the people' would no longer be an abstract idea but a concrete challenge. Thus the ideologically reformative value inherent in social productive labour was the moral basis of social integration.

Given the above principle, it is not surprising that students and staff were often assigned what had formally been considered to be the most menial kind of labour. Students of civil engineering, for instance, began their education by digging earth[61] and students in the machine building industry were made to cut metal rods.[62] One might sympathise with those students who complained that they could 'learn nothing by doing such coolie work',[63] but only the most malicious would argue that it was a way to exploit cheap labour. Yet, however much we might sympathise with students' complaints, the purpose was very clear. In the words of one worker: 'We ask you to dig up earth in order to cultivate within you the feeling of the working people and to help you criticise the doctrine of going to school in order to become officials'.[64]

5. Education in the Humanities

As might be expected, the principle of combining education with productive labour and theory with practice was more easily implemented in agriculture, medicine and the natural sciences than in the humanities and press comment leaves us with the impression that it was in the former fields that reform was most thorough. Such had been the case even before the Cultural Revolution, as Mao remarked in 1964:

> Generally speaking, the intellectuals specialising in engineering are better, because they are in touch with reality. Scientists, pure scientists, are worse, but they are still better than those who specialise in arts subjects'.[65]

Later in 1968, in his famous directive to the effect that colleges were still necessary, he cautiously avoided mentioning the humanities: 'I am mainly saying that colleges of science and engineering should be run'.[66] Commenting on the directive a few days later he was more explicit:

> I deliberately worded my talk in such a way as to leave ample room for flexible interpretation. I said colleges of science and engineering should still be run. I didn't say liberal arts colleges should not be run. [But] if you can't make a success of them, why not just leave them alone.[67]

Despite Mao's reservations, a number of humanities departments in the universities did, in fact, reopen after the Cultural Revolution with Mao's works as basic teaching material. Quite clearly, Mao's works were chosen because they provided guidance in how to understand the old society and how to handle contemporary problems. One cannot but suspect, however, that sometimes teachers opted for Mao's works out of reluctance to put forward their own views after the criticisms of the Cultural Revoluton, especially since much of the teaching material used in humanities departments had been severely denounced as anti-Marxist.

In addition to their role in providing teaching material, the works of Mao played a major role in the general criticism of bourgeois thought which continued in humanities departments with undiminished intensity. This criticism was carried on under the slogan 'destruction takes precedence over construction'. The study of Mao Tsetung Thought was held to be inseparable from class struggle[68] which, in the context of humanities departments, meant continuing with the, as yet inadequate, denunciation of 'Liuist' economic theories and policies, 'bourgeois' theories in literature and art and erroneous works of historiography. It was felt that the danger of the imminent revival of these theories was ever present.[69]

As for the 'workshops' to which humanities students might be sent, Mao designated nothing short of the 'whole of society'.[70] Consequently, students and staff went far and wide to factories and communes to be re-educated by workers and peasants, to run courses for them and to carry out social surveys. One university, for example, set students and staff the task of carrying out an investigation in a particular factory which had been the setting of a pre-1949 account written by a 'reactionary writer' about the life of contracted female workers.[71] Another organised a history course, within an agricultural production brigade, to provide background material for cadres' study of Mao's essay 'The Chinese Revolution and the Chinese Communist Party'.[72]

In these endeavours, the humanities students and staff claimed success. Those peasant cadres who attended the history course declared that they had learned 'the glorious tradition of the Chinese people's revolutionary struggle' and understood that 'it was the peasants' uprisings that constituted the real motive force of historical development'.[73]   A student of literature wrote a 'most convincing' account of the heroic deeds of an old peasant, in refutation of a 'reactionary writer' who had distorted the image of the peasantry.[74]

A group of worker-students in a workshop, long beset with unsolved problems, 'made living study and application of Chairman Mao's viewpoint concerning classes and class struggle', wrote an article 'On Class Struggle in the Workshop', located the key to those problems and brought about general improvements.[75] Granted all the reports are true, one is still left wondering whether that particular student of literature could not have written an article just as convincing had he lived and worked in the countryside long enough to know the peasants well without ever going to university. One is not at all sure in what particular way the study of the humanities helped the workers of that hapless workshop in their 'living study and application' of Mao Tsetung Thought; after all, this is what the Chinese press claimed many workers and peasants had been doing all the time without the benefit of a higher education – and with no less impressive results.

6. Worker-Peasant-Soldier Teachers

The educational revolution of 1969-71 involved students in university administration to an unprecedented degree. Yet it cannot be denied that reforms in the content of teaching and in general attitudes towards education depended primarily upon the teachers. Insisting on this is not making concessions to Confucian or 'bourgeois' notions that the role of the teacher is central or that he deserves respect solely because of his institutional position. In fact, when Mao remarked that 'the problem of educational reform is primarily a problem of teachers',[76] he might merely have meant that most teachers, as intellectuals with 'bourgeois tendencies', could constitute the most formidable obstacle to the educational revolution unless they were effectively reformed.

Reports as to the effectiveness of attempts to reform the teaching staff in higher education varied in tone. Sometimes, it was claimed that the ideological regeneration of intellectuals resulted in more effective professional work. Students and teachers of medical colleges, for example, were said to have discovered effective indigenous cures after working with peasants and realising how badly the peasants needed them.[77] At other times, it appeared that the morale of teachers was low. This was particularly the case with teachers in the humanities who felt that they should quit the profession in order to avoid future criticism.[78] On still other occasions, teachers were said to be so steeped in the values of the old system that they could do little else but embark once again on the well-worn path.[79]

Though most intellectuals agreed on the need for reform, they did not manifest the same degree of support for the many and varied

proposals that were put forward. There was no consensus on the extent
to which courses might be cut and the degree to which students and
staff should participate in manual labour. Such 'dissensus' was undoubtedly
a curb on enthusiasm and new formulae had to be |adopted to remedy
the situation. One such widely adopted formula, was the 'three thirds'
system whereby one third of the original university teachers was sent
to be re-educated in the communes and factories, one third was
assigned jointly to manual labour and scientific research (or, in the
case of the humanities, social research) whilst the remaining third
undertook normal teaching duties. By rotating these 'thirds', it was
hoped that most would be remoulded to various degrees through the
baptism of the 'three struggles'.[80]

It was evident that the above reforms would take a considerable
amount of time and Mao was fully aware that effective changes would
not be brought about by 'a few lessons and a few meetings'.[81] To speed
up the whole process, therefore, new blood had to be infused into the
education system in the form of worker-peasant-soldier teachers. Though
a few of these new teachers were employed full-time, the majority were
released from factories and communes on a part-time basis. Their
functions were twofold. First, they were required to assist the
re-education of students and teachers by undertaking classes in politics.
This was usually done by the new teacher recounting his own sufferings
in the past and relating those experiences to 'the history of class
struggle and the struggle between the two lines'. Secondly, the new
teachers were to ensure that technical training was not divorced from
'the correct political orientation'. At Tsinghua University, for example,
the worker-teachers initiated criticism of a new programme of
mechanical engineering which was felt to isolate theory from practical
experience.[82]

Both of the above functions should be seen in the context of the
political but one should not assume that these new teachers, rich in
practical experience, had nothing to offer in the way of technical
training. Indeed, they proved themselves particularly invaluable in
the fields of agricultural science and engineering. A forge-hand, for
example, was cited as providing guidance in the writing of text books on
forging and stamping technology.[83] The job of these new teachers,
however, was to complement rather than replace the theoretical
training of the more professional teachers, the more easily to forge a
new unified teaching staff.[84]

Twists and Turns 1971-3: 'Red' Versus 'Expert'

By 1971, higher education in China had experienced its most radical changes since 1949. Following the collapse of the old Ministry of Higher Education and the major reorganisation of the power structure in most tertiary institutions, it seemed that Mao's blueprint for educational reform had been unanimously endorsed by the Party leadership at all levels.

Such a harmonious picture, however, soon proved to be deceptive. Following the alleged coup attempt by Lin Piao and his followers in September 1971, policies in almost every field were subjected to re-evaluation. Subsequent chapters in this book, which deal with the economy, will discuss the most important of these and we shall see that items previously hailed as 'socialist new things' were occasionally criticised as ultra-leftist and attributed to Lin Piao. The educational revolution of 1969-71 was, of course, no exception to this trend and it soon became apparent that opinions were divided both at the centre and at the grass-roots.

Central to this controversy was the perennial issue of how to combine 'redness' and 'expertise', or more specifically the relationship between politics and academic study. One group of leaders, headed by Premier Chou En-lai, the Minister of Education Chou Jung-hsin and later the newly reinstated Vice Premier Teng Hsiao-p'ing, were concerned that an overemphasis on political study and manual labour in institutions of higher learning might lead to a lowering of academic standards. As we shall see, this group showed particular skill in initiating and cautiously guiding discussion in the fields of foreign languages, science and engineering. Opposed to them was that group of Party leaders, now designated the 'Gang of Four', whose position was neatly summed up by Chang Ch'un-ch'iao:

> Bring up exploiters and intellectual aristocrats with bourgeois consciousness and culture, or bring up workers with consciousness but no culture: which do you want? I'd rather have workers without culture than exploiters and intellectual aristocrats with culture.[85]

For the sake of brevity, I shall refer to the former as the 'expert' group and the latter the 'red' group, instead of the current but highly misleading terms 'moderates' and 'radicals'. There must be, however, one important caveat. These terms do not indicate the attitude of each group to the general social relationship between politics and

professional competence; they refer merely to the relative priority given
by each group, at that particular time, to the twin goals of education.

Immediately after the downfall of Lin Piao, the 'expert' group
appeared to have gained predominance. A perusal of the official
literature on higher education in 1972 reveals a subtle shift in emphasis,
in line with the current criticism of 'ultra-leftism'. Formerly, the
dominant theme underlying all the reforms in education had been
'politics should take precedence over everything else'. A qualification
was now added: 'if political work is not integrated with vocational
work, this is tantamount to giving up political leadership in
vocational work'. Furthermore, the notion that 'politics can overrule
everything else' was repudiated as a fallacy advertised by 'swindlers
like Liu Shao-chi'i'[86] (which, we have seen, was a code name for Lin
Piao).

Such a shift in emphasis seemed to fly in the face of Mao's constant
exhortations to 'put politics in command'. Yet, to a certain extent,
Mao had helped bring this change about. In the course of criticising
Lin Piao, he had made it clear that he disapproved of the personality cult
built around him by the former Vice Chairman.[87] He expressed also
many grave reservations about the 'four good' 'five good' slogans
propagated in the Army since the early 1960s,[88] the gist of which was
that being good at politics not only took precedence over other
qualities but was said to guarantee automatically that one would be
good at other things.[89] Though we cannot be precise as to the nature
of Mao's reservations, it is clear that his position might easily be
interpreted as a criticism of the overemphasis on politics. At least,
that was how those who wanted to give greater stress to academic
performance in education interpreted it.

There can be no doubt that at times the particular *interpretation*
given to the injunction to place 'politics in command' might result
in unsatisfactory teaching. Such was apparently the case with
foreign languages. The teaching material compiled in 1970
frequently introduced political vocabulary at the expense of vocabulary
used in everyday life and the oversimplification of grammar (in the
supposed interest of minimising the teaching of abstract theory)
resulted in very poor sentence structure.[90] Students sometimes
found that they had learned the phrase 'to take the road of socialism'
and not the elementary verb 'to walk'.[91] Sometimes, simple words
like 'summer' and 'winter' had to be taught in connection with
'singing praise to the beautiful landscape of the fatherland'.[92] In such
a situation, those in charge of foreign affairs could not but be alarmed,

and no less a person than Premier Chou En-lai personally conducted a discussion of these problems with some teachers of foreign languages from Peking University. The results of this discussion were embodied in an article written by the Educational Revolution Unit of that university in the summer of 1972, in which the above excesses were attributed to a narrow interpretation of the primacy of politics stemming from the influence of 'swindlers like Liu Shao-ch'i'.[93]

All those who experienced the changes in this area of teaching would attest to their dramatic nature. The English textbook, compiled by Peking Teachers' College in 1971, based mainly on a number of political slogans such as 'Long Live the Communist Party of China' and 'Long Live Chairman Mao' and upon quotations from the works of Chairman Mao, was totally rejected in 1972 in favour of more academically-oriented textbooks. Once again, teachers busied themselves shaking the dust from pre-Cultural Revolution textbooks to look for 'useful materials to inherit'.

Chiang Ch'ing's position in the controversy is of particular interest. She has usually been identified with the total rejection of traditional and foreign influence in art and literature. Yet now she approved the invitation of Western orchestras to tour China. She instructed music departments that arias from the old Peking operas and works by Western composers might be used as teaching materials because they embodied useful technique. Even more remarkable, she was said to have recommended ten Western novels as essential for art and literature workers; these included titles such as *Gone With the Wind* and *The Count of Monte Cristo*[94] which could hardly be justified on political grounds. Such a glaring discrepancy between word and deed makes one wonder whether there is not some truth in the current accusation that she merely gave prominence to politics to damn her opponents. Anyway, whatever her motives, there is no doubt that her moves were taken by many to be official endorsement for the revival of less politicised art and literature. Thus, she was in part responsible for bringing about what she later denounced as 'the resurgence of the revisionist line'.

The debate was, of course not confined to foreign languages, literature and art. A similar debate took place in departments of science and engineering. It was sparked off by suggestions made by a visiting distinguished American scientist of Chinese extraction. These suggestions, echoed by other visiting Chinese-American scientists, maintained that the current emphasis on practical rather than theoretical training would, in the long run, lower the quality of technical manpower.[95] It might be assumed that such distinguished visitors reflected the views of Chinese scientists with whom they were in close contact. Furthermore, since the suggestions had allegedly been released by order of Chou En-lai, it was assumed that the Premier did not entirely disagree with them.

The cleavage between the 'red' and 'expert' groups came to the surface in a series of four articles in the Ninth issue of *Red Flag* in 1972. The 'red' position was taken by the July Twenty First Workers University of the Shanghai Machine Tools Plant (the model held up by Mao for emulation by all universities). It maintained that theories could only be studied in repeated practice and that the only criterion for judging the level of theoretical knowledge of a student was whether that knowledge could solve the practical problems of production. Tsinghua University and Peking University, once the vanguards of the educational revolution, unexpectedly took the 'expert' position. Complaining that it was 'a short sighted view' which maintained that 'fundamental theoretical subjects are useless', they criticised new teaching material which went to the extreme of 'discussing only particular phenomena without general principles and only formulae without logical deduction', with the result that students found them illogical and difficult to understand. It was subsequently alleged that a few opponents of the Cultural Revolution in both these universities were responsible for this relapse.[96] They were never mentioned by name in the official press but we, at least, know one such person to be the physicist Chou P'ei-yuan, the Vice Chairman of the Revolutionary Committee of Peking University. In unequivocal terms, he further developed the Tsinghua-Peking position in an article which became both influential and highly controversial. After citing examples of past scientific discoveries, he argued:

> Some important discoveries in natural science . . . were made principally through scientific experiment . . . and not due to the direct needs of production. Care, therefore, must be exercised in dealing with some specialties which are more or less abstract and for which no application can be found at present. These must not be written off lightly.

Questioning the desirability of linking teaching too closely with production, he went on:

> Although production is composite in character and involves many

special subjects, the area of each subject is pretty narrow, so that
the students so trained will not meet the requirement that
scientific personnel have a broad theoretical basis.

Chou's prescription, therefore, was for universities to take care of basic
courses in theory and, only after those were taught, were students to
proceed to factories and villages to learn the techniques relevant to
particular fields of production.[97]

Chou's article constituted an open challenge to the basic policies
of the educational revolution, namely 'open-door' management,
integrating theoretical training with productive labour, enrolling
workers and peasants with practical experience and employing veteran
workers and peasants as university teachers. The fact that such an
article could be printed in a major national newspaper with no
unfavourable editorial comment indicated that Chou's position was
not only supported by a substantial number of people in the universities
but was also backed by people high up in the leadership.[98]

The 'expert' position was by no means merely confined to words. In
some universities the time allotted to manual labour was cut. In Peking
Teachers' College, where I taught, the foreign Languages Department
changed its former policy of devoting half of each day to work on a
college farm to merely one afternoon of manual labour within the
campus. In places as far apart as the Ninghsia Agricultural College[99]
and the East China Petroleum College in Shantung, class-room
teaching became the norm. Indeed, in the latter institution, some
college-run factories were either closed down or suspended production.[100]
Tsinghua University, which usually represented authoritative views, now
began to justify this in terms of efficiency:

> At the present stage, the differences between mental and manual
> labour exist objectively and have to be eliminated over a fairly
> long period of time. Any rigid demand for uniformity would
> lower work efficiency and harm the development of the socialist
> cause.[101]

Once again it was in Shanghai, the power base of the 'red' group,
that the challenge of the 'expert' group was taken up. The newspaper
Wenhuibao countered sharply:

> At no time must we reverse the relationship between practice and
> knowledge. If anyone were to misunderstand or abandon this

principle, he would very easily take the beaten track of the bourgeoisie.[102]

Neither was the counter-attack merely confined to words. In Shanghai's T'ungchi University, for example, some people had branded as 'ultra-leftist' the 'May Seventh Commune' where teaching had been closely integrated with production. Their charge, however, was refuted by the workers' propaganda teams and the worker-teachers who maintained their support for the educational revolution and pointedly criticised the 'ultra-right' nature of Lin Piao's line.[103] Similarly, in the Chaoyang Agricultural College of Shenyang, another stronghold of the 'red' group, a charge that the policy of taking students from the communes and returning them to the communes was 'ultra-leftist' was rebutted by the Party committee.[104]

There was also sharp disagreement over the policy for admission to universities. Out of consideration for academic standards, some people opposed the policy of selecting students from among workers and peasants.[105] Others argued that, since all candidates for university admission had been 'recommended by the masses' and approved by the appropriate leadership, their political desirability had to be treated as uniform. Consequently, selection from among them ought to be determined by the results of an entrance examination.[106] In such a climate, entrance examinations were gradually reintroduced. It was alleged that candidates were sometimes subjected to repeated examinations according to the old techniques of 'surprise tests' and 'tests with difficult and strange questions'.[107] As examinations became more important, potential candidates were required to spend less time in productive labour in order to prepare for them.[108]

The 'national hero' who protested against the gradual reversion to the old examination system was one Chang T'ieh-sheng a rusticated youth from Liaoning. As leader of a production team, Chang had felt compelled to work an eighteen-hour day, which did not leave him much time to prepare for the entrance examination. When finally faced with the exam in chemistry and physics, unable to answer many of the questions, he chose instead to write the following answer in the form of a letter to the examinations board:

To tell the truth, I have no respect for the 'college fanatics' who for many years have been taking it easy and have done nothing useful. I dislike them intensely. I think the examination is being monopolised by these 'college fanatics'. During the busy season of

summer hoeing, I just could not bring myself to abandon my
production task and shut myself up in a small room to study. That
would have been very selfish. If I had done that, I would have
been guilty of being unworthy of the revolutionary cause . . .
and I would have been condemned by my own revolutionary
conscience . . . What saddens me is that a few hours of written
test could mean the loss of my qualifications for admission . . .
I am sure if two days had been allowed me for reviewing my
lessons, I could have scored full marks . . .I have a clean record
as far as my own political outlook, my family background and my
social connections are concerned. Especially in my thinking and
feeling, and in the remoulding of my world outlook, I can say I have
experienced a 'leap'.[109]

Chang's letter was first carried in the Liaoning provincial Party
newspaper *Liaoning Daily*. When it was finally reprinted by *People's
Daily*, it signalled the ascendency of the 'red' group. A discussion of
enrolment policy was not slow to develop. In that discussion,
although most people agreed that political criteria should take
precedence over academic criteria and that academic criteria should
focus on a candidate's ability to locate and solve practical problems, no
one went as far as to suggest the complete abolition of examinations.[110]
As might be expected, in condemning all those who tried to gain or
had already gained admittance into universities and colleges as 'college
fanatics who had done nothing useful', Chang alienated many of his
peer group. If, however, all he had meant was that combining
political recommendation with academic assessment did not necessarily
ensure the selection of people with genuine political and ideological
commitment, he could not have been more correct. Certainly, there
was no provision to enable one to distinguish an opportunist who had
acquired a veneer of political conformity from a sincere political
activist. But this important issue raised by Chang's letter was largely
ignored in the subsequent discussion.
The crux of the matter lay in 'mass recommendation' which, in
some cases, had become a mere formality. Evidently, some cadres
had treated 'mass recommendation' as 'nothing but so much noise in
which nothing can be achieved' and the masses themselves were
often too busy with production tasks to care about who was to go to
college.[111] When such was the case, what really mattered was the
approval by the appropriate leadership and this rendered the
enrolment system highly susceptible to nepotism.

It soon became clear that the problem of nepotism was quite widespread, following the publication of an application by one Chung Chih-min to withdraw from study at Nanking University. Chung, it appeared, owed his place at the university to the influence of his father, a veteran Army cadre. At first, Chung considered this his due by virtue of his father's contribution to the revolution. With the campaign against Lin Piao and Confucius in 1973, however, he began to realise that favouritism might lead to the growth of a privileged class which could come to exploit the common people. He consequently withdrew from the university and applied to become a private soldier in the Army.[112] The repercussions of Chung's action were startling. One after another, those who had been admitted 'through the back door' withdrew from the universities[113] and this touched off a nation-wide campaign against favouritism and nepotism. Such practices were denounced as manifestations of 'bourgeois right' which led to social cleavage but no suggestion was offered as to how the admission procedure might be reformed to guard against such abuses. Yet, in the last resort, no legal provision could be adequate; the remedy had, in the spirit of Mao Tsetung Thought, to be ideological.

As Young's chapter has pointed out, there was one body of which the very *raison d'etre* was ideological rather than administrative and that was the newly reformed Party. By 1972, articles on educational reform, formerly written by workers' propaganda teams, were now attributed to Party committees or revolutionary committees and educational revolution groups (both under Party leadership). Clearly the importance of the propaganda teams had diminished with the reconstruction of the Party. It is true that some Party members of the propaganda teams were incorporated into the new Party committees but they were less experienced in university administration than the old Party cadres and tended to recede into the background. As for non-Party members of the propaganda teams, they felt that they had fulfilled their role and were keen to return to the factories or military units where they could still be useful.[114] Furthermore, as Woodward has noted, an immediate consequence of the Lin Piao incident of 1971 had been the sharp curtailment of military involvement in civilian life and this did nothing to prolong the effectiveness of worker teams which maintained close links with their PLA counterparts.

In 1972, therefore, the workers' and PLA propaganda teams were but shadows of their former selves. They consisted often of merely one

worker and one soldier, in striking contrast to the ten to twelve
member teams of 1968-71 which had exercised real power. In 1972,
it was the Party committee that gave instructions on important
matters such as the assignment of teachers and the choice of teaching
materials. Thus, the propaganda teams were usually by-passed and
were not effective instruments to combat retrogression. Yet it was
to the propaganda teams that the 'red' group turned once again in
1974, just as Mao had done in 1968, in the belief that they could
articulate working class leadership to combat 'revisionist
retrogression'.

In early 1974, therefore, a number of provinces began to take
measures to strengthen the role of workers' propaganda teams.[115] Most
noteworthy was the decision taken by the Party Committee of the
Sinkiang Uighur Autonomous Region, *for the first time,* to move
workers' propaganda teams into all four institutions of higher
learning in Urumchi.[116] It has never been clearly explained why no
teams had been formed in Sinkiang prior to that date but we may
surmise that it was due to the fact that the growth of the Cultural
revolution had been stunted in that region because of its sensitive
strategic position. Indeed, even what little Cultural Revolution there
had been in Sinkiang had met with the opposition of the Party's
First Secretary, Wang En-mao, who rallied both workers and Army
behind him in opposition to rebel Red Guards (largely students).[117]
If such had been the political orientation of Sinkiang's workers and
Army, they were not ideal candidates for inclusion in propaganda
teams – at least until 1974.

Conclusion

Following the intense mass criticism and struggle of 1966-8 against
what were seen as vestiges of 'capitalism and revisionism' in
education, a whole series of reforms were instituted. Changes were
made to the structure of power in educational institutions, the
distribution of educational opportunities, the examination system
and teaching methods and materials. At first, reforms went unhindered
in the name of implementing 'Mao's educational line', opposition
was muted and reservations were kept in check. It soon became
apparent, however, that Mao himself took issue with some of the
assumptions underlying the reforms, notably the extent politics
should 'take command' of professional work and the desirability
of totally abolishing examinations.[118] Mao's reservations provided an
opportunity for those who were concerned about academic standards

and who wished to modify the politicisation of higher education to put forward their views. This group, headed by Chou En-lai (and later Teng Hsiao-p'ing who took over some of the ailing Premier's duties) became dominant in 1972 and early 1973. Their position reflected the interests of several social groups who still held considerable sway in China's political, economic and social life. First were the academics and many university students, in whose interest it was to stress academic performance. Second were many cadres in educational institutions who had been criticised in the Cultural Revolution for neglecting politics and since rehabilitated. They perhaps saw in such a position a vindication of their former stance. Third were the scientific, technical and managerial personnel in agriculture, industry and research who were sensitive to the difficulties caused by the inadequate input of highly qualified expertise. It will be remembered that four years had elapsed since tertiary institutions had turned out their last batch of graduates and the effects of such a hiatus must have been acutely felt by 1972. Thus, in that year, there were complaints about the low quality of industrial production and this was generally attributed to an insufficiently trained work force.[119] Manifestly, the improvement of academic standards was a widespread concern.

The publication of Chang T'ieh-sheng's letter in *People's Daily* heralded a campaign in which the 'red' group became dominant. In denouncing the 'expert' line as 'revisionist', however, the group did not enjoy unqualified success. Its most bitter disappointment was perhaps the failure of its attempt to discredit Chou En-lai, the main protagonist of the 'expert' line. This failure had two consequences. First, it became very difficult to discredit people at lower levels in the Party. Chou P'ei-yuan, for instance, though criticised in wall posters, retained his post as Vice Chairman of Peking University's revolutionary committee. Secondly, the official media could only criticise the 'expert' line in moderate tone. It was usually conceded that people promoting the 'expert' resurgence were merely 'comrades . . . not accustomed to socialist new things':[120] the remedy, therefore, was education rather than supression.

As for concrete measures to counter the resurgence, the campaign was unimpressive. Chang T'ieh-sheng's letter, full of sound and fury, probably served to play down the importance of formal written examinations but there is no evidence that it initiated reforms in admission procedure any more radical than those which came into existence after 1968, nor is there any indication that entrance examinations were abandoned. Chung Chih-min's application for withdrawal from the university had nation-wide repercussions in terms of limiting 'bourgeois right' but such a limitation was not central to the debate on the educational front. Furthermore, the revamped workers' propaganda teams provided no effective guarantee that the 'red' line would be implemented. There was little basis to assume that workers were uniformly sympathetic to that line and, in any case, after the reconstruction of Party leadership at all levels, such teams could not but be pawns at the service of Party committees.

The first round of the campaign (subsumed under a more general movement to 'Criticise Lin Piao and Confucius') achieved no more than stalemate. Much of what the 'red' group wanted to achieve had to wait until the next round which began towards the end of 1975. With the second downfall of Teng Hsiao-p'ing and the dismissal of Chou Jung-hsin, one would have imagined that the 'red' group had triumphed and future developments would be charted by them. Yet their discrediting after the death of Mao highlights the danger of premature conclusions.

A crucial question remains. In view of the current criticism of the 'Gang of Four', will the educational revolution started in the Cultural Revolution be as short-lived as that of 1958? Events are, of course, unpredictable and any answer may only be tentative. What is clear at present is that the 'expert' line is once again asserting itself. Chang Ch'un-ch'iao's theory that 'redness' and 'expertise' are mutually exclusive is criticised and it is argued that 'redness' cannot stand without the complement of 'expertise'.[121] Neglect of study in schools and universities is said to be a vice encouraged by the 'Gang of Four' and their followers,[122] and academic achievements are acclaimed by the official media.[123] The reason is all too obvious. The present leaders' earnest commitment to modernising the country within the century has left them little option but to stress heavily the 'expert' goal of education. This might compel them to suspend or modify some of the practices introduced in the last few years in higher education which might impede their achieving this goal. For instance, in the field of scientific and technological education, the emphasis now seems to be on theoretical training,[124] and this is likely to be accompanied by a reduction of practical training and manual labour in the curriculum. In the policy of university admission, the criterion of academic performance is likely to receive greater prominence. It is even possible that, in some of the most crucial fields where the lacunae of expertise need to be quickly filled, the present requirements of several years of practical experience and mass recommendation might be waived or given very flexible interpretation. A less dogmatic attitude might be adopted towards past experiences and experiences of foreign countries, so long as they can serve the overall goal of modernisation. That the official media accept Lenin's view on Taylorism as 'a combination of the refined brutality of bourgeois exploitation and a number of the greatest scientific achievements'[125] is one such example. Finally, to co-opt the expertise of intellectuals, a more moderate policy towards them might be adopted, and this would mean a greater representation of these people in the power structure of higher education.

Will all these trends eventually displace many of the anti-élitist and more egalitarian policies, which have been so central to the educational revolution? Much depends on how far the trends are pushed and how adeptly the present leadership is able to balance the twin goals of education. As yet, it is too early to tell. Even with the passing of time, we will still need more factual information and more reliable data than we are ever likely to get from China to draw any definitive conclusion.

It must, however, be pointed out that certain constraints on policy formulation will continue to exist, and these will, to a large extent, determine the future development of higher education. First, the Chinese leadership is anything but a monolithic political body, a fact well borne out by the events of the last decade. It would, therefore, be rash to assume that, with the downfall of the 'Gang of Four', the division between the 'red' position and the 'expert' position within the leadership no longer exists. So long as there is still division at the top, the development of education will be characterised by a continuation of what the Chinese call 'the struggle between the two lines'. Since this kind of struggle seldom resolves itself in a complete domination of one line over the other, as has been well demonstrated by the struggles in the last decade or so, it would be difficult for whichever group that gains predominance not to make some kind of concession to the position of the other group or groups. This would probably mean that the guidelines for education will be a result of compromise between various leading groups, the nature of which will vary from time to time with the fluctuation of the balance of power among them.

Secondly, given the heterogeneous nature of Chinese society, with so many social groups and so many diverse group interests, one might assume that divisions in sympathy for the two lines in education will be less clear-cut and more diverse at the grass-roots level. We have already discussed which social groups rallied behind the 'expert' line in 1972-3. On the other hand, it is not difficult to see that the anti-élitist and egalitarian implications of the 'red' line would have great appeal to the underprivileged and the less sophisticated among the populace. Already, they are the beneficiaries of the educational revolution. Their direct participation in the educational revolution has opened their eyes to entirely new possibilities of a revolutionised system of education and this has produced an immense social impact. It would be difficult for any policy-maker to ignore the aspirations of this part of the constituency altogether, without having his own communist credentials called into question. The educational revolution started in 1958 and was revived and invigorated during the Cultural Revolution. It has left such an indelible imprint that it is inconceivable that education could ever return to its former élitist, formalistic and anti-social state, however much individual policy-makers might prefer to 'take the capitalist road'.

Notes

1. This idea is implicit in many of Mao's writings: e.g. 'the people and the people alone are the motive force in world history' *SW* English edition, Vol.3, p.257.
2. See above pp.20-27.
3. See Nee 1969. For accounts of the student movement in other places in Peking see Hinton 1972, *Hundred Day War* (in my opinion the best account); Hunter 1969 and Collier 1973.
4. See above pp.27-30.
5. See e.g. the role played by Ch'i Pen-yu, in Hinton 1972, *Hundred Day War.* Stories of how different *PLA* units supported different Red Guard factions fill most Red Guard publications, especially during the Wuhan Incident of July 1967.
6. The 'February Adverse Current' is discussed in Esmein 1973, pp.155-6.
7. Ch'i Pen-yu was a member of the Central Cultural Revolution Group and afterwards the alleged head of an 'ultra-leftist' faction known as the 'May Sixteenth Group'. See Hinton 1972, *Hundred Day War.*
8. The case of Yang Ch'eng-wu is discussed in Brugger 1977, pp.334-6.
9. Mao Tsetung 22 July 1966, *Wansui* 1969, pp.646-7. (Schram 1974, pp.256-7).
10. Mao Tsetung, 10 March 1967, in *CB* 888, p.19.
11. Mao Tsetung, 1 May 1967, *Wansui* 1969, p.676 (*JPRS* 1974, p.459).
12. Ibid., p.675 (*JPRS* 1974, p.458).
13. Hinton 1972, *Hundred Day War,* pp.185-233.
14. *Hongqi* 2, 1968, p.1.
15. See above, pp.41-56.
16. *RMRB*, 9 August 1966, p.1 (point 8)
17. Li Chih-hua, *Hongqi* 10, 1970, p.32.
18. *Hongqi* 6, 1971, p.89.
19. Li Chih-hua, *Hongqi* 10, 1970, p.32.
20. *PR* 26, 24 June 1966, pp.18-20.
21. State Statistical Bureau 1960, p.200.
22. Tsang 1968, p.200.
23. *RMRB*, 31 March 1969, p.1.
24. *RMRB*, 29 March 1969, p.1.

25. *RMRB,* 22 July 1968, p.1.
26. *Hongqi* 8, 1970, p.15.
27. *RMRB,* 11 October 1970, p.3; Kui Yu-p'eng, *RMRB,* 22 August 1970, p.3.
28. On the civil service exam as a stepping stone to officialdom, see Franke 1960.
29. *GMRB,* 12 September 1972, p.2.
30. *Hongqi* 6, 1971, pp.60-61.
31. Mao Tsetung, 13 February 1964, *Wansui* 1969, p.460 (another trans. in *JPRS* 1974, p.331).
32. Name of a well-known Chinese novel written in the 18th century.
33. Mao Tsetung, 13 February 1964, *Wansui* 1969, p.460 (another trans. in *JPRS* 1974, pp.331-2).
34. *RMRB,* 28 August 1969, p.3.
35. *Hongqi* 6, 1971, p.82.
36. *RMRB,* 9 August 1966, p.1 (point 10).
37. Bastid 1970, pp.16-45.
38. Mao Tsetung, *SW,* English edition, Vol.3, pp.17-25, 35-51, 53-68, 69-98 and *Wansui* 1969, pp.624-9.
39. Mao Tsetung 1967, *Mao Zhuxi Yulu,* pp.36-7.
40. Hinton 1972, *Hundred Day War,* p.25.
41. *RMRB,* 5 April 1970, p.2.
42. *RMRB,* 17 August 1970, p.3.
43. *RMRB,* 18 January 1970, p.2.
44. Lindsay 1950. See especially the appendices, pp.51-139.
45. Lu Ting-i, in Fraser 1965, pp.283-300.
46. *PR* 47, 17 November 1967, pp.9-11; *PR* 20, 17 May 1968, pp.11-12 and *Hongqi* 6, 1971, pp.89-97.
47. *Hongqi* 6, 1971, p.77.
48. *RMRB,* 25 July 1970, p.2.
49. Ibid.
50. *RMRB,* 7 August 1970, p.2.
51. Mao Tsetung, May 1941, *SW,* English edition, Vol.3, pp.17-25; and 1 February 1942, ibid, pp.35-51.
52. Schram in Schram (ed.), 1973.
53. E.g. *RMRB,* 7 August 1970, p.2 and *RMRB,* 5 September 1970, p.3.
54. *RMRB,* 5 September 1971, p.3.
55. *RMRB,* 5 April 1970, p.2.
56. *RMRB,* 5 September 1970, p.3.
57. Marx 1867, p.484.
58. Mao Tsetung, 27 February 1957, in Mao Tsetung, *SW,* Chinese edition, Vol.5, p.385 (trans., Mao 1971, p.459).
59. Mao Tsetung, 2 May 1942, *SW,* English edition, Vol.3, p.73.
60. *Hongqi* 13, 1964, pp.31-2.
61. *RMRB,* 8 June 1969, p.2.
62. *RMRB,* 29 October 1969, p.3.
63. Ibid.
64. Ibid.
65. Mao Tsetung, 29 August 1964, *Wansui* 1969, p.569 (another trans. in *CB* 891, p.46).
66. *RMRB,* 22 July 1968, p.1.
67. Mao Tsetung, 28 July 1968, *Wansui* 1969, p.693 (another trans. in *JPRS* 1974, pp.474-5).
68. *Hongqi* 1, 1970, pp.46-50.
69. This was one of the most important themes of the 9th Party Congress. See Lin Piao, 1 April 1969, in *PR* Special Issue, 28 April 1969, pp.11-30.
70. Mao Tsetung, 29 August 1964, *Wansui* 1969, p.575 (*CB* 891, p.47).
71. Terrill 1971, pp.127-8.
72. *RMRB,* 15 October 1969, p.5.
73. Ibid.
74. *RMRB,* 18 January 1970, p.2.
75. *RMRB,* 15 October 1969, p.5.
76. Mao Tsetung, 5 July 1964, *Wansui* 1969, p.470 (Schram 1974, p.248)

77. *RMRB*, 25 July 1970, p.2.
78. *Hongqi* 6-7, 1969, pp.24-7.
79. *RMRB*, 17 August 1970, p.3.
80. These are, according to Mao 'class struggle', 'the struggle for production' and 'scientific experiment'. See note 60.
81. Mao Tsetung, 12 March 1957, in *SW*, Chinese edition, Vol.5, p.415 (trans. Mao 1971, pp.493-4).
82. *PR* 3, 15 January 1971, pp.7-8.
83. *Ibid.*, p.9.
84. *RMRB*, 5 April 1970, p.2.
85. *PR* 8, 18 February 1977, p.11.
86. *RMRB*, 13 May 1972, p.2.
87. Mao's talk with Edgar Snow on the personality cult was officially released after the Lin Piao incident. See Snow 1971, pp.168-70. See also Mao Tsetung's letter to Chiang Ch'ing, *Issues and Studies*, Vol.9, No.1, January 1973 pp.94-6.
88. CCP CC *Zhongfa* 1972/12 in *Issues and Studies*, Vol.8, No.9,1972,pp.64-71.
89. See above, p.27.
90. *RMRB*, 24 August 1972, p.2.
91. *Hongqi* 7, 1972, p.2.
92. *RMRB*, 24 August 1972, p.2.
93. Ibid.
94. *RMRB*, 7 February 1977, p.2.
95. *Qishi Niandai Zazhi She* 1974, p.249 and pp.294-5.
96. *Hongqi* 5, 1974, p.66.
97. Chou P'ei-yuan, *GMRB*, 6 October 1972, pp.1-2.
98. This was confirmed by *RMRB, 16 March 1977*, p.2.
99. *GMRB*, 22 January 1974, p.2.
100. *SWB*, FE/4546/B11/4.
101. *Hongqi* 10, 1972, p.27.
102. *SWB*, FE/4185/B1/17
103. *Xuexi yu Pipan* 7, 1975, p.75.
104. *Hongqi* 5, 1975, p.69.
105. *SWB*, FE/4546/B11/4.
106. *RMRB*, 28 July 1973, p.2.
107. *RMRB*, 22 September 1973,p.2.
108. *RMRB*, 28 July 1973, p.2.
109. *RMRB*, 10 August 1973, p.1.
110. *RMRB*, 22 September 1973, p.3; 1 December 1973, p.2.
111. *RMRB,,* 20 June 1973, p.3.
112. *RMRB*, 18 January 1974, p.1.
113. *SWB*, FE/4521/B11/1; FE/4534/B11/12.
114. *RMRB*, 9 December 1971, p.2.
115. *SWB*, FE/4590/B11/27-30.
116. *SWB*, FE/4590/B11/30.
117. Rice 1974, pp.384-5; Hinton 1972, *Hundred Day War*, pp.87-94; *CB* 855, pp.3-4.
118. CCP CC *Zhongfa* 1972/12, in *Issues and Studies*, Vol.8, No.9, September 1972, pp.64-71: See also Mao Tsetung in ibid, Vol.11, No.2, February 1975, p.92.
119. *Hongqi* 5, 1972, pp.40-44; *SWB*, FE/4022/B11/1-7; *RMRB* 14 November 1972, p.2 and 19 November 1972, p.1.
120. *Hongqi* 1, 1974, pp.7-8, 9-13, 53-8.
121. *PR* 8, 18 February 1977, p.11.
122. *Hongqi* 3, 1977, pp.48-54, 60-65.
123. *RMRB*, 26 February 1977, p.1.
124. *RMRB*, 16 March 1977, p.2; *Hongqi* 4, 1977, pp.68-76.
125. *PR* 14, 1 April 1977, p.25.

4 STRATEGY FOR ECONOMIC DEVELOPMENT

Joseph (Yu-shek) Cheng

In the Introduction to this book, great stress was laid on that seminal document of the mid 1950s — 'On the Ten Major Relationships'.[1] It was pointed out that, of these ten relationships, five constituted 'contradictions'[2] central to China's development strategy. They were:

1. the relationship between industry and agriculture and between heavy and light industry
2. the relationship between industry in the coastal regions and industry in the interior
3. the relationship between economic construction and defence construction
4. the relationship between the state, the units of production and the individual producers
5. the relationship between the centre and the regions.

Though put forward as a response to the unsatisfactory consequences of following a Soviet model, these five contradictions have remained central to all economic debates during the past twenty years. It is probably no exaggeration to say that the crystallisation of two antagonistic 'lines',[3] to which all the contributors to this book continually refer, stem from disagreements on how exactly to handle precisely the above five contradictions. Indeed, it is these five contradictions which will determine the pattern of socialist transition.

There is probably little disagreement amongst the Chinese leaders that all positive elements and all available forces must be mobilised to build a socialist society in a 'faster, better and more economical way'. Struggles concerning Liu Shao-ch'i's 'revisionist' economic policies in the 1960s, the importation of foreign technology in the 1970s,[4] Teng Hsiao-p'ing's alleged re-imposition of direct and exclusive ministerial control over enterprises shortly before Mao's death[5] and the activities of the 'Gang of Four'[6] even more recently do not hinge on considerations of the absolute growth rate of China's GNP but on the process of socialist transition, with the attendant danger of capitalist retrogression. It is therefore, a concern for the qualitative dimensions of the above five contradictions that will inform this chapter.

126

General Strategy

In 1969, when the intense political activities of the Cultural Revolution gradually gave way to normalisation, two important statements on Chinese industrial policy were released. The first appeared in the form of a *People's Daily* editorial on 21 February 1969,[7] and the second in the tenth issue of *Red Flag* in the same year.[8] Both statements re-affirmed the policy of 'agriculture as the foundation, and industry as the leading factor', the principles of 'self-reliance', 'walking on two legs' and fostering technological innovations.

In this context, three trends, deserve considerable attention. First, in view of the Soviet invasion of Czechoslovakia, the enunciation of the Brezhnev doctrine and the Sino-Soviet border clashes, there was a predictable emphasis on integrating industrial construction with preparation for war. Secondly, the strategy of taking 'agriculture as the foundation, and industry as the leading factor' received much greater clarification and elaboration. All units were called upon to support agriculture, and an industrial network was to be established to serve it. Mechanisation of agriculture was regarded as vital, and workshops for the manufacture and repair of agricultural machinery were to be established in every *xian*. Thirdly the *People's Daily* editorial demanded that, when formulating production plans, 'it is necessary to mobilise the masses and see to it that there is enough leeway (*yudi*)'. The concept of 'leeway' was defined, in a Shanghai newspaper the following day, as drawing up plans in such a way that 'the masses can reach or surpass the new production targets by active efforts and that plans can be fulfilled or overfulfilled'.[9] It was not intended that targets should be set too low, for 'a plan which leaves enough leeway is a fruit which can only be picked by jumping and reaching up, not one which can be taken by stretching out one's arm from a lying or sitting position'.

The introduction (or in fact reintroduction) of the concept of 'leeway' at this stage suggested that a compromise might have been reached between planners who were calling for limited goals and cautious planning and those who claimed that the Cultural Revolution had released incalculable productive energies which should be allowed free rein. 'Leeway' would cover the interests of the latter without, at this stage, affecting the plans of the former. More significantly, the concept of 'leeway' had first been used in August 1960, by the then Chairman of the State Planning Commission, Li Fu-ch'un, as one of the measures to restore balance in the economy after the Great Leap Forward.[10]

The theme of integrating industrial construction with preparation for war was clearly spelled out in the *Red Flag* article as follows:

> With a view to preparedness against war, every area, province and
> city should pay attention to rational geographical distribution and
> appropriate multi-purpose development of industries in line with
> Chairman Mao's instruction: 'Various localities should endeavour to
> build up independent industrial systems. Where conditions permit
> (set up) co-ordination zones, and then provinces should establish
> relatively independent but varied industrial systems.' When
> circumstances permit, we must encourage co-operation between
> nearby units for industrial production and increase their capacity
> to turn out whole sets of industrial products. In addition, we must
> pay attention to producing industrial goods needed in both peace
> time and war time and for civilian and military use. Should US
> imperialism and social imperialism impose a war on the Chinese
> people, we shall have many big and small reliable industrial bases
> which provide us with more room for manoeuvre, so that all
> parts of the country can fight the war on their own, become
> impregnable, wipe out the enemy and win victory . . . [11]

A rational geographical distribution of industries would certainly be
concerned with the proper handling of the relationship between
industry in the coastal regions and industry in the interior. Chinese
industries were and still are far too concentrated in the North East and
along the coast. By the early 1970s, a few major cities — Shenyang,
Tientsin, Anshan, Lushun/Talien, Tsingtao, Peking, Shanghai and
Kwangchow produced almost half of the country's total value of
industrial output; and Shanghai alone produced about 15.5 per cent of
the total.[12] On the other hand, the vast interior — the North West, the
South West and Inner Mongolia — had very few industries; this
imbalance surely had to be redressed. But it involved much more than
that. In preparing for war against the Soviet Union, logic would
suggest that heavy industrial plants in the North East and North West
should be moved to Central and South China. The heavy concentration
of industries in a few urban centres along the coast, both from the
military viewpoint and that of a rational geographical distribution,
therefore, required appropriate adjustment. Thus, in late 1969 and early
1970, there appeared considerable speculation regarding the
re-distribution of China's industries.

It was said that the Chinese government planned to move industrial
plants from 'the first line' (east of Chengchow and including Shenyang,

Tsingtao, Shanghai, Foochow, Kwangchow. etc.) to the 'second line' (west of Chengchow including Sian, Chungking, Kweiyang, Kunming, etc.).[13] It was also reported that new industrial centres were to be established in the five provinces of Hunan, Hupei, Honan, Hopei and Anhwei and that industrial plants were to be gradually transported to these new centres from the coastal areas and the North East.[14] These reports have never been substantially confirmed, though there is sporadic evidence in support. For example, a new industrial centre emerged near the Tayeh iron mines in Hupei; this was the city of Huang Shih.[15] Szechwan also has become an important industrial centre serving the South West, and new industries are being built in Yunnan, Kweichow and Tibet.[16]

To implement such a rational geographical distribution of industries, certain measures of inter-regional resource redistribution had to be imposed by the centre. Highly industrialised areas such as Shanghai and Liaoning remit to the centre well over half of this annual revenue while less-developed regions typically not only retain all of their revenue but also frequently receive additional direct subsidies from the central government. In the least developed provinces and autonomous regions, these subsidies finance over half of all provincial and local expenditure.[17] The central government not only redistributes substantial fiscal resources, but also systematically transfers skilled labour and technical and managerial manpower from more developed regions (particularly Shanghai) to less-developed areas. By the early 1970s, Shanghai had supplied over half a million skilled workers to inland industry.[18] Though these measures had been carried out since 1949, it seems that the pace was speeded up after the Cultural Revolution.

Besides preparing for war and striving for a better inter-regional balance, a rational geographical distribution of industries also aimed at correcting a number of anomalies. In the first place, many Chinese industrial centres were too far away from the sources of raw materials and fuels as well as from the consumers. For example, Shanghai, the largest textile centre with a production capacity of 40 per cent of the Chinese total, had to import about 60 to 70 per cent of the cotton it needed from Hunan, Hopei and Shantung. In addition, Shanghai had to import millions of tons of coal from North China.[19] It was only logical, therefore, to develop textile centres in the cotton growing areas in North China to minimise costs and to reduce their reliance on textile products from Shanghai; at the same time, it also paid to develop small collieries near Shanghai to increase its self-sufficiency in fuel. In view of the bottlenecks in transportation, these investment plans appeared all the more urgent. Moreover, even within the same region, imbalances still existed among the various sectors of the same industry. The mining of iron ore was well developed, for example, in the North East, largely due to the legacy of Japanese occupation. Consequently that region's mining capacity exceeded that of steel-making, and the latter exceeded that of rolling; steel, therefore had to be imported from Japan while iron ore and cast iron were exported to the same country. Simultaneously, the rolling mills and machine-building plants in East China had to bring in cast iron and finished steel from outside the region. To remedy the situation, industrial plants, wherever possible, were to be established near the sources of raw materials and fuel and the population centres where the industrial products were consumed. This would help to ensure the full utilisation of natural resources, the elimination of unnecessary transport costs and the acceleration of economic turnover. Secondly, in order to reduce the differences in living standards between peasants and industrial workers and between urban and rural areas, new industrial centres were to be built in rural areas; these industrial centres would also help to improve agriculture by supplying much-needed inputs such as tractors, farm machinery, chemical fertilisers, pesticides, etc. Thirdly, to speed up the economic development in national minority areas (largely in the North West and South West), priority was to be given to industrial development in those areas. This was essential not only to raise the low living standards in minority areas, but to help implement Mao Tsetung's policy of eliminating 'Han chauvinism' and the centrifugal tendencies among certain national minorities, particularly those living near the Sino-Soviet border. Finally, while striving to achieve self-sufficiency, each region and locality was at the same time to specialise in products most appropriate to its factor endowments.

Thus, the above policy of decentralisation, though influenced by an external military threat, was part of the general policy laid down in 'On the Ten Major Relationships'. A reassessment of the relationship between centre and regions, moreover, had important implications for the structure of ministerial control. Already attenuated after 1957, the power of central ministries was further reduced after the Cultural Revolution. This was accompanied by a decrease in the number of central ministries through amalgamations and by a reduction in the size of their staff.[20] Premier Chou En-lai stated in December 1970 that the number of cadres in organs of the central government numbered only 10,000 compared with 60,000 before the Cultural Revolution.[21] Few productive enterprises seemed to remain directly under central ministries; even the huge Anshan Iron and Steel Company appeared at that time to be controlled by Liaoning province.[22] By the end of 1970, in the words of a Yugoslav correspondent in China, 'countless independent or relatively independent production centres (were) being set up throughout the country'.[23] This development probably demonstrated an awareness that the ability of at least some local authorities to co-ordinate individual enterprises would be greater than that of the centre, and it surely reflected Mao Tsetung's insistence on relying on the enthusiasm, will-power and initiative of the masses.

The establishment of independent industrial systems in local areas meant also a solid implementation of Mao's policy of 'walking on two legs' and an emphasis on local small-scale factories. Back in the Great Leap Forward, the development of local industries had received special attention and plans were made to establish factories in every *xian* and every commune. Due to mismanagement and financial losses, however, most of these factories were closed down after the Great Leap; the '70 Guidelines For Industry', authorised by Liu Shao-ch'i, in fact, ordered all local factories incurring losses to be abandoned.[24] The revised policy is best illustrated by the following example, taken from many similar ones singled out for praise in the official Chinese press. A colliery in Tungshan *xian,* Hupei was opened during the Great Leap in 1958 which:

> originally had over 1,000 workers, but the agents of Liu Shao-ch'i ordered it to be closed. However, eighteen revolutionary workers kept the mine in operation . . . The mine's equipment is now valued at more than 80,000 *yuan* and it produces 3,500 tons of coal a year. In nine years the miners have never asked the state for aid.[25]

This exemplifies the expansion of a local enterprise through ploughing back profits and its ability to improvise out of its own resources, rather than relying on state investment grants.

The growth of enterprise self-sufficiency was particularly marked with regard to machinery. Accounts appeared in press and radio of numerous factories in all branches of industry which made or even invented their own equipment rather than getting outside help. This process has been criticised by Audrey Donnithorne as 'unnecessarily extravagant' since time and effort were spent discovering what was already known in larger and more modern enterprises.[26] Nevertheless, since local plants had to rely on local resources, the known technology usually had to be imported into the locality. It might itself be in short supply in the

advanced industrial sector. Such inputs, moreover, might not be
suitable for local needs. The principle of self-reliance required local
industries to be based on technology which made optimal use of natural
resources, manpower and equipment which were available locally.
Furthermore, the immense educational value of developing local
technology was not to be underestimated, particularly in view of the fact
that educated youth from the urban areas would almost inevitably
be involved.

As indicated by Jon Sigurdson, two measures were important in
fostering technology, appropriate for local industries and rural
economic development.
1. The development of 'entirely' new technologies in research and
   design institutes as exemplified by the design of chemical fertiliser
   plants.
2. The use of old designs and processes and second-hand machinery
   appropriate to the scale of operations and needs of the localities.[27]

The significance for rural industries of this development and
transfer of technology can best be appreciated by an examination of the
linkages between agriculture, rural and modern industry. Rural industry
was introduced as a transmission belt for knowledge. Initially, the
linkage with modern industry was mainly a one-way relationship, in
which rural industry was provided with much of the necessary
technology and equipment. The linkage between agriculture and
rural industry, on the other hand, was a mutual relationship. Rural
industry, for its part, provided an increasing amount of inputs into
agriculture and was responsible for the formation of technical skills in
that sector. Agriculture in turn, supplied raw materials and capital. As
the level of agricultural production rose and rural industries expanded in
scale and improved in sophistication, the differences between the rural
and modern industrial sectors would gradually be reduced.[28]

Under normal circumstances, a local industrial system would be best
able to serve the local rural sector. Indeed, the division of labour
within local industrial systems revealed that local industries were
chiefly designed to serve agriculture. In Kiangsi, for example, major
items of development at the provincial level were the manufacture of
tractors, automobiles and machine tools and the generation of electric
power; at *xian* level, the emphasis was on chemical fertiliser production
and the manufacture and repair of agricultural machinery; and at the
production brigade level, the chief aim was the establishment of
agricultural machinery repair shops.[29] The plans of other provinces
appeared to be similar. In Hunan, it was reported, in December

1969, that over 90 *xian* and municipalities (*shi*) had developed
medium- and small-scale collieries, over 40 per cent of the *xian* and
municipalities had established chemical fertiliser factories, and every
xian had its own rural machinery factory and hydro-electric power
station. The number of tractors in the province increased by 300 per
cent over the pre-Cultural Revolution figure; the annual production of
chemical fertilisers, 200 per cent; and mechanical pumping capacity,
almost 100 per cent.[30] In each of the eight provinces publicly praised
for outstanding achievements in local small-scale industries, workshops
were set up in every *xian* for the manufacture and repair of agricultural
machinery.[31]

The Rural Sector

In the agricultural sector, the campaign to expand and merge communes
and production brigades, which started in October 1968,[32] and the talk
of a 'flying leap' in agricultural production, which reached its peak in
late 1969,[33] gradually gave way to a more cautious approach as China
entered the 1970s. An important article on agriculture appeared in the
February issue of *Red Flag* in 1970; it was subsequently republished in
People's Daily and repeatedly broadcast, thus indicating that it was
intended to reflect official policy. The emphasis of the article was
entirely on gradual development with no sudden changes in the
existing pattern of commune organisation:

> Chairman Mao has taught us: 'The method we are using in the
> socialist transformation of agriculture is one of step-by-step
> advance.' The advantage of this method is that it is 'possible for the
> peasants gradually to raise their socialist consciousness through their
> personal experience and gradually to change their mode of life, thus
> lessening any feeling of abrupt change' . . . We cannot and should
> not try to achieve this process by a single stroke . . . The step-by-step
> realisation of the mechanisation and electrification of agriculture
> on the basis of agricultural collectivisation is the road for the
> development of China's socialist agriculture . . .[34]

This step-by-step approach was confirmed as the official policy in the
following years. Revolutionary committees and Party committees were
gradually established and re-established, but the fundamental organisation
of the communes remained unaltered; and, in the new Constitution
promulgated in 1975, it was clearly stated that the production team would
be the basic accounting unit.[35] In rural areas, major efforts were

concentrated on water conservation works, mechanisation, electrification, and small chemical plants. Such developments were made possible by the official requirement for industry to support agriculture. Although the principle of self-reliance was given much emphasis, and almost all investment funds had to come from the communes themselves, it was also obvious that very considerable resources in the industrial sector were devoted to supplying agriculture with the modern inputs that it required. As revealed in Premier Chou En-lai's 'Report on the Work of the Government' delivered at the Fourth National People's Congress in early 1975: while China's gross industrial output for 1974 was estimated to be 190 per cent more than 1964, electric power was said to be 200 per cent more, chemical fertilisers 330 per cent more, and tractors 520 per cent more.[36] A significant proportion of the electric power, chemical fertilisers and tractors did not come from the advanced industrial sector, but was produced by small plants in the *xian;* nonetheless these plants still required machinery, equipment, spare parts and other inputs from the advanced industrial sector. More important still, precious foreign exchange was spent in the US and Japan in the early 1970s.[37]

A major campaign to build water works started in the winter of 1968-9, and in eleven provinces (Liaoning, Hopei, Hunan, Kwangsi, etc.), 37 million people were mobilised.[38] The operative slogan was 'conservation, smallness of scale and self-reliance'; and this resulted in the construction of numerous small reservoirs. Just in the suburbs of Peking, about 190 small reservoirs were built in 1969 alone;[39] and, in Kiangsi, over 20,000 small-scale water conservation projects were completed in the same winter.[40] Certain large-scale projects, however, were financed by the State, as in the case of the Kiangtu irrigation project in Kiangsu.[41]

As Chairman Mao pointed out: 'The fundamental way out for agriculture lies in mechanisation'.[42] Progress in this field was not to be neglected; and we have discussed the significance of establishing a farm machinery repair shop in every *xian.* Thus, after a few years of relative quiescence in the design and manufacture of new farm machinery, an exhibition was held in Nanning, in May 1969 to introduce a new rice transplanter.[43] There followed many other similar exhibitions in the years which followed, which indicated a continuing concern with rural mechanisation.

The rural electrification scheme was based mainly on the development of hydro-electric power. The construction of small hydro-electric power stations in the countryside was coupled with a severe criticism of Liu Shao-ch'i's 'revisionist' policy of discouraging rural electrification in favour of electrification in the urban sector.[44] Most of these small hydro-electric power stations were financed by the communes and the production brigades, and usually had a generating capacity of between 20 – 100 kilowatts.[45] In the use of electricity, priority had to be given first to irrigation networks, then rural industries, and last of all domestic consumption.

The chemical fertiliser industry was perhaps the most successful of all the small-scale rural industries. According to an estimate by Chao Kang in 1974, 45 per cent of the total chemical fertiliser output in China came from these small rural plants.[46] This increase in production in the rural areas, plus the importation of modern plants could significantly reduce China's purchases from abroad, notably from Japan. Indeed, China might perhaps achieve self-sufficiency in the near future.

Since all these developments were largely to be financed locally, the problem of accumulating local funds became very serious. Here there are dangers as well as bright prospects. It appeared, in most cases, that grain production alone could not raise sufficient funds to provide for these developments; there was a need to generate further income from sideline production. The importance of sideline production and the need to pay appropriate attention to such sectors as forestry and animal husbandry (particularly pig raising both collective and private) became apparent. Yet over-emphasis on these activities, it was feared, would 'give rise to capitalism'; consequently some local cadres became 'hesitant, gave no strong leadership, and lacked enthusiasm'.[47] On the other hand, there was also a genuine and legitimate concern regarding 'spontaneous' rural capitalism and possessiveness among peasants. The peasants had to be reminded that pursuit of profit, even for socialist construction, could easily stray out of acceptable bounds.

In this respect, the relationship of the Tachai model to mechanisation became clearer. As a production brigade – though in size no larger than most production teams – Tachai, being the basic accounting unit, already represented a higher level of collectivisation than would be found in most parts of China. With no private plots and the individual pursuit of wealth de-emphasised, Tachai was able to generate sufficient funds for basic mechanisation without any sacrifice of ideological values. The individual would benefit indirectly as the brigade's living standards improved. Thus, Tachai served as a model to counter the excess concern for profit engendered amongst other things by mechanisation.

The almost total reliance on the local accumulation of funds meant that the richer communes would be able to do much better than the poorer communes and this might help to perpetuate and even sharpen the disparities in wealth between communes, *xian* and larger regions. This danger, of course, would be remedied by the state contributing to the financing of such projects in the poor regions; but there was no evidence to show that this was being done, except perhaps in the national minority areas.

Both the need to finance local projects and to employ rationally the income derived from rural industries might help to increase the status of brigade and commune as economic units. Nevertheless, as indicated above, there appeared no signs that the Chinese wanted to speed up the process. Anhwei, for example, set 1980, as a target for raising the percentage of commune and brigade — level incomes to about 30 per cent of the total.[48] Commune and production brigade enterprises in a more developed *xian* in Shanghai municipality already accounted for 49 per cent of the income of the three-level rural economy in 1975 and the *xian* Party committee set the goal of raising this total to 52 per cent in 1976.[49] Perhaps a more typical case in this period, however, may be found in Lingyun *xian* in Kwangsi where the commune and production brigade enterprises only generated 10.6 per cent of the total income.[50]

When viewed against Mao's statement that movement from production team ownership to commune ownership should not occur until the latter's own income was greater than one half of the gross income of all three levels,[51] the above percentages and targets provided some indication of both the distance that collectivisation had to travel and the measured pace at which it was intended to proceed.

Though the evidence is far from conclusive, there were signs that development and expansion of commune and brigade enterprises also helped the development of poorer units within the commune. As explained in a *People's Daily* article, an important aspect of the question of raising poor production brigades to the level of richer ones was the 'development of the economy of the commune and production brigades and the creation of a more powerful material base for supporting poor production brigades'.[52] In illustration, it cited a commune in Shantung which provided six of its poor production brigades with 'eight tractors, six diesel engines, and 258 other farm machines from funds accumulated from commune and brigade-owned enterprises'.

The Industrial Sector

After the political upheavals of the Cultural Revolution had abated, the

Chinese leadership, confronted with problems of restoring labour discipline and incentives, was hard pressed to increase industrial output to make up for the losses of previous years. To promote production, a campaign of socialist emulation was launched by the Peking Iron and Steel Corporation in September 1969.[53] In this campaign, though stress was placed on 'revolutionary spirit', it was quite clear that the aim was to minimise waste, to economise on raw materials and fuel and to utilise, to the full, existing productive capacity.[54] At the same time, various enterprises were encouraged to take advantage of the presence of their representatives in Peking for the National Day celebrations to learn from the advanced experiences of industrial units in the capital.[55]

The problem of waste, to which Lin Piao alluded in this Report to the Ninth Party Congress,[56] was tackled boldly. In November 1969, Shanghai's industrial sector was said to have saved 900,000 tons of coal and vast amounts of electricity, steel, timber and petroleum in the previous ten months.[57] Efforts were made too to recycle waste. This was facilitated by large-scale programmes of inter-factory co-ordination with the waste of one factory being used by another. Such co-ordination was developed further in 1970 when production units, research units and schools combined to accomplish specific industrial projects — to manufacture a new product or develop a new technology. This was to be the precursor of independent regional industrial systems. Here again, Shanghai achieved notable results when, in March 1970, over three hundred units in various enterprises co-operated to produce, in a short space of time, a vast array of equipment needed by small fertiliser plants.[58] The aim was not Liu Shao-ch'i's 'revisionist' policy of rigid specialisation but co-ordinated industrial complexes based on such single major industries.[59]

Technical innovation and improvements in product quality also received due attention. Though many technicians, removed during the Cultural Revolution, returned to their posts,[60] this did not necessarily mean that there was a return to the former policy of reliance on 'experts'. Workers were now to be involved in industrial design and technical innovation and former specialists were required to undergo re-education through participation in collective labour. Groups and committees responsible for such innovations were set up, based on a 'triple combination' of veteran workers, cadres and specialists and such innovations were examined by review committees in which workers participated. Workers were enjoined to supervise the implementation of new designs and to avoid the previous blind reliance on foreign blueprints; care also was to be taken to ensure that new products went into production within one year of their being formally adopted.[61]

The improvement of product quality was, therefore, of prime importance. According to *People's Daily,* it was not just an economic question but also a political question.[62] It would remain a problem so long as the factionalism and 'anarchism' noted in previous chapters, remained and so long as cadres had not regained sufficient confidence to take bold initiatives.[63] It was also, perhaps, a consequence of emulation campaigns which stressed quantity rather than quality. To deal with this problem and the factionalism which helped to cause it, a number of measures were taken which will be the subject of a subsequent chapter by Andrew Watson. Suffice it here to summarise the main items. First, as Young's chapter has indicated, Party leadership at enterprise level was greatly strengthened. Secondly, efforts were made to draft new 'rational rules and regulations' for management which were said to be significantly different from those which pertained in 1965.[64] Thirdly, these rules were accompanied by a tighter system of accounting which was to encourage sound business procedure without 'putting profits in command'.[65] Fourthly, attempts were made to specify the limits within which cadres might participate in manual labour.[66] Fifthly, a moderate wage reform was carried out which raised the average wage by about 10 per cent.[67] Finally, welfare expenditures were greatly increased and occasionally reached 36 per cent of the wage bill.[68]

Rural Incentives and Rural Commerce

While labour discipline in rural areas remained largely unaffected by the Cultural Revolution, and the re-structuring of leadership at the commune level and below was not much more than a matter of formality, the question of 'rational incentives' was nonetheless an important one. In the Constitution, adopted in January 1975 at the Fourth National People's Congress, it was made clear that certain concessions to peasant thrift were to remain: private plots, individual sideline production and private ownership of livestock in pastoral areas were to be permitted. In institutionalising people's communes, moreover, the Constitution also protected the accounting rights of production teams.[69] Since a draft of the Constitution had been presented to the Second Plenum of the Ninth Central Committee in 1970, and since the sections of this draft which dealt with the rural sector were largely retained, it seems safe to conclude that rural policy was quite well defined by the end of 1970.[70] Added evidence is provided by the *People's Daily* editorial of 18 February 1971 on China's rural policy, which gave particular emphasis to the correct handling of the relationship between the state, the collective and the individual and did not differ in any important respect from the relevant sections of the Constitution adopted in 1975. In another report at the end of 1971, *People's Daily* praised a production brigade in Kiangsu for good distribution work after the autumn harvest.[71] It was said that the production brigade carried out Mao's instruction on increasing production and increasing individual income annually, so that both the food rations and cash income of brigade members were increased.

The priority attached to the development of agriculture and the channelling of industrial output to support it certainly helped to raise the income of the communes and, therefore, the peasants. Relaxation of restrictions on sideline production and the development of rural industries naturally also contributed to increasing rural income. Likewise, the greater concern given to the rural sector by commercial departments and the restructuring of the rural commercial network, was of significant importance to the support of agriculture and improvement in rural living standards. On 19 October 1970, *People's Daily* published a long article entitled 'The Orientation of China's Socialist Commerce' by the Writing Group of the Ministry of Commerce which probably served as a guideline for commercial activities in China. One of the major principles raised in the article was:

> With regard to the peasants, only the system of exchange and not expropriation can be used. This is a basic viewpoint of Mao Tsetung Thought. Apart from the small amount of agricultural tax, the overwhelming amount of agricultural and sideline products needed by the state are obtained through the exchange of commodities ... Socialist commerce follows the policy of stabilising prices; the policy of making little profit and selling more is carried out as regards industrial products; and the policy of the exchange of equal values or approximately equal values is adopted in exchanging industrial products for agricultural produce. These policies ... have aroused the peasants' enthusiasm for socialism, stimulated the urban and rural economy and consolidated the socialist base ...[72]

The strengthening of the rural commercial network was mainly reflected in the reliance on representatives of poor and lower-middle-class peasants to run rural commercial co-operatives[73] and the expansion of the commercial network into the remote communes and brigades.[74]

The aim was to provide a better service, but this was not to be limited merely to an increase in the amount of goods. It also included new supply schedules and the provision of a greater variety of products suitable for local needs.[75] The expansion of sideline production in rural areas naturally implied that rural demands would become increasingly complex and that more sophisticated purchasing plans would have to be devised to absorb these sideline products. The rural commercial network even extended its service to providing advice on the proper handling of the relationship between grain production and sideline production, the local accumulation of investment funds, the introduction of new agricultural inputs and new technology, and the training of technical personnel.[76]

Foreign Trade

China's foreign trade showed a slight reduction in 1967 and 1968 but the second half of 1968 already witnessed a marked recovery.[77] It may be noted that a sharp deterioration in China's exports to Hong Kong in these two years was a major reason for the relatively poor trade performance[78] and China's overall trade pattern was, in fact, not much affected. On the whole, it did not appear that the Cultural Revolution had any significant impact on China's trade policy. A *People's Daily* article on 14 October 1969 more than hinted that China was not against foreign trade; it stated that 'economic mutual-aid and cooperation between friendly countries, with each supplying what the other needs, is necessary on the basis of the principles of mutual respect for state sovereignty and independence, complete equality and mutual benefit'.[79]

Apparently, China's foreign trade increased rapidly after the Cultural Revolution from US$3,860 million in 1969 to US$14,090 million in 1975.[80] With the notable exceptions of 1974 and 1975 in which very considerable trade deficits were incurred, China roughly maintained a balance in its annual trade accounts.[81] The expansion in trade was due to the increasing capacity to export rice, textiles, handicrafts and petroleum, and the intent to import foreign plants and technology to speed up economic development. Success in establishing trade relations with practically every part of the world obviously also contributed to this expansion, though China'a major trading partners remained more or less the same as in the 1960s, with the United States being the only new partner of any significance.[82]

By 1977, however, previous forecasts of a spectacular expansion of China's foreign trade had been largely disproved: China's oil exports did not increase significantly but remained stagnant for two years; [83] Sino-American trade dropped sharply as China became more self-sufficient in grain after the recent good harvests;[84] and even Sino-Japanese trade showed only moderate increases.[85] China remained adamant in rejecting all proposals of joint economic ventures and in refusing to accept any long-term credit. Like Saudi Arabia, it became increasingly wary of exploiting its natural resources solely for export. Its concern for trade balances also meant that imports would only increase as its capacity for exports grew, which, incidentally, partly depended on acquiring techniques of promoting sales in the capitalist world.

The most interesting aspect of China's foreign trade, as far as development strategy was concerned, was perhaps the acquisition and diffusion of advanced foreign technology. Since 1970, the Chinese leaders looked outwards once again for the acquisition of capital equipment and know-how on a substantial scale. They purchased large numbers of complete plants to increase output in a number of basic industries, primary metallurgy, petro-chemicals and energy. From December 1972 to the spring of 1975, contracts worth between US$2.2 and 2.5 billion were made, principally with Japan, France and West Germany, with deliveries extending through 1977.[86] Imports of plant and technology, therefore, rose more rapidly in recent years than in any previous period.

How should this large-scale import of foreign plants and technology be evaluated? The significance or the 'weight' of this technological import in the Chinese development strategy and the problems associated with its unprecedented scale surely merit attention. There was no doubt that the principle of self-reliance continued to be stressed with at least three objectives in view: (1) to minimise China's strategic and financial dependence on foreign countries; (2) to create a self-confident generation of Chinese and guard against contamination by foreign influences; and (3) to mobilise local savings so as to economise on scarce foreign exchange and state investment funds. The pursuit of self-reliance in these terms in past decades enabled the Chinese to achieve a high degree of technical and economic independence; thus, according to one estimate in 1975, 'China's own production of machinery and equipment is now so large that imported technology represents only a small fraction (perhaps 6 to 8 per cent) of its overall technology accretion'.[87]

It may also be noted that, throughout the history of the People's Republic of China, foreign trade lagged behind economic growth so that the Chinese economy was actually becoming less oriented to foreign-trade. According to Alexander Eckstein, trade as a proportion of GNP dropped from an estimated 8 per cent in the 1950s to perhaps around 5 per cent in the mid-1970s.[88] Assuming that this ratio is maintained in the near future, the import of foreign technology might still increase as changes occur in the composition of imports. As the newly imported plants come into operation, the output of chemical fertilisers and steel might be expected to increase dramatically. Thus, when China achieves a greater degree of self-sufficiency not only in grain but also in these two items, a much larger amount of foreign currency will become available for further technological imports. In fact, the recent increase in such imports rather reflects China's increased import capacity than a deliberate change in policy in favour of foreign plants and technology. After all, China has looked to the West for such imports ever since the early 1960s.

In Chinese industry as a whole, the highly structured process of internal diffusion certainly appears to be far more important a source of technological advancement than the technology acquired from abroad. The Chinese leadership, moreover, seems willing to accept some short-term retardation of growth, in order, in the long run, to attain the social goals of mass participation and self-reliance. In an economy which 'walks on two legs', the major task is surely to raise the technological level of the farm machinery repair shops in the *xian* to that of the tractor plants in Shenyang. In qualitative terms, however, imports of technology will still be an important factor in the develop-ment of the more sophisticated sectors of Chinese industry. In some areas, output based on inefficient and obsolescent plans can be dramatically improved by the importation of modern technology and production facilities: such, indeed, has been the case with Rolls Royce Spey engines.[89] Imports of technology and the industrial exhibitions which go along with them have provided valuable international scientific contacts and information. These exhibitions have provided good opportunities for purchasing display models at favourable prices, for purposes of analysis and copying. Programmes for the importation of complete plants often also include the training of Chinese personnel by foreign firms. The construction of the large steel complex in Wuhan, jointly installed by DEMAG and Nippon Steel, for example, provided a six-month training course in Japan for Chinese technical personnel.[90] Thus, the existence of a highly skilled pool of technical manpower will help the Chinese assimilate sophisticated technology. It has, in fact already done so, as is well demonstrated by the successful shift of industrial priorities which lay behind the recent expansion of the chemical and petroleum industries. Such a shift indicates a new capacity to apply 'technical knowledge, skills and facilities for producing machinery to accommodate the changing requirements of productive activity'. This, Rosenberg identifies as a central characteristic of industrialised, as opposed to backward, economies.[91]

As may be expected, the considerable increase in China's foreign trade and imports of foreign plant and technology − at least in absolute terms − has posed serious problems and political dilemmas. China's increased involvement in the international economy has exposed it somewhat to the uncertainties of the world market, as was clearly demonstrated in 1974. The global recession and double-digit inflation has, therefore, caused Chinese exports to suffer from both a decline in demand and a deterioration in the terms of trade. Since a sizable share of Chinese imports are based on advance commitments, China incurred huge deficits in 1974 and 1975, amounting to about US$1.1 billion and 400 million respectively.[92] In order to finance this trade gap, the principle of 'self reliance' was stretched to dangerous limits. One of the most explicit formulations was the statement by Vice-Premier Teng Hsiao-p'ing in October 1974:

> Only self-reliance is a sure-fire method. Why is there world inflation, with only the *reminbi* [China's currency] not likely to be affected? Because of our reliance on our own resources. We now also accept instalment payment terms for machinery from abroad but only in the knowledge that we are capable of making regular payments. We must remain free from debts, both at home and abroad, and not go further than that.[93]

Such a concern for self-reliance resulted in the employment of a number of devices either to defer payment for goods received or to obtain foreign exchange to pay for them. These ranged from quite short-term 30-day suppliers' credits to 5-year deferred-payment schemes linked to complete plant deliveries. In addition, a number of West European and Japanese banks were invited to place foreign currency deposits in the Bank of China at Eurodollar rates (or at rates approximating these) for periods of up to one year, and renewable annually. These deposits might have amounted to several hundred million dollars in 1974, and they could be considered as loans in disguise.[94] Moreover, the large-scale influx of Western visitors has meant greater exposure of Chinese managers and technicians to capitalist ways, a greater acceptance of the relevance of foreign expertise and technology to Chinese development, and, therefore, a greater threat of back-sliding into a 'slavish comprador philosophy' and 'revisionism'. It is, therefore, small wonder that in the campaign to Criticise Lin Piao and Confucius, foreign technology was a hotly-debated issue and the Chinese were warned against the evil Liu Shao-ch'i/Lin Piao 'revisionist' line of 'worshipping foreign things', trumpeting the 'slavish comprador philosophy and promoting the mentality of trailing behind at a snail's pace'.[95]

Since the arrest of the Gang of Four, visiting delegations have been told that China would expand its imports;[96] yet no major expansion appears likely in the near future. Due to the huge trade deficits incurred in 1974 and 1975, China will not be fiscally able to engage in a substantial buying programme until 1978 or 1979 without getting into debt; and the present Chinese leadership shows no signs that it will accept long-term credit. Nevertheless, eventual trade expansion seems very likely. China will not become a colossal market for foreign capital equipment, but neither will it entertain complete economic autarchy. So long as China insists on the maintenance of its long-held policy of paying for imports with export earnings, the size of its technological and other imports will have to depend on its export capabilities.

Conclusion

In the evolution of the Chinese development strategy, the proper handling of the relationships between industry and agriculture, between industry in the coastal regions and industry in the interior, between the state, the units of production and the individual producers, etc. have been, at least, as important as economic growth. The assurance of a minimum standard of living and the narrowing of income inequalities are stated objectives of economic programmes in most developing countries. In China, however, in contrast to many Third World countries, these objectives, together with the preservation of socialist values, have been assigned a high priority in deed as well as in word.

Though a contentious point, many would agree that the experiments with an original Chinese development strategy embodied in the Great Leap Forward ended almost in economic disaster. The direction of economic policy after the Cultural Revolution however, suggests some kind of synthesis of elements of the Great Leap and concessions to the materialistic demands of peasants and workers. The groundwork for this new course seems to have been laid and management of the economy appears more decentralised, with considerable emphasis on the development of small-scale rural industry.

In the agricultural sector, the continued improvement of the water control system and the general increase in agricultural inputs constitute key elements in the long-term upward trend of farm output. Though many water control projects are only partly finished and major rivers and large tributaries remain to be harnessed, irrigation and water control in the more distant future will surely show diminishing returns. Mechanisation, chemical fertilisers and improved seeds, on the other hand, will assume increasing importance. Hua Kuo-feng's report to the First National Conference on Learning from Tachai appears to have demonstrated this awareness.[97] Chinese agriculture has also benefited from the broadening of education and training in rural areas, the increased experience of the work force with fertilisers and machinery and the assignment to the countryside since 1968 of nearly 10 million secondary school graduates from urban areas.[98] The policy of 'walking on two legs' continues to satisfy short-term and long-term rural requirements. For example, simple seed selection and crossing have been practised by peasants and limited scientific capabilities have been devoted to sophisticated varietal development. The problem, of course, is to ensure that these activities complement rather than hinder each other. Similar problems exist, of course, in rural industries, and guidelines have been set so that they do not absorb more than 5 per cent of the labour force of any *xian*.[99]

According to Eckstein's estimates, only 28 per cent of China's national product in 1970 derived from agriculture, as compared with 45 per cent in 1952.[100] The agricultural sector is, therefore, of diminishing significance in China's economic development, and the emphasis on the agricultural sector in the Chinese development strategy is largely based on social and political factors. If Chinese leaders had not adopted the policy of deliberately favouring the rural sector, the country would almost certainly have developed a dual economy. The problem is still far from solved. Although agricultural output has been increasing steadily in the past fifteen years or so, its growth rate has been vastly outstripped by that of industry. There is no indication that the proportion of the total work-force engaged in agriculture (75 per cent) has diminished,[101] and the migration of secondary school graduates from the urban to the rural areas continues to be strongly encouraged. The development of rural industries and the increase in supply of modern inputs from the industrial sector are, of course, aimed at eliminating the very considerable differences in living standards between the two sectors; fiscal means have also been adopted to improve the terms of trade for peasants. Using 1952 prices as base figures, Nicholas Lardy has estimated that, between 1952 and 1974, the prices of farm products paid by the state increased by 64.4 per cent while prices of industrial goods sold in rural areas increased by a mere 0.3 per cent.[102] These fiscal measures achieved fast results, but ultimately they depend on the amount of resources devoted to the support of the rural sector.

It is of interest to note that much of the tremendous increase in contracts for Western industrial plants in 1973 and 1974 (US$1.2 billion in 1973 and $850 million in 1974, compared with only $60 million in 1972) was not designed to increase the machine-building or mining capacity but rather to expand several fold the capacity to produce chemical fertilisers and artificial fibres.[103] Between November 1972 and May 1974, China bought 13 large urea plants from Japan, Western Europe and the United States at a total cost of US$500 million.[104] Output from these plants, if supplemented by improved water control facilities and increased supplies of other types of fertiliser, will boost agricultural output considerably by 1980 and the need for imports of grain and nitrogen fertilisers might be eliminated, even in poor crop years. To what extent these plant purchases will continue is, of course, difficult to estimate, but the amount of foreign exchange spent is a good indication of the Chinese leadership's determination to tackle the problems of the rural sector.

Performance in the industrial sector has been satisfactory in the post-Cultural Revolution period, as confirmed by the figures released by Premier Chou in early 1975.[105] The policy of supporting agriculture in the past years, as analysed above, has probably set the stage for a break-through in agriculture in the early 1980s and this break-through, in turn, will boost industrial production. In the first place, the increased production of agricultural raw materials will provide more inputs for light industry. Secondly, the foreign exchange currently needed to purchase grain and fertilisers will be freed for industrial investment.

More balanced efforts to promote growth will be required so as to correct the existing structural flaws in industry. The recent shortages of coal, iron ore, etc. reflected fundamental imbalances in extractive, processing and finishing industries. In metallurgy, for example, investment has been concentrated too heavily on the development of crude steel capacity at the expense of mining and finished steel.

To deal with the unbalanced distribution of industries, the Chinese undertook a deliberately phased policy of regional development beginning with the First Five-Year Plan. The specific provisions governing the geographical distribution of industrial capital construction were as follows: (1) expansion of existing industrial bases, especially in North East China, in order to support the construction of new industrial areas; (2) construction of new industrial bases in North China and Central China, centring around two new iron and steel complexes to be built in Paotow and Wuhan; and (3) the construction of a new industrial base in South West China.[106] According to the rates of provincial industrial growth between 1949 and 1974, provided by Lardy, many of the least-industrialised interior regions of China, such as Kansu, Tsinghai, Ninghsia and Inner Mongolia, actually sustained the highest rates of growth.[107] On the other hand, many of the provinces which were highly developed in 1949 grew relatively slowly. China's leading industrial centre, Shanghai, for example, was one of the slowest growing areas. South West China, however, seems to have lagged slightly behind; though it is likely that the recent investments in the infrastructure in that region, particularly in the transportation sector (symbolised by the completion of the Chengtu-Kunming railway) would start to pay off in the near future.

Since the early 1970s, there has been a series of small improvements in the quality, variety and availability of consumer goods; and the extent of improvement is probably most noticeable in the ownership of consumer durables — bicycles, watches, transistor radios, cameras, and sewing machines. This phenomenon reflects the amount of resources devoted to light industry. Such commodities, however, are still largely available only to industrial workers and to members of well-to-do communes. The problem, therefore, is whether the increasing availability of such commodities at cheaper prices will, in fact, aggravate real income differentials. In many ways, such might well be a temporary and necessary evil since the expansion of consumer goods industries will inevitably be a lengthy process.

Finally, any discussion of China's development strategy must consider population growth. Estimates of the Chinese population in the mid-1970s ranged from 800 to 920 million;[108] and the seriousness of the problem is well illustrated by the following statement made in mid-1971 by Vice-Premier Li Hsien-nien to a journalist from Cairo: 'We have been racing against time to cope with the enormous increase in population. Some people estimate the population at 800 million and some at 750 million. Unfortunately, there are no accurate statistics in this connection.'[109] The present population control programme, which is much more vigorous than the campaigns of 1956-8 and 1962-6, has only been in operation since the Cultural Revolution and has only just begun to take effect in the rural areas. Although its importance is appreciated, cadres at all levels probably have a host of other programmes competing for their attention. If the highest priority is given to curbing the birth rate in the next decade, the Chinese have the organisation, the technology and a changing social climate which could make the programme a success. Indeed, some encouraging signs emerged in early 1977. It was revealed that in Hopei and Kiangsu, the population growth rate had declined from 25 per thousand in 1965 to around 10 per thousand, and Shanghai and Peking had managed to keep their population growth to below 6 per thousand.[110] The major task in the future is to bring the rates in the rural areas down to the level of those in Peking and Shanghai.

As revealed in Premier Chou's Report to the Fourth National People's Congress in January 1975, China aims initially to build an independent and relatively comprehensive industrial and economic system before 1980, and after that, to accomplish the comprehensive modernisation of agriculture, industry, national defence and science and technology before the end of the century.[111] There appears to be no reason why it should not succeed.

In this general survey of the Chinese strategy in the post-Cultural Revolution period, the significance of the purge of Lin Piao, the campaign to Criticise Lin Piao and Confucius, the campaign to Study the Theory of the Dictatorship of the Proletariat, the criticisms of Teng Hsiao-ping, and the arrest of the 'Gang of Four' have all been conspicuously neglected. An easy way out, of course, is to say that the scope of the chapter does not allow a detailed analysis of the impact of these events. But, several additional points may be made. In the first place, the broad outline of the development strategy discussed above appears to have been confirmed both at the Tenth Party Congress in August 1973 and at the Fourth National People's Congress in January 1975. The major thrust of the sharpening 'struggle between the two lines' in recent years was chiefly directed at things like educational policy, the restoration of former cadres and the neglect of class struggle. With the exception of the role of foreign technology, the broad outline of the development strategy has never been an important issue of debate.

Secondly, the arrest of the 'Gang of Four' revealed that its influence was limited to control of the mass media, and to a lesser extent, Shanghai. The purge of Lin Piao had little impact on development strategy and the so-called 'electronics versus steel' debate proved to be a non-issue.[112] Thus, throughout this period, the Chinese development strategy does not seem to have been substantially affected by such crises. Even during the campaign to Study the Theory of the Dictatorship of the Proletariat, the rights of peasants to private plots and individual side-line production were never actually in doubt. Both 1974 and 1975 began with political campaigns which were called off by the mid year as industrial production declined and factional fighting erupted among workers. Both years continued with massive emphases on unity and order as prerequisites for meeting production goals.[113] The expansion of trade and the introduction of foreign plants and technology, which once stretched the self-reliance principle to its very limits, especially in the field of foreign credit, did give cause for criticism. Nevertheless, the growth of China's shipbuilding industry and improvement in port facilities continued at a rapid pace.[114] Precious resources would definitely have been channelled elsewhere if China's trade policy and development strategy had encountered serious domestic opposition.

One may only conclude that the Chinese development strategy is the result of years of experimentation and learning; and there have been no signs in recent years that difficulties have been experienced so enormous that a major revision was required, as was the case at the end of the First Five Year Plan and during the difficult post-Leap years of 1959-61. Moreover, the period since the Cultural Revolution has been characterised by a very considerable degree of policy diversity and experimentation. Some communes practised the Tachai system of politicised remuneration and brigade-level management whilst others continued with piece-rate work points and team management. Some factories gave bonuses whilst others mounted campaigns against 'economism'. Similarly, educational institutions experimented with various admission procedures and teaching materials.[115] Such an argument does not aim to deny the importance of the 'struggle between the two lines', but this survey, in attempting to sketch the broad outline of the Chinese development strategy, covers in most cases ground that appears to have remained largely unchallenged.

Notes

1. Mao Tsetung, 25 April 1956, in *SW,* Chinese edition, Vol. 5, pp.267-88 (translated *PR* 1, 1 January 1977, pp.10-25). A slightly different version in *Wansui* 1969, pp.40-59 (translated Schram 1974, pp.61-83).
2. Ibid., (Schram 1974, p.62).

3. See Gray 1973.
4. See e.g. Tien Chih-sung, *RMRB,* 22 March 1974, p.2.
5. See e.g. *RMRB,* 31 May 1976, pp.1-2 and 4.
6. See e.g. Chi Wei, *PR* 11, 11 March 1977, pp.6-9.
7. *RMRB,* 21 February 1969, translated in *PR* 9, 28 February 1969, pp.4-6.
8. Writing Group of the Peking Municipal Revolutionary Committee, *Hongqi* 10, 1969, translated in *PR* 43, 24 October 1969, pp.7-13.
9. *Jiefang Ribao (Liberation Daily),* Shanghai, 22 February 1969.
10. *CQ* 38, April-June 1969, pp.185-6.
11. *PR* 43, 24 October 1969, p.12.
12. For an analysis of the 'weight' of each province in the gross value of industrial output, see Field, Lardy and Emerson 1975, pp.421-34.
13. Taipei, *Central News Agency,* 12 February 1970, in *Sing Tao Wan Pao,* Hong Kong, 13 February 1970; cited in Hsu Tak-ming 1974, pp.256-7.
14. *Sing Tao Jih Pao,* Hongkong, 7 December 1969, p.4.
15. *RMRB,* 18 April 1968, p.4.
16. Hsu Tak-ming 1974, pp.609-11, 613-14. See also *RMRB,* 1 June 1971, p.1; 19 June 1971, p.1; 5 October 1971, p.1; 9 January 1972.
17. Lardy 1976, pp. 8-9.
18. *Eckstein 1975, China's Economic Development,* p.364.
19. Hsu Tak-ming 1974, p.259.
20. Donnithorne 1972, p.605.
21. Chou En-lai, Interview with Edgar Snow, *Epoca,* February 1971, p.23.
22. *RMRB,* 15 January 1972, p.1.
23. *SWB,* FE/3506/B/3, quoting Tanjug correspondent Stjepan Pucak, Peking, 9 October 1970.
24. *RMRB,* 25 October 1969, p.2. See also Hsu Tak-ming 1974, p.254.
25. *SWB,* FE/w557/A/10. See also *NCNA,* 30 January 1970.
26. Donnithorne 1972, p.610.
27. Sigurdson 1973, pp.223-4.
28. Ibid, pp.203-9.
29. *RMRB,* 18 April 1969, p.2.
30. *RMRB,* 26 December 1969, p.3.
31. *RMRB,* 14 October 1969, p.4; 25 October 1969, p.2; 10 November 1969, p.1; 14 December 1969, p.1; *GMRB,* 24 December 1969, p.1; *Economic Reporter,* Hong Kong, 1 January 1970, p.35.
32. Hsu Tak-ming 1974, pp.417-18.
33. At the end of 1969, a number of provincial revolutionary committees organised agricultural, financial and industrial conferences. In most of them, a 'leap forward' or 'flying leap' was said to be imminent or being planned. See e.g. *SWB,* FE/3222 (Changsha); *SWB,* FE/3266 (Sining); *SWB,* FE/3263 (Kwangchow); *SWB,* FE/3266 (Harbin). Similar conferences in early 1970, held in Yunnan, Kirin, Chekiang, etc., also made reference to a 'flying leap'.
34. Writing group of the Honan Revolutionary Committee, *Hongqi* 2, 1970, trans. in *PR* 7, 13 February 1970, p.5 and 7.
35. *PR* 4, 24 January 1975, p.14.
36. Chou En-lai, 13 January 1975, in ibid., p.22.
37. Ashbrook 1975, p.29.
38. *RMRB,* 15 February 1969, p.2.
39. *RMRB,* 8 December 1969, p.4.
40. *RMRB,* 15 May 1969, p.4.
41. *RMRB,* 25 September 1969, p.1.
42. See note 34.
43. Hsu Tak-ming 1974, p.407.

44. Ibid., p.408.
45. *RMRB,* 24 September 1969, p.2 and 8 December 1969, p.4.
46. Chao Kang 1975, p.713.
47. Hallford 1976, p.8.
48. Ibid., p.10.
49. Ibid., p.10.
50. Ibid., p.10.
51. Mao Tsetung 1960 (or 1961-2), *Wansui* 1969, p.343 (*JPRS* 1974, p.267)
52. *RMRB,* 17 October 1975, p.1.
53. Challenges were issued to other iron and steel corporations in Wuhan, Paotow, Taiyuan and Chungking. *RMRB,* 11 September 1969, p.1 and 14 September 1969, p.1 and 3.
54. *RMRB,* 11 September 1969, p.1.
55. *RMRB,* 2 December 1969, p.1. See also Hsu Tak-ming 1974, pp.262-4.
56. *PR* Special Issue, 28 April 1969, p.20.
57. *RMRB,* 24 November 1969, p.4.
58. *RMRB,* 28 November 1970, p.2.
59. Hsu Tak-ming 1974, pp.564-6.
60. Howe (in Schram) 1973, pp.249-50.
61. *GMRB,* 30 August 1970, p.2; *RMRB,* 2 December 1970, p.1 and 4 and *RMRB,* 14 August 1970, p.3.
62. *RMRB,* 11 January 1970, p.1.
63. *RMRB,* 11 January 1970, p.1 and *RMRB,* 12 July 1970, p.3. See also Hsu Tak-ming 1974, pp.267-8.
64. *RMRB,* 4 February 1972.
65. Ibid.
66. *RMRB,* 20 November 1969, p.1.
67. Howe (in Schram) 1973, p.251.
68. *Hongqi* 7, 1972, p.46. Compare this figure with a 20 per cent level which in 1958 was considered too high. Howe 1973, p.252.
69. See note 35.
70. According to intelligence sources in Taipei, a draft of the Constitution was passed at the Second Plenum of the Ninth CC, in September 1970. For the text of the draft Constitution obtained by these sources, see Liu Ching-po 1973, pp.427-36.
71. *RMRB,* 28 December 1971, p.3.
72. *PR* 50, 11 December 1970, p.4.
73. *RMRB,* 5 December 1970, p.1.
74. *RMRB,* 6 January 1972, p.1.
75. *RMRB,* 5 March 1971, p.2. See also Hsu Tak-ming 1974, pp.800-1.
76. Ibid., see also *RMRB,* 6 January 1972, p.1.
77. For statistics on China's foreign trade, see Chen Nai-ruenn 1975, p.645. On the recovery in the second half of 1968, see *FEER Yearbook: Asia,* 1970, p.107.
78. Ibid., see also Hsu Tak-ming 1974, pp.115-16, 500-2.
79. *PR* 43, 24 October 1969, p.8.
80. Chen Nai-ruenn 1975, p.645, and *FEER Yearbook: Asia,* 1977, p.159.
81. Ibid, See also *FEER Yearbook: Asia,* 1976, p.153.
82. Chen Nai-ruenn 1975, pp.648-50. See also *FEER Yearbook: Asia,* 1977, p.159.
83. Smil 1976, pp.69-74 See also *FEER Yearbook: Asia,* 1977, p.160.
84. Eckstein (in *Foreign Affairs*) 1975, pp.150-2 and *FEER Yearbook: Asia,* 1977, p.159.
85. Chen Nai-ruenn 1975, p.650 and *FEER Yearbook: Asia,* 1977, p.159.
86. Eckstein (in *Foreign Affairs)* 1975, p.140.

87. Heymann 1975, p.679.
88. Eckstein (in *Foreign Affairs*) 1975, pp.138-9.
89. A Reed. *The Times,* 17 December 1975, p.6.
90. Eckstein (in *Foreign Affairs*) 1975, p.145.
91. Rosenberg 1964, p.71. See also Rawski 1973, p.26.
92. See note 81; also Eckstein (in *Foreign Affairs*) 1975, pp.147-8.
93. Teng made this statement at a reception for Overseas Chinese in Peking on 2 October 1974; quoted in *U.S. – China Business Review,* Vol.2, No.1, p.34, cited in Eckstein (in *Foreign Affairs)* 1975, p.148.
94. Eckstein (in *Foreign Affairs*) 1975, p.149.
95. Tian Chih-sung, *RMRB,* 22 March 1974, p.2.
96. *FEER Yearbook: Asia,* 1977, p.160.
97. Excerpts in *PR* 44, 31 October 1975, pp.7-10, 18.
98. Ashbrook 1975, p.30.
99. Ibid.
100. Eckstein 1973, p.236.
101. Ibid.
102. Lardy 1976, p.6.
103. Ashbrook 1975, p.31.
104. Ibid. p.29.
105. Chou En-lai, 13 January 1975, *PR* 4, 24 January 1975, p.22.
106. Field 1975, p.154.
107. Lardy 1976, pp.10-11.
108. Chou En-lai in his Report of 13 January 1975, referred to a population of nearly 800 million' (*PR* 4, 24 January 1975, p.22). Ashbrook (1975, p.35), however, estimated that the population was about 920 million in mid 1974.
109. *FBIS,* CHI – 71-238, 10 December 1971, A8.
110. *PR* 13, 25 March 1977, p.29.
111. Chou En-lai, 13 January 1975, *PR* 4, 24 January 1975, p.23.
112. For the significance of the debate, see Sigurdson 1973, pp. 227-30. For a good analysis of the relationship between Lin Piao and development strategy, see O'Leary 1974, pp.159-62.
113. Winckler 1976, p.741.
114. *FEER Yearbook: Asia,* 1977, p.161.
115. Nathan 1976, p.730.

'TWO LINE STRUGGLE' IN AGRICULTURE

Dennis Woodward

The Effects of the Cultural Revolution

In the previous chapter, Cheng argued that, in both the industrial and rural sectors, 'ultra-leftism' was a consequence of the Cultural Revolution which faded away in the early 1970s. Such a conclusion hides the fact that the progress of the Cultural Revolution in the rural areas was profoundly different from its progress in the industrial areas, with very different consequences for the pace and nature of reform in the period after 1969. This chapter must begin, therefore, with a description of the impact of the Cultural Revolution on the countryside.

Such is by no means an easy task since surprisingly little has been written about changes in the Chinese countryside since the early 1960s. Due to the unavailability of statistics after the Great Leap Forward, most discussions of Chinese agriculture focus on the 1950s.[1] That period provides a rewarding field for research, not only because of the availability of hard data but because many documents released by Red Guards during the Cultural Revolution reveal profound policy differences which relate to that time. The fact that not much has been written about the 1960s has contributed to the view that no really significant changes have occurred in rural institutional structure and organisation since that time and that political movements directed at the villages were concerned mainly with ideological problems. It is rash to make such a judgement. A set of documents relating to Lienchiang *xian* in Fukien, captured by Kuomintang raiders in the early 1960s, reveal the persistence of considerable organisational as well as ideological problems.[2] The Socialist Education Movement of 1962-6, moreover, was not just directed at 'capitalist' attitudes in the countryside (though perhaps that is what some of the more conservative leaders of the Party might have wished). It was also concerned with institutional arrangements which might contribute to 'capitalist' relations. Yet this major movement and the subsequent Cultural Revolution in the countryside have been given scant attention in the literature.[3] Only the works of Baum have attempted to come to grips with the problem[4] and even these are too frequently based on documents which refer to the urban situation transposed on to the rural

153

scene.

Baum's major contention, however, that for the greater part of the period 1966-8, the majority of China's rural areas did not experience 'significant Red Guard agitation' and remained largely insulated from the events of the Cultural Revolution[5] is borne out by what little evidence we have on the subject. For example, a Red Guard refugee reported that his excursions into the countryside revealed that the Cultural Revolution had not really touched the peasants at all.[6] Similarly, the speed with which revolutionary committees were formed in the countryside during 1968 strongly suggests that the existing administration did little more than change its name. Such is precisely what happened in Liu Ling village, as recorded in one of the few studies of a rural village which have appeared since the Cultural Revolution.[7]

In fact, it may even be the case that Baum has overestimated the changes in rural organisation which took place in the latter half of 1968. He lists the following changes:[8]

1. The merging and consolidation of brigades and communes
2. The decentralisation of rural educational, medical and public health facilities
3. The fostering of small-scale commune-run industries
4. The adoption of the Tachai system of labour remuneration and work point evaluation.

Indeed, it is not at all clear whether the above were usually any more than proposals in 1968 and Baum's citing of articles in *Current Scene* in 1969, as evidence of what was occurring in 1968, is somewhat questionable.[9] There is considerable danger in assuming that the agricultural policies advocated in the Chinese media (especially in the highly charged political climate of 1968) accurately reflected what was going on throughout the countryside. Baum, moreover, is not alone in making such an assumption. Wheelwright and McFarlane argue that the production brigade was generally the 'unit of account' after the Cultural Revolution[10] and MacDougall argues that the Tachai system of remuneration was widespread[11] -- views which, I suggest, are quite erroneous. There were, in fact, considerable delays between the promulgation of policies and their actual implementation and advanced models (such as Tachai) were not copied so generally as Chinese publications suggest.

In terms of its impact on organisation, the Cultural Revolution was largely an urban phenomenon and, with the exception of communes on the outskirts of major cities, the countryside did not

suffer major upheavals.[12] Until the latter part of 1968, the impact of
the Cultural Revolution on rural areas was largely ideological. Liu
Shao-ch'i's 'revisionist line on agriculture' (symbolised by *san zi
yi bao* and the 'four freedoms') was, of course, criticised throughout
1967 but it was not until the second half of the following year, when
the Cultural Revolution in the urban sector had begun to abate,
that concrete reforms were initiated in the countryside.[13] At that
time, PLA Mao Tsetung Thought propaganda teams attempted to
extend the campaign of 'struggle, criticism and transformation' into
the villages. They proposed to foster small scale industries, to
amalgamate teams, brigades and communes,[14] to decentralise
educational and other facilities and to reorganise the supply and
marketing network. Farm machinery and tractors, which had belonged
to state-controlled stations, were to be handed down to individual
communes.[15] At the same time, the campaign to learn from Tachai
was greately intensified. But one must be less sanguine than Baum
about the immediate success in implementing these proposals. Indeed,
it was sometimes not until 1969 that anything much was achieved
and the problems created by such implementation were to persist into
the early 1970s.

   Thus, the belated implementation of the Cultural Revolution in
the rural sector produced a climate very different from that of
industry. Within the factories, efforts were directed to overcoming
the turmoil of previous years and consolidating the new situation.
In the villages, the denunciation of old policies often intensified after
1969 with the continued stress on the protracted nature of class
struggle and 'extensive revolutionary criticism'. Whilst the
industrial sector had reached the 'transformation' stage in the
'struggle, criticism, transformation' formula, the rural sector had
only just begun to engage in 'struggle and criticism'.

The Post Cultural Revolution Situation – Introduction

The dearth of studies on rural organisation has continued into the
1970s. References to changes in institutional structure and the
effect of rural campaigns have been all too fleeting. Marianne Bastid
has touched briefly on these questions[16] and Leo Goodstadt has
attempted somewhat more detail.[17] Goodstadt, however, has
ill-digested the material he presents and we still lack a clear picture of
what exactly took place in the countryside. With regard to specific
questions such as fertilisers[18] and rural industry,[19] we are perhaps more
fortunate since travellers accounts, supplemented by the release of

some new official statistics have given us something to work on. It is possible once again to discuss with confidence changes in agricultural output and some mention must be made of these before we return to the central concern with rural organisation.

Since Cheng has already summarised the main items, it will be sufficient here to note that the debates on rural organisation took place within the context of marked agricultural growth. In 1970, official statistics claimed a grain output of 240 million tonnes.[20] Most commentators see no reason to doubt this figure,[21] which was much higher than previously predicted[22] and indicated that previous estimates had been consistently low. In 1971, the official figure was 246 million tonnes[23] (later often rounded up to 250)[24] which was an all-time record. In 1972, output fell to 240 million tonnes[25] which in itself was a remarkable achievement for a year in which crops had been seriously threatened by adverse weather. In 1973, total output exceeded 250 million tonnes,[26] bettering the previous record, and this was again surpassed in 1974.[27] Estimates of the average annual growth rate for agriculture vary from 2.5 per cent to 3.7 per cent (1963-70)[28] through 3.4 per cent (1965-71)[29] to 4 per cent (1963-71)[30] and all estimates show that agricultural production is clearly outstripping population growth (1.7 to 2.1 per cent). Furthermore, the increase in agricultural output since the Cultural Revolution suggests that China has succeeded in fundamentally establishing its agricultural base. Thus, the benefits of land reclamation, capital construction works (particularly irrigation), an expanded fertiliser industry, double cropping, the development and popularisation of new seed strains etc. are now being realised, to the extent that high stable yields might be guaranteed irrespective of weather conditions.

Despite a background of increasing agricultural output, however, it is apparent that betwen 1969 and 1973 the Chinese countryside was the scene of continuing struggle over the nature and implementation of agricultural development. Conventionally, it is argued that 'radical' or 'Maoist' policies were dominant after the Cultural Revolution until the fall of Lin Piao, after which, more 'conservative policies' were followed.[31] Contrary to this view, this chapter will argue that, insofar as agriculture was concerned, the 'radical' phase, commonly associated with Lin Piao was marked by excesses which were antithetical to Mao's position. The correction of these excesses, which began in 1970 and which had been largely completed by late 1972, rather than marking a return to 'conservative' policies, in fact, indicated the re-assertion of Mao's position. The argument, therefore, is that the major political struggles of the early 1970s were inextricably linked with development strategy and were not, as Cheng suggests, outside its scope. Let us, therefore, first summarise Mao's strategy.

Mao's Strategy for Agriculture – A Brief Review

The Introduction to this book discussed the broad outlines of Mao's strategy for economic development and Cheng's chapter is set against that background. Many components, it will be remembered, derived from the experiences of the Communist Party in Yenan. Mass campaigns to increase production, the stress on self reliance, a concern for the livelihood of the people, anti-bureaucratism and a collectivist orientation all owe their origin to the early 1940s.[32] It was not until 1956, however, when the Soviet model began to be rejected, that anything like a comprehensive framework within which to measure qualitative development emerged. As Cheng has demonstrated, Mao's 'On the Ten Major Relationships' was the first attempt at such a framework[33] and, though subsequently there were new evaluations of the relationship between balance and imbalance and on the general speed of development, the overall framework remained. Mao's stress on the complementarity of agriculture and industry and central and local initiative remained constant, as did his concern for a gradual increase in peasant income and welfare.

The speed of development was as contentious an issue in the 1950s as it was to be in the 1970s. Mao could, of course, offer no *a priori* edict on the optimum speed of social change valid for the whole period of socialist transition. Yet he had to offer some way of measuring the 'correct' rate of social change. As the Introduction pointed out, this was to take shape in the 1960s as a theory of stages defined in terms of three criteria – the nature of ownership, the relations between people at work and the pattern of distribution.[34] Land reform, during and after the Civil War of 1946-9, changed the basis of ownership but had less effect on the other two criteria. Because co-operativisation campaigns did not receive sufficient backing, relations between peasants at work remained unchanged. Thus, atomised peasant farming could easily degenerate into traditional patterns of landholding with more and more land concentrated in the hands of richer peasants. Mao's response, in the mid 1950s, was a rapid programme of co-operativisation,[35] which changed the relationship between people at work but created new problems concerning ownership of the means of production and distribution of income. It was not at all clear to what extent the communes of 1958 constituted 'ownership by the whole people', nor how to go about changing the pattern of distribution. Indeed, some people considered that one could contemplate a switch from the 'socialist' principle of distribution according to work to the 'communist' principle of distribution according to needs. After some apparent indecision, Mao was eventually to conclude that, though the ownership-status of communes remained a problem, ownership at lower levels (after 1958 the 'basic accounting units') was still largely co-operative.[36] Thus, the principle of distribution according to need had been prematurely applied to situations where different types of ownership co-existed.

Though Mao became critical of this and some other aspects of the Great Leap Forward of 1958, he held fast to its basic principles. He affirmed the policy of 'walking on two legs'— the simultaneous development of industry and agriculture, of heavy and light industry, of national and local industry, of large and small enterprises and of modern and indigenous methods of production. He also insisted on the efficacy of mass mobilisation to increase production and the decentralisation of economic decision making. Thus, looking back on the Great Leap Forward, Mao seemed to affirm the total strategy and to condemn as 'ultra-left', policies which stressed only one of the three criteria for socialist transition. Thus to strive prematurely for 'ownership by the whole people', which might bring short term benefits to the peasants at the expense of people's work relations and patterns of distribution was 'ultra-leftist'. To change the distribution system to 'payment according to need' without creating a communist system of ownership and relations between people based on communist consciousness was likewise 'ultra-leftist'. Similarly to think that one could change the relationship between people at work without changing the nature of ownership and the pattern of distribution was also 'ultra-leftist'. As Mao said in December 1958.

> We are Marxist-Leninists who hold that revolution goes on continuously. In our opinion, there is no Great Wall and there should not be allowed to exist a Great Wall separating the democratic revolution and the socialist revolution, and separating socialism and communism. We are also Marxist-Leninists who hold that revolution develops by stages. We hold that different stages of development reflect the qualitative change of matter, and that these qualitatively different stages should not be mixed up with each other.[37]

Clearly to confuse qualitatively different stages of development, such
as to introduce communist principles of distribution prematurely, was
condemned. The relevance of this view to the situation in the 1970s was
made explicit in the Chinese press which quoted this statement of
Mao's as central to an article attacking 'ultra-leftism'.[38] Yet one may
not just define 'ultra-leftist' in terms of a stress on only one criterion for
socialist transition. There was one other crucial element in the
definition; policies, however comprehensive and however radical, had
not to transcend the limits of the Mass Line. Any attempt to coerce
the masses into what was believed to be socialism was certainly
'ultra-leftist'. It was not until after the lessons of the Great Leap
Forward that Mao began to think along these lines.[39] Perhaps too much
is being read into his position but the above will provide a useful
point of reference when considering the 'ultra-leftism' of the early
1970s.

   If the above constituted 'ultra-leftism', then it was but the counter-
point of that 'rightist' position which was criticised in the mid 1950s.
The 'rightist' agricultural policy of the early 1950s had also stressed
only one criterion in socialist transition (the nature of ownership)
at the expense of the other two (which would have involved greater
co-operativisation and the modification of market relationships). The
'rightists' believed that one could not change the relationships between
people at work until they were freed from the drudgery of a labour-
intensive rural cycle and one could not change the pattern of
distribution until one had enough surplus to distribute. The magic
wand for the 'rightists', therefore, was mechanisation through state-
controlled tractor stations. No-one in China would ever wish to
oppose mechanisation nor slow it down, but to claim that it was
the pre-requisite for any social change in the countryside was clearly,
from Mao's point of view, 'rightist'. Mao's strategy was that social
change and mechanisation should procede simultaneously.

   We are now in a position to see why Mao considered that the
changes in agriculture made in the early 1960s were 'rightist'. The
objection was not to private plots, making the team the basic accounting
unit or even the temporary growth of market relationships. It was to
a policy which discouraged cadres from advancing to a new stage
defined in terms of all three criteria and which confirmed the partial
retrogression to an earlier stage. We may also see why the Chinese
press so easily associate the 'ultra-left' and the 'right'. We are perhaps
unable to get out of the dilemma, noted in the first two chapters,
whereby this association leads to any target for criticism being

accused of any 'incorrect' policy currently under attack,[40] but at least
we may now look at the early 1970s with a slightly clearer theoretical
framework.

'Line Struggle' in Agriculture: The Continued Criticism of
Capitalist Tendencies (1969-70)

As already noted, the criticisms of 'capitalist tendencies' in agriculture
were most conspicuous in 1969 and early 1970 and it is possible that
the PLA Mao Tsetung Thought propaganda teams played an
important part in mobilising the masses to this end.[41] Of these
'capitalist tendencies', the most frequently criticised was that of
individual sideline production.[42] This sometimes even involved giving
up farming[43] but usually meant just attaching a greater importance to
individual production for profit rather than collective agriculture.[44]
At the same time, there were warnings against 'spontaneous capitalist
tendencies among the small producers'[45] and talk of 'class enemies'
being responsible for corruption, hoarding, theft, profiteering, inciting
peasants to abandon farming for commerce and generally undermining
the collective economy.[46]

Criticisms of such 'capitalist tendencies', however, became less
frequent after mid-1970, although there were still isolated
instances where 'rightist deviations' were criticised. Chuch'eng *xian*
in Shangtung, for example, witnessed a brief re-fixing of output quotas
on a household basis — a 'crime' for which Liu Shao-ch'i had been
roundly condemned:

> This year, at the height of the *gaoliang* (sorghum) harvest, some
> production brigades adopted the erroneous method of fixing
> output on a per capita basis, in order to speed up the process.
> They divided up the *gaoliang* fields by assigning the plot of land
> between each ridge to an individual to harvest, with the heads
> going to the brigade and the stalks going to the individual.[47]

Instances were also cited of the attempts of 'class enemies' to sabotage
the movement to learn from Tachai and to foment clan feuds in the
villages. Utilising what remained of a 'feudal clan outlook' they sought
to undermine the solidarity of natural villages, divided into different
clans, and to incite the labour force to migrate to other places and
engage in commerce.[48] Though fewer than before, criticisms were
still directed to sideline undertakings which were detrimental to
collective production[49] and one whole production brigade was

accused of being obsessed with rope-making at the expense of 'zealous' participation in collective labour.[50]

The Campaign Against 'Ultra-Leftism' in Agriculture: 1970 – mid 1972

Despite the continuing criticisms of 'capitalist tendencies', by far the overwhelming trend for the 1969-73 period was for criticisms to be directed against 'ultra-leftism'. Though this began as early as 1969, it achieved a new momentum in 1971. For example, those who criticised individual commune members for engaging in 'capitalist enterprise' by keeping pigs were themselves denounced as 'class enemies appearing in an ultra-left guise'[51] and numerous articles appeared urging individual commune members to raise one or two pigs in addition to collective pig farming.[52] In fact the right of commune members to raise pigs and keep the 'appropriate rewards' appears to have been one of the key issues in the rural debate and a focus of 'ultra-leftist' pressure.

Another major bone of contention was what exactly constituted 'proper sideline production'.[53] Some kinds of individual sideline production had been roundly condemned as a 'capitalist tendency' but when this condemnation extended to all sideline production, it was felt that an 'ultra-leftist' error had been committed.[54] Clearly a prohibition on all sideline production would harm the rural economy. As one article put it:

> After criticising the capitalist tendencies of 'attaching greater importance to sideline occupations than to farming' and 'putting money in command', a minority of cadres and commune members went from one extreme to the other. Their attitude was a blanket rejection and criticism of all sideline occupations. Taking advantage of this opportunity, a small group of class enemies emerged, in ultra leftist guide, to interfere and conduct sabotage. They spread ideas to the effect that sideline occupations could easily be destroyed.[55]

That all was not well in the countryside at this time may be discerned by the extension into the rural areas of that major rectification campaign known as 'one strike and three oppositions' (*yi da san fan*),[56] which we have already encountered in earlier chapters. Already under way by the time of the Second Plenum of the Ninth Central Committee in September 1970, it gained momentum late in 1970 and continued throughout 1971. It seemed to have all the hallmarks of a typically 'top-down' rectification movement, at least judging from its implementation in Yunnan:

> It is necessary to send out crack Mao Tsetung Thought Propaganda
> teams, [and] by means of . . . struggle-criticism-transformation, to
> rectify [deviant elements] one by one, to wipe out bad elements
> and to promote [suitable] elements to leading posts.[57]

At the same time as this campaign, a new upsurge in the movement to
learn from Tachai was inaugurated by a *People's Daily* editorial in late
September.[58] This editorial called for the *yi da san fan* movement to be
pursued forcefully while adhering to the Tachai model, and talked of
implementing the whole series of Chairman Mao's rural policies. Thus
the movements to learn from Tachai and *yi da san fan* seem to have
merged, as *xian* level cadres were sent down into the communes to
ensure the implementation of Party policy in the twin movements
and to criticise those cadres who had failed to explain policy to the
masses. Such inattention to the masses appeared to have been
commonplace:

> There were . . . a few cadres who were afraid that transmitting
> policies to the masses would shackle them and harm their activism
> and creativity.[59]
>
> . . . some individual leading cadres [of the commune revolutionary
> committee] mistakenly thought that it would be sufficient if only to
> leadership mastered policies and that it did not matter whether the
> masses mastered them or not.[60]

Thus, throughout 1971, there were innumerable articles aimed at
overcoming 'ultra-leftism' and at ensuring that the Party's rural
economic policies were put into practice. In fact, these two aims
were much the same, since the policies which were not being universally
implemented were those which had been particularly designed to
rectify 'ultra-leftist' excesses.

Documents from a provincial conference on rural work in Yunnan
are particularly revealing in this context. Urging the necessity of fully
implementing 'policy', they stress the need to strengthen cadre
education, 'to overcome the anarchical tendency in certain places'
and to counter opposition from both right and left.[61] They argue that,
in overcoming major erroneous tendencies, other erroneous tendencies
might be concealed. Thus, although it was imperative to eliminate the
influence of *san zi yi bao* and the 'four freedoms':

> . . . when there is [a] guarantee and [an] absolute advantage for the
> development of [the] collective economy, commune members may
> be allowed to possess small sized private plots and take sideline jobs.[62]

The documents also spoke of opposing egalitarianism and of restoring flexibility to production teams, noting that production and construction at team level should not be harmed by transferring productive forces elsewhere under the pretext of mobilising the peasants for state construction.[63] Clearly, in Yunnan, some private plots had been collectivised, some peasants had been deprived of spare time jobs and the rights of some production teams had been ignored.

As criticisms of 'ultra-leftism' continued apace, there were renewed calls to allow commune members to raise pigs,[64] to prevent increases in reserve funds to the detriment of peasant income[65] and to distinguish correctly between 'spontaneous capitalist tendencies' and permissible sideline production where the collective economy was not threatened.[66] It was even noted that occasionally there occurred that paradigm case of 'ultra-leftism' where the socialist principle of payment according to work was disregarded and peasant enthusiasm was dampened:

> . . . some cadres considered that the consciousness of commune members had been raised and no longer evaluated work points. Thus, they abolished some of the systems for the rational evaluation of work.[67]

As has been noted, the above was an example of altering the pattern of distribution without regard for the nature of ownership and the relationship between people at work. Another 'ultra-leftist' policy was to alter the nature of ownership without regard for the other two criteria. Thus, the 'three level ownership' system in the communes was tampered with. As already noted, there is some evidence to suggest that, at least in some areas, moves were made to shift the unit of account from team to brigade level,[68] with the result that both production and income at team level suffered. Even more serious was the suggestion that attempts were made to institute immediate 'ownership by the whole people', so that communes would become, in effect, state farms:

> When on the side of the 'left' they (Wang Ming, Liu Shao-ch'i and other political swindlers) went so far as to call for the abolition of the production of commodities, negate the principle of value and *advocate the immediate enforcement of the 'system of ownership by the whole people' in rural people's communes and the destruction of the system of ownership at three levels*

with the team as the foundation.[69]

Just as attempts to curtail distribution according to labour were
rebutted by renewed calls for the acceptance of 'reasonable assessment
of work and the recording of work points',[70] so the attempt to
accelerate prematurely the transition to 'ownership by the whole
people' was rebutted in terms equally stern. 'The system of three level
ownership in people's communes with the production team as the base
. . . must be implemented resolutely.'[71]

Delay in Implementing the Party's Rural Economic Policy

One might have imagined that an 'ultra-leftist' zeal, which sometimes
reached the point of forbidding individual commune members to gather
herbs[72] or which contemplated the confiscation of trees planted by
peasants around their houses,[73] could easily have been dealt with.
In fact, the actual rectification of excesses at the basic level was a very
slow process and the need to implement seriously the Party's economic
policy was constantly re-stressed:

> Implementing the Party's economic policy for the countryside at
> the present stage is certainly not a minor matter which one can
> take or leave. *It is a major matter with which one must come to
> grips.*[74]

The same theme was taken up in a Central Committee Directive in
December 1971[75] which, whilst criticising certain 'rightist' tendencies,
directed its main thrust at persistent 'ultra-leftism'. Its main points
were now all too familiar. It warned against accumulation policies
which prevented annual increases in peasant income and excessive
grain purchases by the state. It re-affirmed the injunction that
production brigades should not draw upon the public accumulation
fund which belonged to the production teams. It opposed
'egalitarianism' in the current stage and insisted, yet again, that
remuneration should be on the 'socialist principle' — 'to each
according to his work'. Once more, the right of peasants to engage
in sideline production was confirmed:

> They should make a fine line between multiple business and
> 'money takes command', and should not mistake multiple
> business, which is allowed by the Party's policy, for the
> capitalist inclination, which must be criticised and repudiated.[76]

Party policy could not be more clear and yet it apparently took some months for the Central Committee directive of December 1971 to be implemented in certain areas. A document of the Ssumao district Party committee in March 1972 revealed that only then was the directive being put into effect in that part of Yunnan.[77] Here, 'ultra-leftist' excesses had been particularly virulent. The local leadership had not just contemplated confiscating the fruit trees round peasants' houses but had actually done so:

> Commune members are permitted and encouraged to operate proper domestic side [line] occupations, provided that the development and superiority of the collective economy is ensured. *Those collectivised fruit trees, bamboo and other kinds of tree planted by commune members around their houses and in their private plots must be returned to commune members.*[78]

In learning from Tachai, moreover, egalitarian methods of remuneration had been imposed regardless of the objective conditions:

> In some . . . production teams, the Tachai way of evaluating work can be continued, because it has been experimented (with) and is accepted by the masses. However, most of the production teams . . . should not fully copy Tachai's method.[79]

Consolidation: Mid 1972-1973

Directives and articles continued in the same vein throughout the first half of 1972 though there was a discernible shift in emphasis away from a simple condemnation of 'ultra-leftism' to the need to reassert Party authority. This is what Young's article on Party building might have led us to expect. It is not at all clear, however, whether the eventual success in implementing Party policy in the second half of 1972 reflected more the strengthened link between the centre and Party branches or the results of the various campaigns of 1971. It is probably the case that the criticism of 'ultra-leftism' and the process of strengthening the Party organisation were mutually reinforcing, but such had not always been the case as the history of the early 1960s shows.

By mid and late 1972, success in countering 'ultra-leftism' led to model *xian* being held up for emulation.[80] These had long since rectified 'ultra-leftism' deviations and were prospering under the Party's policy. It was apparent that this had been the result of extensive propaganda work carried out by 'policy investigation teams' sent down to the lower levels to examine the conditions under which policy was being implemented.[81] The experiences of these teams reveal quite clearly what a protracted task rural rectification had been. One Mao Tsetung Thought propaganda team, for example, consisting of over one hundred cadres of *xian* or commune organs, went to the lower levels no less than five times in eight months to propagate Party policy and check up on its implementation.[82]

Attempts were made by these teams, moreover, to explain policy in theoretical terms. This was in line with the current stress, noted in previous chapters, to study Marxism 'seriously'. It was explained that, although the ideological level of the broad masses of the people had been greatly raised, it was still far from communist consciousness.[83] The Party's policy had to take this level of consciousness into account[84] and it was 'ultra-left' to introduce measures more appropriate to a future 'communist' stage such as the egalitarian distribution of income.

> The whole series of rural economic policies laid down by Chairman Mao both embodies the major orientation in which the Party leads the peasants on the socialist road and also takes into consideration such many sided factors as the current level of agricultural output and the level of peasant consciousness.[85]

Thus, the debate on 'ultra-leftism' was brought to an end. The above conclusion was clearly in line with Mao's thinking on socialist transition in the early 1960s though one might have wished for more discussion on all three criteria for socialist transition outlined above.' Nevertheless, there is sufficient evidence to refute any claim that the campaign against 'ultra-leftism' constituted a departure from Mao's line and a reassertion of more conservative policies.

The sequel to the debate was a renewed campaign in March 1973 to learn from Tachai. In order to avoid the mechanical adoption of the entire Tachai system, however, the campaign was conducted with restraint and in accordance with the above Party line.[86] This line was confirmed once again in the new state Constitution of 1975, which stipulated that commune members were allowed to farm 'small plots for their personal needs' and to 'engage in limited household sideline production', so long as the collective econony remained dominant and its development was not impaired.[87] Once again, the production team was confirmed as the basic rural unit of account.[88]

Thus, after a period of confusion, in which the system of ownership and distribution were characterised by 'ultra-leftist' excesses, it was firmly decided that, for the immediate stage of development, policy should follow 'socialist' principles (with limited concessions to what was called 'bourgeois right') and not 'communist' principles.

Conclusion

The emphasis in this chapter has been somewhat different from that of Cheng's preceding chapter in that far greater attention has been paid to the question of 'line struggle'. Nonetheless, there is substantial agreement with Cheng's contention that the early 1970s saw a reassertion of Mao Tsetung's rural policy articulated in 'On the Ten Major Relationships'. The focus here has been the relationship between the state, the units of production and the individual producers. Cheng's chapter has focused mainly on the other four of Mao's 'relationships' which deal directly with the question of economic development. Of these, the most important in the 1970s have been the relationships between agriculture and industry and centre and regions. Since Cheng has dealt at length with the development of rural industry, it is sufficient here merely to point out that success in this field has greatly surpassed that of the mid and late 1950s and represents one of the hallmarks of Mao's economic strategy.

In terms of Mao's theory of 'continuous revolution' (with its stress on the development of revolution within the period of socialist transition), the period 1969-73 can be seen both as a step forward and as a period of consolidation. That is to say, the increases in agricultural output, the proliferation of small scale local industries, the re-affirmation of the primacy of the collective and the general extension of welfare services (education, health, etc.) to the countryside, all marked a step forward in the goal of developing a socialist countryside and in narrowing the 'three major differences' between town and countryside, mental and manual labour and between workers and peasants.

It was a period of consolidation in the sense that, rather than push ahead with further changes, regularisation was the rule. Attempts to forge preciptiously ahead were resisted, branded as 'ultra-leftist' and finally defeated. This 'ultra-leftism' included such practices as the confiscation of privately-owned pigs, land and trees, a prohibition on private sideline production, the implementation of egalitarian income policies (often accompanied by excessive collective accumulation) and arbitrarily raising the unit of account from team to brigade level. While many of these policies are in themselves admirable, their forced generalisation *at that stage* was sufficient to categorise them as 'ultra-leftist'. They might be so defined because they stressed only one criterion in socialist transition, that they were in advance of mass consciousness, that they were in advance of existing objective conditions and that they sought to leap from the stage of socialism prematurely into communism. Policies of excessive accumulation and egalitarian income distribution, moreover, adversely affected the livelihood of the peasants and were a clear violation of Mao's line.

Thus the recognition of the right of peasants to continue to own a limited amount of land, to raise a few livestock and to carry out certain sideline activities was not a result of the 'conservatives' in the Party triumphing over the 'radicals' but was, in fact, the result of the triumph of Mao's line for the socialist development of agriculture. Similarly the policy of promoting local industries, to which Cheng gives much attention, was consistent with Mao's strategy for self reliant, decentralised development.

Notes

1. Buck 1966; Wu 1966. See also Tang 1968.
2. See Chen and Ridley 1969.
3. See Baum and Teiwes 1968 (one of the few works specifically on the subject).
4. See Baum 1971.
5. Ibid., p.367.
6. Bennett and Montaperto 1972, p.212. See also p.103.
7. Myrdal and Kessle 1973, p.100, *et.seq.*
8. Baum 1971, p.451, *et.seq.*
9. Ibid.
10. Wheelwright and McFarlane 1970, p.193.
11. MacDougall 1969 (in *FEER*).
12. The fact that it was possible to suspend all political campaigns in rural China in late 1966 suggests that mass mobilisation and mass participation were not at a high level. Baum (1971, p.385) has argued that this suspension was put into effect in order to get in the harvest.
13. Baum 1971; MacDougall 1969 (in *FEER*).
14. MacDougall 1969 (in *Current Scene*).
15. See e.g. *SCMM* 643, 1969, p.17.
16. Bastid 1973, p.173, *et.seq.*
17. Goodstadt 1972, p.223, *et.seq.* and p.244, *et.seq.*
18. See Chao Kang 1975.
19. See Riskin 1971; Sigurdson 1972.
20. First reported by Chou En-lai to Edgar Snow, January 1971. See Snow 1971, p.49.
21. Rawski 1973, p.2.
22. See e.g. Klatt (1970) who estimated a total grain output of only 200 million tonnes. US Department of State estimates ran between 215 and 220 million

tonnes. See Eckstein 1973, p.217.
23. *PR* 1, 7 January 1972, p.10.
24. *Hsinhua Selected News*, 5 January 1973, p.11.
25. Ibid., p.10.
26. *PR* 1, 4 January 1974, p.8.
27. *PR* 1, 3 January 1975, p.8.
28. Eckstein 1973, p.218.
29. Rawski 1973, p.8.
30. Perkins 1973, p.4.
31. See e.g. Bradsher 1973.
32. Mao Tsetung December 1942, *Economic and Financial Problems*. A translation of this book by A. Watson is awaiting publication. Part of the work is included in *SW* English edition, Vol.3, pp.111-16. See also *SW*, Vol.3 pp.131-5 and pp.153-61.
33. See pp.17-18 and 126.
34. See p.23 and Levy 1975.
35. Mao Tsetung, 31 July 1955, in Mao 1971, pp.389-420 (*SW* Vol.5, pp.168-91).
36. See p.22.
37. CCP CC, in URI 1971, p.132.
38. *RMRB* 12 August 1972, p.2.
39. The above is based largely on Mao Tsetung 1960 (or 1961-2), *Wansui* 1969, pp.319-99 (*JPRS* 1974, pp.247-313). See also the Introduction.
40. See p.88.
41. See *NCNA*, Hangchow, 8 October 1969, in *SCMP* 4520, pp.5-7; *RMRB*, 18 March 1972, in *SCMP* 5104, p.138.
42. *NCNA*, Hangchow, 8 October 1969, in *SCMP* 4520 pp.1-4; *RMRB* 7 January 1970, in *SCMP*, 4586, pp.58-60.
43. *RMRB*, 26 January 1970, in *SCMP* 4597, pp.6-10.
44. *RMRB*, 12 February 1970, in *SCMP* 4602, pp.8-10.
45. *RMRB*, 18 January 1970, in *SCMP* 4594, pp.29-33.
46. *RMRB*, 7 March 1970, in *SCMP* 4615, pp.129-131.
47. *RMRB*, 28 November 1971 p.4 (emphasis added).
48. *RMRB*, 10 April 1972, in *SCMP* 5119, p.54 *et.seq.*
49. *RMRB*, 14 July 1972, p.4.
50. *RMRB*, 31 May 1972, in *SCMP* 5155, p.131.
51. *RMRB*, 20 August 1969, in *SCMP* 4487, pp.9-12.
52. *RMRB*, 16 May 1969, in *SCMP* 4425, p.10; *SCMP* 4443, pp.9-10.
53. 'proper sideline production' encompassed both collective and (to a lesser extent) individual sideline production, undertaken *without causing collective agricultural production to suffer* as a result.
54. *RMRB*, 17 June 1970, in *SCMP* 4695, pp.8-11.
55. *RMRB*, 24 October 1970, p.2.
56. I.e. 'strike counter-revolutionaries: oppose corruption, oppose speculation and oppose extravagance and waste'.
57. Minutes of the Yunnan Provincial Conference on Rural Work (draft) 24 December 1970, in *Issues and Studies*, Vol.8, No.2, November 1971, p.106.
58. *RMRB*, 23 September 1970, p.1.
59. *RMRB*, 14 March 1971, p.4.
60. *RMRB*, 21 June 1971, p.4.
61. Minutes of the Yunnan Provincial Conference on Rural Work (draft) 24 December 1970, in *Issues and Studies*, Vol.8, No.2, November 1971, p.106.
62. Ibid.
63. Ibid., p.107.
64. *RMRB*, 14 January 1971, in *SCMP* 4829, pp.44-6.
65. *RMRB*, 24 February 1971, in *SCMP* 4854, p.91.

66. Ibid, pp.92-3.
67. *RMRB*, 21 June 1971, p.4.
68. *RMRB*, 22 October 1972, p.2.
69. *GMRB*, 11 August 1971, in *SCMP* 4961, p.72 (emphasis added).
70. *RMRB*, 21 March 1971, in *SCMP* 4871, p.226.
71. Writing Group of the Ministry of Agriculture and Forestry, *RMRB*, 13 April 1971, p.2.
72. *RMRB*, 12 December 1971, in *SCMP* 5043, pp.117-20.
73. *RMRB*, 7 November 1971, in *SCMP* 5017 pp.131-5.
74. *RMRB*, 30 October 1971, p.3 (emphasis added).
75. CCP CC, *Zhongfa* 1971/82 in *Issues and Studies,* Vol.9, No.2, November 1972, pp.92-5.
76. Ibid., p.95.
77. CCP Ssumao District Committee, Document 22 (26 March 1972), in *Issues and Studies,* Vol.9, No.6, March 1973, pp.91-7.
78. Ibid., p.96 (emphasis added).
79. Ibid., p.92.
80. *GMRB* 22 May 1972, in *SCMP* 5146, pp.159-62.
81. *RMRB*, 14 July 1972, p.4.
82. *RMRB*, 20 May 1972, in *SCMP* 5146, p.165.
83. *RMRB*, 26 June 1972, in *SCMP* 5171, pp.50-7.
84. Ibid.
85. Liu Yueh-wu, *RMRB* 12 August 1972, p.2.
86. *RMRB,* 31 March 1973, p.1.
87. *PR* 4, 24 January 1975, p.14.
88. Ibid.

6 INDUSTRIAL MANAGEMENT – EXPERIMENTS IN MASS PARTICIPATION

Andrew Watson

Analysis of industrial mangement in China has to a large extent been guided by the theoretical framework developed by Franz Schurmann in his *Ideology and Organization in Communist China*.[1] This framework has grown from sociological research on the nature of organisations and their methods of operation, and has attempted to interpret the organisation of industry in China in terms of the theoretical constructs that research has produced. The key issues identified by this approach are the relationship between ideology and organisation, the nature of leadership and its articulation, the problems of vertical control and horizontal integration, and the role of the mass of individuals within an organisational structure. A large number of the particular problems of industrial management are subsumed under these general considerations, including such things as the method of planning, the degree of centralisation, the relationship between staff and line management,[2] the number of organisational levels, the forms of remuneration and incentive, the methods of maintaining discipline and so forth. The contrasting policies that can be implemented in each of these areas are interpreted as deriving from the contrasting nature of the alternative general theoretical models. Schurmann distinguishes between organisations relying on technological solidarity and organisations relying on human solidarity, that is on relationships within the organisation that are based on technical roles and relationships that are based on the links between human beings.[3] Organisations based on technological solidarity are typified as being led by the modern manager (western or Soviet), and organisations based on human solidarity are typified as being led by the ideal 'cadre', described in the writings of Mao. In respect of the particular industrial issues listed above, the modern manager in China is associated with economically and technically determined planning, firm centralised control, complex regulation of staff and line relationships with clearly defined channels of command and methods of operation, complex organisational structures, remuneration and incentives based on material reward for technical competence, and strict discipline defined by the technical demands of the production process. By contrast, the 'cadre' is associated with flexible planning which takes account of political and social factors beyond the economic and technical, decentralisation of control, a less rigid line management structure with more integration of staff functions at the level of production, fewer organisational levels with greater mass participation in management, and methods of remuneration, incentives and discipline based on ideological commitment rather than technical performance. Seen in this perspective, the evolution of industrial management in China since 1949 has been the product of a continuous interaction and conflict between these two fundamentally contradictory organisational forms. Thus Brugger[4] and Andors[5] develop their analyses in terms of a series of cycles or alternating trends between the dominance of either form. Brugger identifies the period from 1949 to late 1950 as one in which the manager began to take over from the 'cadre', 1951 and early 1952 as a period of the resurgence of the 'cadre', and 1952 and 1953 as a further marked shift towards the manager. Andors, using different definitions and timing, describes a period in the early part of the 1950s in which the two models existed side by side in different parts of the country, followed by the period of the First Five-Year Plan in which the Soviet managerial style gained partial ascendancy, a transition to the Great Leap Forward which was an attempt to move rapidly to the 'cadre' style of leadership, a subsequent period of confused conflict between the two models, and finally a further attempt to assert the dominance of the 'cadre' during the Cultural Revolution. While both are careful to underline that the opposing trends in industrial management have been present simultaneously in different parts of the country, that the size, nature, technological sophistication, and economic or military importance of a particular enterprise has had an important bearing on the organisational form found within it, and that members of the central leadership in China cannot always be identified as being simplistically and constantly associated with one or the other of the organisational models,[6] nevertheless, the compelling dualism of the underlying theoretical approach has ultimately produced a picture of Chinese industrial management which poses two sharply distinct alternatives. To a greater or lesser extent these alternatives have been accepted by most observers of the Chinese political economy, though with different emphases derived from their own organisational preferences. Thus Richman, for example, contrasts 'ideological extremism' (i.e. 'cadre' style leadership) with 'managerial, technical and economic rationality' (i.e. modern manager style leadership) and describes a 'cyclical wavering' between the two since 1949,[7] and both Gray[8] and Selden[9] contrast a Soviet or Stalinist model of managerial leadership with a Yenan or cadre model which derived from the Chinese communists' experience of economic and organisational work in their base areas before 1949.

The dualism of this approach and the chronological periodisation of developments in industrial organisation in China that derive from it parallel the Chinese leadership's own analysis of the 'two-line struggle' between the capitalist and the socialist roads since 1949. This close relationship is inevitable since the two types of leadership examined by Schurmann are defined in terms of the Soviet model of the First Five-Year Plan and the 'cadre' model of the Great Leap Forward. Nevertheless, while China's description of the 'two-line struggle' does give a coherent picture of the two alternative approaches to the problems and methods of industrial management, the level of analysis that is adopted tends to simplify the interpretation of past policy decisions and the roles of various individuals in the discussions that led up to them. It gives less emphasis to the immediate context and to the ambiguities of some of the policy positions ascribed to various leaders.[10] It is also a level of analysis that requires a constant re-evaluation of previous events as each stage of the struggle unfolds.[11] This had led some critics in China to point out that, at times the official picture of the 'two line struggle' does not penetrate deeply enough to give a full account of the social origins and nature of the political divisions in China and of the reasons why struggles continually develop within the Chinese Communist Party.[12] Nevertheless, the differences between the industrial management policies of the two sides in the 'two-line struggle' have been sufficiently clearly contrasted to enable some analysts such as Bettelheim to accept them as reflecting the opposing positions of Liu Shao-ch'i and Mao, as well as the differences between capitalist and socialist industrial management.[13]

On the whole, therefore, the dualistic model adopted by Schurmann and others and the Chinese analysis of the 'two-line struggle' have provided the basic framework with which events in China since 1949 and the problems facing the Chinese in the transformation and development of their society have been analysed. The experiments of the Great Leap Forward and the debates of the Cultural Revolution have shown that, whatever other factors may be involved and whatever compromises may be worked out, the implications of the two methods of leadership are a central concern of China's leaders, no matter which of the two they individually prefer. Events since the Cultural Revolution have, however, raised many questions as to the extent to which foreign perceptions of the 'two-line struggle' are the same as those of the Chinese and the extent to which the official Chinese analysis of the 'two-line struggle' is at any one time an accurate picture of the practical differences between the two sides. For example, Bettelheim ascribes the roots of 'revisionist' industrial management in the Soviet Union to Lenin's retreat to capitalist techniques and his adoption of some aspects of the Taylor system (i.e. scientifically determined technical management).[14] He also interprets the Cultural Revolution as a new discovery in the process of socialist transformation.[15] If one accepts these arguments, then presumably the adoption of Lenin's view of Taylorism by the current Chinese leadership[16] might also be seen as a retreat and, in Bettelheim's terms, an even more serious one since it comes after the watershed of the Cultural Revolution. Nevertheless, one might also conclude that the account of the 'two-line struggle' given by Bettelheim does not entirely reflect the areas of principle that divide the Chinese leadership or the details of the practical struggle waged in industrial management since 1949. Furthermore, even if the current moves did mark a partial retreat, might it not be possible for some aspects of the two models to exist side by side? Need one assume that all the innovations in industrial management in China made since 1956 will automatically be swept aside? Bettelheim's conception of the dividing line between socialist and 'revisionist' management may not coincide with that of the Chinese leadership. Similarly, the dramatic confrontation between the management policies of the two sides that is presented in the Chinese media's description of the 'two-line struggle' may well have been as much the product of manoeuvering between opposing groups within the leadership (as is implied by criticisms of the 'Gang of Four's' manipulation of the press) as of actual shop floor practice. It has tended to obscure the extent to which practice at any one time has been a product of both lines. The concentration on goals as dictated by line has overshadowed the importance of resources as the other determinant of management practice. Thus the dualism of the framework has tended to disguise the many areas of detail and practice in which the two approaches have shared a common ground.[17]

Another problem is that we still lack a clear picture of the social basis for the continued struggle between the two sides in China. As is discussed by Brugger in the Introduction, should the conflict be seen as a remnant of the old society or a creation of the new? What factors in society have led to the re-emergence of some aspects of the managerial approach to leadership after the Great Leap Forward and

the Cultural Revolution? Is it sufficient to argue that the remnants of
bourgeois classes and ideas within society continually generate
renewed conflict and that leaders such as Liu Shao-ch'i, Lin Piao and
Teng Hsiao-p'ing are expressing this legacy from the past? Is the
conflict, as Mao has argued, created by the division of labour and
contradictions growing therefrom that exist in the transitional society?
Or is it the inevitable consequence of the nature of Party and state
structure that was attacked in the Cultural Revolution and which, as
Young shows, has in many ways regrown since? Is there a closer
relationship between the stage of China's industrial development
and the technology it uses on one hand, and the nature of managerial
leadership it demands on the other? Is it perhaps inevitable that
industrial enterprises of different sizes and different technological
complexity demand different types of management, thus creating a
continuum of management methods from the 'cadre' model in a
small factory run by a neighbourhood collective to the manager model
in a large integrated plant? At a different level, which elements in
society were disposed to support Lin Piao's and the 'Gang of Four's'
encouragement of 'ultra-leftism' including industrial anarchy, striking
out at all leading cadres, and the elimination of all industrial rules and
regulations? Why were they able to generate so much support?
Conversely, what elements in society supported Teng Hsiao-p'ing's
appeal in 1975 to reintroduce many of the policies that had been
attacked during the Cultural Revolution? Much of the information
which might enable us to answer some of these questions is not
available. For example, to what extent can managers and technicians
in China be distinguished from other social groups by their patterns
of consumption, access to education, housing and welfare advantages
and so forth? Despite the Cultural Revolution, do they still see
themselves as a group with common interests distinct from those of
the workers? Do the workers form an homogeneous group or does
the difference in income according to the eight-grade scale affect
their relationships to one another? Do differences in income levels
and skill levels give rise to differences in attitudes towards the
system of industrial management? To what extent do the workers
regard the innovations of the revolutionary committees and various
forms of participation in management introduced during the
Cultural Revolution as giving them real access to decision making
and to what extent do they see them as formal structures with
little real meaning? While the answers to questions like these need
not negate the validity of the general dualistic framework of

analysis, they would considerably enrich our understanding of the
way the conflict operates in China and of the way it is being resolved.
They might also mitigate to some extent the polarity implied in the
'two-line struggle' and thus give a clearer picture of the extent to
which industrial management practice has had some persistent
features over the whole period since 1949, perhaps achieved as a
series of compromises between the extremes of the two models. With
these reservations in mind, the following sections will look at
developments in industrial management since 1968 and the role of
the workers in management over that period.

The Legacy of the Cultural Revolution

In 1968, Chinese factories slowly began to emerge from the destructive
phase of the Cultural Revolution with a clear outline of those areas
where reform was believed necessary in order to escape the
influence of the consolidation policies of the early 1960s. Many of
these areas were succinctly defined in terms of opposition to Liu Shao-
ch'i's alleged policies of 'profits in command', 'production first', 'experts
running factories', 'technique first', 'control, restrict and suppress
the workers', and 'material incentives'. The key areas of policy above
the enterprise level have been dealt with in detail by Cheng, above.
There was a renewed commitment to the general economic strategy
of balanced sectoral growth outlined in Mao's 'On the Ten Major
Relationships'.[18] The decentralised structure of control first introduced
in 1957/8 was confirmed again and the centralising tendencies of the
early 1960s were rejected. The system of 'trusts' which consisted of
closely integrated corporations operating as self-contained economic
units expanding according to the demands of vertical integration and
increased profits was to be broken up. The importance of continuing
the consultative system of planning, which required close contact
and agreement between upper and lower levels and allowed for a certain
amount of flexibility and 'leeway' was to be continued. There was,
however, to be a change in target priorities with the profit target given
less importance so that the profit motive, while not entirely
eliminated, ceased to be in command of the whole plan, and overall
requirements received greater emphasis. Thus the pressure on
factories to make profits, some of which could be retained for internal
investment or bonus payments, was removed.[19] Within enterprises
there was a renewed attack on any vestiges of the Soviet 'one-man
management' system which had been officially withdrawn in 1956 but
still had its adherents. There was also criticism of the dual system of

'managerial responsibility under the unified leadership of the factory
Party Committee' which had replaced the Soviet model in 1956 and
to a large extent characterised industrial management after the retreat
from the Greap Leap Forward.[20] In practice this had often, though
not universally, resulted in the Party committee being relegated to
ensuring that the manager's orders were carried out. In place of this
system, the primacy of the Party's leadership was to be affirmed in
accordance with the Anshan Constitution put forward by Mao in 1960.
This stated:

> Keep politics firmly in command; strengthen Party leadership;
> launch vigorous mass movements, institute the system of cadre
> participation in productive labour and worker participation in
> management, of reform of irrational and outdated rules and
> regulations, and of close co-operation among workers, cadres
> and technicians; and go full steam ahead with the technical
> innovations and technical revolution.[21]

Allied to this constitution were demands to reduce the numbers of
administrative personnel not engaged in productive work and for the
use of collective and moral incentives rather than individual bonus
systems. In effect, this was a revival of the 'two participations and one
reform' and 'triple combination' slogans of the Great Leap
Forward.[22] As the above list has made clear, many of these issues
had already been the centre of earlier attempts at reform and
elements of these reforms were still present in industrial organisation
up until 1966. Nevertheless, while the issues were clear in theory, the
Cultural Revolution had not, by 1968, produced any formulae for
their practical resolution. In many ways, therefore, the period
since then has been an extended debate over how the reforms could
be translated into realities, and what should be jettisoned and what
retained of industrial management practices before the Cultural
Revolution. Before this process could begin, however, the immediate
problem was to overcome the legacy of factionalism and division that
had dominated the Cultural Revolution for most of 1966 and 1967,
and which, as earlier chapters have shown, was a prominent feature
in most areas of social reform in the years that followed.

In practice, the Cultural Revolution had been a very complex
and confusing struggle for China's workers. Although the overall
theoretical goals were soon clarified, events within individual
factories and towns often served to obscure the local situation and

added to the difficulties of deciding which factory cadres supported which policies and how to put things right.[23] In many places the workers at first identified their interests with those of the managers and Party cadres who were later to be denounced for following Liu's line. In others, differences of opinion which might have been settled by debate were exacerbated by violence and abuse. Still other factories remained relatively unaffected for long periods. Overall, groups with various political allegiances and goals manoeuvered against each other and attempted to pull events in a direction favourable to themselves. The mass factions rapidly spread beyond individual institutions to become large alliances, almost like political parties, with links throughout the country and a clear sense of separateness from each other. Since each of these factional groups claimed to be the 'true revolutionaries' and denounced their opponents as 'reactionaries and revisionists', there was no organisational basis for carrying out reforms and the first problem was one of rebuilding unity. This involved breaking down the factional links between groups from different enterprises so that reform within each unit could be dealt with separately rather than as part of a generalised debate, and reconciling the mass organisations within each factory so that neither side could claim a monopoly of truth or the accolade of being declared the 'true left'. Since the mass organisations could not be relied upon to reform themselves, the only resort was to fall back on the Army and eventually a rebuilt Party. Thus, the possibility, that Mao appeared to have raised, of abandoning the Leninist vanguard Party and its state structure in favour of 'extensive democracy' (as might have been realised through an experiment like the Shanghai Commune) was firmly rejected, and the process of rebuilding state, Party and factory organisation was begun.[24] The first steps in this direction came early in 1967 with the call for the Army to 'support the left' and for the formation of revolutionary alliances based on a triple combination of masses, revolutionary cadres and soldiers. Subsequently, these became formalised as revolutionary committees which were then able to turn to the practical issues of reforming their individual factories. The programme was outlined in a statement by Mao in 1968 in which he said:

Establish revolutionary committees with triple combinations. Carry out widespread criticism, purify the class ranks, rectify the Party, simplify administration, reform irrational rules and regulations, send down technical personnel; the movement

for struggle, criticism and transformation within factories will
in general go through these few stages.[25]

During the following years, this programme was often quoted as the
guideline for action in factories.[26] Those factories relatively unaffected by factionalism could make progress along these lines
reasonably quickly; those whose problems were 'old, big, and difficult'
required a much longer period. Furthermore, the whole process was
subject to the influence of continued disputes between groups
within the central leadership.

The first stage, the formation of revolutionary committees, began
in 1967 and was completed formally during 1968.[27] However, the
realisation of true unity within many factories lagged far behind the
formal process. Factions manoeuvered to get equal representation
on the new committees for themselves and the cadres they supported,
and the soldiers helping to cement the new unity were forced to
be carefully even-handed when dealing with the opposing groups.[28]
Even after the Ninth Party Congress of April 1969 with its call for
unity and the reconstruction of the Party, the legacy of factionalism
still continued to cause problems within factories. One article by a
worker in the Peking Iron and Steel Corporation entitled 'Sectarianism
is the Great Enemy of the Proletarian Nature of the Party'[29]
underlined the fact that some revolutionary committee members had
been using their postion to advance their own clique and strive for
hegemony. The rebuilding of the Party was affected in the same way
as the establishment of revolutionary committees. Some factions
wanted to control the process and ensure that their members were
elected into the Party, or insisted on competing with the Party for
leadership.[30] It is not surprising, therefore, that Party branches were
only slowly reformed during 1969 and the first factory Party
committees only emerged during the latter half of the year.[31]

A related problem which slowed down and hindered the growth
of unity and the reform of factory management was the anarchic
tendency associated with the extreme rejection of all forms of
authority that had been so pronounced in 1966 and 1967. This
problem was at its worst in 1968 and 1969 but continued to have an
influence in later years and was often cited as a stumbling block in
the drawing up of new factory rules.[32] In many discussions it was
related to the problem of organising and disciplining the young
workers who had spent their last years at school absorbed in the
Red Guard movement and were among the most deeply affected by

lack of social discipline. Some articles pointed out that the youths had been brought up under the Liuist educational system and were therefore susceptible to bad influences but that, nevertheless, their revolutionary rebelliousness was good and should be channelled into positive work.[33] Be that as it may, the evidence suggests that the main factor in shaping their behaviour was their experience during the Cultural Revolution when 'rebellion was justified'. Waste, losses in production, and organisational problems were all attributed to this anarchy and the main remedy was seen in ideological education. At first, specific bad elements in factories were blamed for causing the trouble but later it was ascribed to the May 16 Group, Lin Piao, and more latterly the 'Gang of Four'.[34] Nevertheless, during the period of the Anti-Confucius campaign, Lin was also accused of attempting to control the workers by means of the oppressive disciplinary methods used by Liu Shao-ch'i.[35] Since the whole of the Anti-Confucius campaign is now open to question because of the role of the 'Gang of Four' who are accused of using it as a lever to attack Chou En-lai, it appears likely that the earlier criticisms of Lin for fomenting 'ultra-left' tactics in factories are the more credible.[36] Whatever the real nature of the divisions at the central level at that time, however, the problem within the factories was one of persuading the rebels of the Cultural Revolution that not all leadership was bad, that not all rules were irrational, that not all technique could be ignored, and that production should not be counterposed to political work.

In the context of these difficulties, it is not surprising that, as Young has shown, consolidating the revolutionary committees, 'purifying the class ranks', and rebuilding the Party throughout the country lasted well into 1971. The demands of production, however, inevitably meant that subsequent stages in the process, those of simplifying administration and reforming rules and regulations, had to start as soon as possible. During 1968 and 1969, therefore, a series of model institutions began to receive regular coverage in the media and each stage of development would invariably be summed up by reference to the achievements of one of them. These were the famous 'six factories and two schools', all led by soldiers from 8341 unit and all in Peking.[37] Thus, from 1968 onwards, Chinese factories were subject to increasing pressure to accept more discipline and to carry out reforms. The extensive freedoms of 1966 and 1967 in which Party and government authority was minimal and 'operational units acted on their own decisions'[38] gave way to leadership through revolutionary committees, at first based on Army leadership and then on a rebuilt Party.[39] As the revolutionary and Party committees gained in authority, the mass organisations had to accept a lesser role and submit to Party leadership, eventually being reformed as workers' congresses during 1970 and 1971. Over the same period and in the context of widespread criticism of extravagance, waste, poor quality, economic corruption, lack of concern for production and for technical skills,[40] there was a drive to restore and advance levels of production, a drive that was often referred to as a new 'flying leap'. Technicians and former managers were gradually returned to work, though often in different capacities and with a different emphasis on their role than formerly[41] and revised systems of rules and regulations were reintroduced. As a whole, this entire process of reconstruction fell into two stages. The first, lasting up until the fall of Lin Piao in 1971, placed reconstruction firmly within the context of the criticisms of Liu Shao-ch'i. The role of ideological education and mass participation was paramount and all new regulations stressed the importance of self-conscious discipline and equal relationships among workers and staff.[42] The second stage, lasting from the fall of Lin Piao until the Anti-Confucius campaign in late 1973, had as its background criticism of anarchy and the 'ultra-left'.[43] While the role of political consciousness in industrial management was not denied, there was a much greater emphasis on strengthening managerial administration and building up complete sets of rules and regulations with which to guide industrial relationships.[44] A report from Kwangchow in June 1972 summed up these changes as follows:

> [leaders] must actively readjust and perfect the organs of enterprise management, augment management personnel, strengthen the system of production command, give full play to the role of professional departments, and integrate mass management with professional management.[45]

By the middle of 1972, pressures such as these had, in some places, led to the reintroduction of systems of material rewards and punishments that had been so roundly denounced during the Cultural Revolution.[46] Thus, although there were many innovations in terms of organisation and mass participation, by 1972 management practices in Chinese factories resembled those of 1965 much more closely than might have been thought likely when the Cultural Revolution was at its height. While the two stages of reconstruction can be seen as distinct both in context and content, the overall trend was one of continuous development towards greater discipline, greater professional leadership and less emphasis on such things as mass participation and ideological education. Indeed, such developments became an important area of attack during the campaign against retrogression that was launched under the banner of criticising Confucius in 1974. Criticisms in that year listed such things as bureaucratic systems of management, disregard of the masses, the use of incentives and punishments, disregard of politics and the withdrawal of cadres from systems of physical labour.[47] The introduction of worker-theorists into factories later in 1974 was presented as a means of ensuring that ideological goals were not subsumed by professional ones.[48] It is now alleged that this campaign was a distortion by the 'Gang of Four' directed at disrupting production and smearing cadres who were following the correct line.[49] Yet, whatever the real basis for this claim, the criticisms voiced in 1974 did indicate that systems of industrial management had moved a long way back towards the pre-Cultural Revolution situation and some distance away from the reforms called for in 1967 and 1968. The end result, however, has not been a complete reversion, as the following discussion of factory revolutionary committees and new systems of rules and regulations illustrates.

The Revolutionary Committee, the Party Committee, and the Mass Representatives

The revolutionary committee, which now forms the standard administrative committee of industrial enterprises, has changed considerably since the first experiments of 1967. Initially, it grew from an alliance of mass organisations, held together by a core group of military representatives and included some veteran cadres.[50] It was thus the sole source of authority, and, as the above discussion of factionalism has indicated, it was very responsive to the opinions of the rank and file mass organisations. Once the process of Party rebuilding began, however, it was necessary to define clearly the relationship between Party and revolutionary committee and the nature of their different functions, especially as the division between Party leadership and managerial leadership had been one of the subjects of debate during the Cultural Revolution. Almost immediately, therefore, it was declared that the new Party committees should exercise unified leadership of the revolutionary committees. This was made clear in the descriptions of the model for enterprise Party rebuilding, the Peking Hsinhua Printing Works (one of the six factories).[51] These reports stressed that the new Party committee led the revolutionary committee, that most members of the revolutionary committee were in fact also members of the Party committee, and that the administrative organs of the revolutionary committee were simultaneously organs of the Party committee. Thus, there was no division of personnel, and there was close organisational unity between the people making the decisions (the Party) and the people executing those decisions (the revolutionary committee). In this way any potential divisions between the two functions might hopefully be obviated. Although the Party rectification was itself carried out in an 'open-door' manner and subject to mass discussion, the Party increasingly stressed its independence of the masses and its internal authority, as the discussions of factionalism and anarchy in 1970 indicated.[52] Thus, although the masses still retained representation on the revolutionary committee, they were now a step away from the ultimate source of authority.[53] This shift in the source of authority for the revolutionary committee was thus a decisive one.

Until the fall of Lin Piao, the military component in factory revolutionary committees remained important, though the soldiers' role as a disciplinary agent grew less necessary as factionalism receded. After Lin's death, however, the Chinese media quoted many examples of instances of where Army cadres had taken on too much power and had been unwilling to form part of a collective leadership.[54] This also led to further discussion of the relationship between the Party committee and the revolutionary committee. A report from Anhwei of 9 November 1971[55] pointed out that the dual role of leading personnel in the Party and the revolutionary committee had led to some confusion of function and a decline in the importance of the revolutionary committee. The report argued that instead of the close overlap there should be a division of labour, with the Party deciding on the main policies and plans, and the revolutionary committee taking charge of general affairs and day-to-day operations, reporting back to the Party. Specific tasks could be given to the special offices of the revolutionary committee which were, in any case, headed by Party members. The report concluded by pointing out that the new relationship between the Party committee and the revolutionary committee was an attempt to escape from the competition between Party and administration that had existed before the Cultural Revolution, and that neglecting the revolutionary committee meant neglecting the role of the masses in the

leading organs. Thus the problem was not only one of the relationship
between the overall leadership and the practical administration
but also involved the relationship of both to the masses. Nevertheless,
the division of labour suggested as a solution in this report, in many
ways, echoes the formula of 1956, 'managerial responsibility under the
unified leadership of the Party Committee'.

After the military representatives on revolutionary committees
were gradually phased out, the sole authority of the Party over the
revolutionary committee was confirmed. Thereafter, the division of
labour between Party and revolutionary committees, described in the
report from Anhwei above, continued and, as the following experience
in the Shanghai Watch and Clock Factory shows, in some places
became formalised in different roles assigned to different people:

> A party committee must grasp major issues. The leading group
> of the factory Party committee consists of a secretary, two
> deputy secretaries and four committee members. One deputy
> secretary, who is a veteran cadre, concurrently serves as vice-
> chairman of the factory revolutionary committee. He is in charge
> of production throughout the factory. The other deputy secretary,
> a new cadre, is in charge of trade union work as well as of study
> and criticism in the factory. The number one leader of the Party
> committee who is free from any administrative work of the
> revolutionary committee, concentrates his energy on grasping
> major issues.[56]

In this more formal situation, the fact that the Party secretary and
the production manager served on both committees can be seen as an
attempt to mitigate any possible conflict of interests between them,
as arose before the Cultural Revolution. It is interesting to note that
the 'new cadre', who might well have come to the fore because of
activism in the mass organisations during the Cultural Revolution, is
assigned to mass work. The report also gives more details on the way
the Party and revolutionary committee divide the work:

> Should a Party Committee grasp issues involving production and
> enterprise management? The factory Party committee holds
> that it should not only grasp such issues, but strengthen its
> leadership in this regard. But how should it exercise leadership
> in this respect? The factory Party committee has not grasped
> concrete issues in production, but has grasped issues concerning

the orientation and the political line. For instance, the factory works out its annual production plan at the beginning of the year, reviews this plan in the middle of the year, and sums up its fulfilment at the end of the year. The number one leader of the Party committee should concern himself with such matters, and the Party committee should discuss them. It is necessary to bring the role of operational units into full play. For instance, the production section is responsible for the planned use of manpower. However, it reports to the factory Party committee on its plan before putting it into practice.[57]

Thus, major policy decisions were taken by the Party but operational work was prepared and implemented by specialists. In this way, the long-standing distinction between the political role of the Party and the functional role of the administration was fully maintained.

Throughout these developments in the nature of the revolutionary committee, the presence of the mass representatives was retained, though the actual personnel changed according to the circumstances. But, as noted above, their importance declined with the revival of Party authority. This decline may also have been reflected by a decline in their numerical representation as the table on p.186 indicates, though the size of the sample makes such a conclusion far from certain.

Thus, in 1971 the average percentage of people on factory revolutionary committees reported as workers was around 57 per cent and in 1976 it was around 36 per cent. An additional problem, on which there is little statistical information, is the relationship between the revolutionary committee as a whole and its standing committee. For example, the Shanghai Docks Fifth District reported in 1971 that it had a revolutionary committee of 23 with a standing committee of 9. The committee itself met at least once a month in full session but might meet more often if the situation demanded it. The standing committee met once or twice a week or whenever necessary. Presumably the standing committee was responsible to the full committee but it seems likely that it consisted of the leading Party and administrative cadres with a lower proportion of worker representatives, the relationship between the two being very similar to the relationship between the Politburo and the Central Committee of the Party. Thus in day-to-day work, the mass representatives may have played a less important role. This certainly seems likely in the situation since 1972 when professional management

Table I: The Composition of Enterprise Revolutionary Committees

1971[a]	Total	Workers	Cadres	Techs	PLA	Workers (in per cent)
Peking No.1 Machine Tool Factory	33	8	15		10	24
Peijung Yuetan Peking	9	6	3			66
Nanking Artificial Fibres Factory	19	12	5		2	63
Peking Petrochemicals Factory	36	17	11		8	47
Shanghai Metal Products Factory	11	7	3		1[d]	63
Shanghai Watch Factory	22	13	7		2[d]	59
Minhang Electrical Equipment Factory	48	30	12		6[d]	62
Feichan Porcelain Factory	11	6	3		2[d]	54
1971[b]						
East is Red Silk Mill, Hangchow	17	9	6		2	53
Red Flag Paper Mill, Hangchow	21	12	5		4	57
Shanghai Machine Tool Plant	43	23	14	5	1	53
Nanking Chemical Fertiliser Plant	27	17[e]	7		3	63
Sian Arts and Handicraft Factory	8	6	2			75
No. 1 Printing & Dyeing Mill, Sian	21	12	6		3	57
1976[c]						
Changchun Film Studios	15	4	11			20
Changchun Hsinhua Printing Works	13	8	7			61
Tientsin No.1 Carpet Factory	19	5	14			26
Tientsin No.1 Machine Factory	27	10	17			36

1a. *Source: L'essor économique de la Chine depuis la révolution culturelle, rapport de la délégation de la commission économique Belgique-Chine après son voyage en République Populaire de Chine en Novembre 1971.;*
b. *Source:* Personal notes, April 1971.
c. *Source:* Personal notes May 1976.
d. Militia and not PLA.
e. Figure given as workers and technicians, not differentiated.

came to receive much greater emphasis than before.

Management Reforms

The administrative structure under the revolutionary committee has varied, depending on the size and complexity of the enterprise itself. At first, committees had a small number of specialist departments, usually four but sometimes more.[58] This was considerably fewer than the number of departments associated with factory managers' offices before the Cultural Revolution.[59] Using military-style terminology, the four departments were usually known as the political work department, the production department, the rear services department (welfare, personnel, etc.) and the general office (research, planning, statistics, etc.). All the personnel in these departments and on the committees themselves were required to take part in collective manual labour for set periods, either by rotation or at regular intervals and this has remained a consistent principle of management since 1967. Although the criticisms voiced in 1974 suggested that in some places the practice had been discontinued or curtailed,[60] most reports since then have indicated that it is being maintained.

Until 1972, most descriptions of systems of management and factory organisation stressed the reduction in the number of administrative personnel not engaged directly in production. Indeed, drives to reduce the number of office workers and administrative levels in industry have been a recurrent feature since 1949 and have led Brugger to posit the existence of a 'bureaucratic cycle' with alternations between periods of bureaucratic growth, typical of managerial style leadership, and campaigns to simplify administration, associated with 'cadre' style leadership.[61] The calls of 1972 to strengthen management and build up complete sets of rules and regulations, however, suggested that the extent of simplification carried out immediately after the Cultural Revolution was having a bad effect on production. Thus, in the middle of the year, many articles were published on the need to employ fully the talents of old cadres and to bring them back into factory work again.[62] Since calls of this kind had already been made in the drive to improve output in 1971[63] the implication was that the increasing complexity of administrative procedures (on which, see below) meant an ever greater need for experienced administrative staff.

Although there has not been a great deal of information on changes in the complexity, numbers and kinds of specialist departments attached to a factory revolutionary committee since 1972, it seems probable that after a period of sharp reduction, the number of administrative personnel in Chinese factories began to grow again. Nevertheless, the work situation facing such personnel in 1972 had a number of important differences from that of before the Cultural Revolution. First, they were expected to participate in collective labour on a more regular basis than before. Second, they had to work alongside representatives of the workers elected to participate in the mass management systems. Third, the independence of staff departments from the Party, line management and the workers had been much curtailed. Whereas previously they had enjoyed considerable autonomy as defined by factory rules,[64] they were now more directly subordinate to the revolutionary committee at the upper level, less organisationally complex at intermediate levels, and combined more closely with the production unit at the lower levels. This transformation was most widely and consistently realised in the deployment of technical personnel. Using the Great Leap Forward formula of 'triple combination', during 1967 workshops formed teams consisting of cadres, technicians and workers which worked together on problems of design, innovation, research, technical reform and so forth. Descriptions indicated that these teams were formed either on permanent basis or *ad hoc* as required. Furthermore instead of a strict division of technical personnel between workshops and sections, there were now arrangements to enable them to be moved flexibly about factories as the situation demanded.[65] Technical administration has thus proved one of the more successful areas for attempts to integrate staff functions with productive activity on the shop floor. The stress on expertise, however, that emerged in 1972 and more latterly since the fall of the 'Gang of Four', indicates that even here there are pressures within Chinese industry to give a more authoritative role and greater independence to technical staff.

Below the factory revolutionary committee level, factories may be divided into branch factories (if big enough), workshops, shifts and production groups.[66] Experiments in organisation at these different levels have taken a variety of forms across the country. The complexity of Party organisation depends largely on the number of Party members so that a branch factory might form a general Party branch or just a Party branch. Similarly, a workshop might have a Party branch or a Party cell. In administration, branch factories have established revolutionary committees and workshops revolutionary leading groups. The latter is headed by a workshop supervisor assisted by some special officers and advised by a workers' management committee. Shifts and production groups are led by heads with a committee of assistants each assigned to do specific tasks. These assistants include specialist staff transferred down during the Cultural Revolution from staff departments, and elected workers.[67] As outlined above, this system evolved in two stages. The first, with its emphasis on mass participation and simple rules and regulations, was characterised by fewer administrative procedures and attempts to make managerial staff more responsive to mass supervision. A model for these innovations was the Shenyang Locomotive and Rolling Stock Plant described in *Red Flag*, No.12, 1970.[68] This report underlined the fact that the new rules were drawn up under the guidance of the principles of the Anshan Constitution and detailed the stages of evolution. Apparently, immediately after the Cultural Revolution, one of the plant's workshops abolished parts of the original rules and regulations that were necessary (such as the system of economic accounting), found that some of the irrational ones it abolished were in fact still used in practice, and did not set up any new rules. The result was confusion and waste, and it was alleged 'class enemies' took the chance to engage in corruption, cause accidents and sabotage production though, from the discussion, some of these problems may simply have been determined by the uncertain management structure. The revolutionary leading group of the workshop, therefore, launched a mass campaign to discuss and set up new rules and regulations. Throughout, the stress was on the role of the masses in deciding and implementing the rules, and in their self-conscious adherence to discipline and to acceptable norms of quality and output. This self-consciousness, which was attributed to political awareness heightened by the Cultural Revolution, was seen as an important reason for being able to simplify rules and rely on the creativity of the masses. The new rules were set up as follows:

> They formulated six sets of rules for governing production planning, technical work, quality control, safety equipment, economic accounting, and welfare services. In respect of production planning, they established a system whereby the leadership issues production targets for mass discussion, there is unified direction with cooperation between work shifts and production teams, and the masses fix the target and manage production. In respect of quality control, they set up a system of combining self-inspection, mutual inspection and professional inspection. In respect of technical work, they established a technical innovation system in which leading cadres, the masses of workers, and technical

personnel together set tasks, do design work, conduct experiments, and engage in production. In respect of economic accounting, they have set up a two-level system of accounting by the workshop and accounting by the shifts and teams, with the latter as the basic level.

The report pointed out that, before the Cultural Revolution, accounting was done at workshop level by a specialist staff of six accountants who did not take part in production. It then described how the new system operated.

Now the workshop only has one specialist accountant and each shift has established one person in charge of economic accounting who is not divorced from production. All the masses of the workers participate in accounting work. They reckon accounts before they do a task and while they are doing it. Every month the workshop publishes the records and results of the various accounts, and it regularly calls meetings to analyse economic accounting, in which the workers take part . . .

Under the leadership of the Party branch, the workshop established two levels of management, the workshop revolutionary leading group and the shift committee. Each of these combined leading cadres, workers and technical personnel in a conscious attempt to escape the influence of the 'one-man management' system and the problem of 'experts in control of the factory'. Mass participation in management of the shift was described as follows:

. . .each shift has a shift committee which has the shift leader (concurrently head of the shift Party cell), deputy shift leader(s), and worker representatives as its core, and also six 'supervisors from the masses' who are responsible for various items of work. This committee exercises comprehensive leadership of revolution and production for the whole shift. The supervisors from the masses are elected democratically by each shift and approved by the Party branch. Re-elections are held at fixed intervals in conjunction with the 'four good' evaluations. The six supervisors from the masses of each shift (there are ten shifts in the workshop, giving a total of sixty people) set up 'mass management networks' for each shift with workers as the core and partici- pation by technical personnel. Under the leadership of the Party breach, this takes responsibility for managing production and standard operating procedures and planned accounting.[72] The implication of these developments was that industrial organisation based on ideological education and motivation was not sufficient to ensure production and that operations had to be governed by formal rules and regulations. The reference to Taching also indicated how new policy themes were grafted on to established models. Since that time, the Taching slogan of the 'three honest and four strict' (honest people, honest words and honest deeds, and strict demands, strict organisation, strict behaviour and strict discipline) has become a code word for improved management policies.[73] Perhaps the most significant aspect of this change was the renewed emphasis on individual responsibility for production tasks and the reintroduction of rules of discipline. Both implicitly entailed a system of rewards and penalties that could be applied at an individual level. Not unexpectedly, this provoked resistance or confusion among those who were most influenced by the extreme expression of the ideals of simplified rules and mass management of the Cultural Revolution. Much discussion in the media reflected this by urging people to distinguish clearly between grasping production for the sake of the revolution and the reactionary theory of 'production first', between economic accounting for the revolution and 'profits in command', between learning techniques and professional work for the revolution and 'professional work in command', and between observing labour discipline for the revolution and the old system of 'controlling, restricting and suppressing' the masses of workers.[74] Obviously, for many people, the practical effect of the new rules was much the same as that of the old, and they needed persuading that the social context had changed sufficiently so that the new rules did not imply a complete return to the old system. By the middle of the year, it was also necessary to distinguish clearly between reasonable rewards and the 'reactionary theory of material incentives'.

The Period since 1973

Despite the above problems of definition, the reforms of 1972 appear to have gained considerable acceptance until they were questioned during the Anti-Confucius campaign. Information on the effects of that campaign, however, is still limited and it is currently the subject of re-analysis in the light of the criticisms of the 'Gang of Four'. Andors argues that the ensuing disturbances in Hangchow were in fact caused by workers' perceptions of the erosion of the equalities with management that they had fought for during the Cultural Revolution.[75] Others have argued that the sporadic disturbances on the daily life in the workshop without being divorced from the shifts and teams, from the masses, and from labour. The mass management network has a supervisory function and management authority.

The report concluded by stressing that cadres all take part in labour, including the seven specialists at workshop level, and that the basis for the success of this system was constant political and educational work, which depended on the leadership of the Party and the activism of mass organisations.

In terms of the managerial and 'cadre' styles of leadership described at the outset, this system does represent a considerable shift away from leadership based on a technical definition of roles as expressed in complex rules. Instead, there is a shift towards leadership based on a sense of ideological unity which guides the integration of technical roles at lower levels. Nevertheless, just as practice before the Cultural Revolution did not entirely deny the importance of politics or such things as cadre participation in labour, the new system did not entirely deny the need for some technical rules, defining tasks to be done and the relationship between man and man, and man and materials. This latter aspect, moreover, began to receive much greater prominence during the second stage of development after the fall of Lin Piao. Thus articles, like the one from Kwangchow noted above[69], stressed the complexity of management work and the need to combine mass management with professional management. Reports began to detail more extensive systems of rules and procedures than those listed in 1970. One, in January 1972 from Changsha, noted that a factory had established nine systems for production planning, technical work, quality control, safety, financial work, materials, equipment, tools, and labour.[70] Another from a Nanchang factory stressed that strengthening of management was based on the Taching model which represented high output, high quality, low consumption of raw materials, and a good safety record. Taching was also seen as the model for management and accounting, with personal responsibility in one's work post, the use of efficiency ratings, and so forth. The Nanchang factory reported that it had set up initial rules for assembling production statistics, consumption of raw materials, quality inspection, computation of production costs, records of material requisitions, reporting of accidents, publication of profit made for the state, and comparison of the efficiency of different teams.[71] Still other reports listed rules for discipline, labour attendance, railways and in cities like Hangchow were caused by worker dissatisfaction with the removal of bonus systems again, and with material conditions. More recently, the Chinese media have alleged that they were the result of anarchy and factionalism stirred up by the 'Gang of Four' in the face of necessary rules and regulations.[76] The situation since 1973 has thus been a confused one with perhaps wider variations in the systems of management used in different parts of the country than previously. On the one hand, not all of the innovations in mass management have been swept aside. In May, 1976, for example, the Changchun No.1 Automobile Works reported mass participation in management committees at all levels with concentration at workshop and production team levels.[77] Most workshops in the Changchun plant had a workers' management committee which advised the workshop supervisor. Thus the formal structure, described by the Shenyang Locomotive and Rolling Stock Plant, still existed in Chinese factories. On the other hand, rules and regulations were prominently displayed on boards throughout the workshops. In the Chassis Workshop, management regulations were listed under the headings of production assignment (*diaodu*), technical quality, equipment work-rate standards, economic accounting, tool administration, safety and fire precautions, work attendance and technical education. The regulations for relationships between shifts detailed such things as clearing up ten minutes before handing over shifts and formal exchange of shifts between shift heads, including reports on output and the current situation. The responsibilities of the heads of production teams included supervision of workers before and after shifts (covering such things as political and technical education, safety and so forth), organisation of production, dealing with all problems, organising the use of labour, implementing technical rules, guiding work improvements and so forth. Finally boards listed the duties of individual production workers. Those for the assembly line workers listed obedience|to discipline, fulfilment of production assignments, care for tools and products, political study, care in the use of raw materials, and attention to safety regulations. Thus, the existence of mass participation in management was complemented by precise detailing of work duties, and definition of roles according to technical responsibilities.

Changes in the Workers' Environment and Status

At first the Cultural Revolution brought many changes to the workers' status and their relationship to their enterprises.[78] In their political life, the immediate influence and pressure of the Party completely

disappeared and the trade unions and Communist Youth League
ceased to function. In the place of these organisations, there grew up
mass organisations with their own channels of affiliation and leadership.
Socially the result was a breakdown in the dominance of the unit of
employment as the centre of all political, social, and cultural activity.
Workers mingled and united with workers in other industries and trades
and with students, office workers and other social groups, discussing
and viewing social problems in a much wider context than their own
unit. They also developed divisions within their ranks based not on class
distinctions but on perceived attitudes towards particular leaders or
particular policies. Within factories, administrative and technical
authorities were downgraded and workers gained considerably in status.
Systems of discipline and work procedures were abandoned or
considerably simplified and, along with these, bonuses and incentives
were stopped. Thus the years 1966 and 1967 saw considerable changes
in the workers' environment, and their improved social status was
underlined in the middle of 1968 with their entry into educational
institutions as members of worker propaganda teams inspired by Mao,
and the publication of Yao Wen-yuan's article, 'The Working Class Must
Lead Everything'.[79]

Since that time, the reconstruction of the Party and the developments
in management described above have significantly limited the extent of
these changes and brought back many features of industrial life that had
been removed. The reconstruction of the Party has returned authority
to that organisation as the interpreter of the ideas of Marxism-Leninism
and Mao Tsetung Thought. The trade unions and Communist Youth
League have been rebuilt, explicitly under the leadership of the Party
and with political and educational duties. The former role of the trade
unions in economic and welfare activities has been discontinued and this
is now placed entirely in the hands of revolutionary committees.[80] Thus,
there is no suggestion that the workers might have interests which
are not expressed through the leadership of the Party or the revolutionary
committee. During the process of the reconstruction of the Party and
trade unions, the mass organisations formed during the Cultural
Revolution were broken up. Initially, the emphasis was on breaking
down the factional divisions between them and on uniting them into
workers' congresses. By 1971, these congresses were being established
through the country.[81] Their main task was to do political work, and
representatives of the workers on revolutionary committees were
appointed through them. These congresses were renamed trade unions
in 1973. The other innovations such as the 'Red Sentinels', described

by Bettelheim,[82] in 1971 and the worker-theorists of 1974 have essentially been means of mobilising political activists to ensure Party policies and principles are explained and realised. Control over the work force is thus again exercised through a variety of forms. Major decisions are taken by the Party which also exercises ideological control through its organisation and through activists. Formal functional control is expressed through the management structures in which the workers are represented and through the codes of rules and regulations.

Socially, the decline of the mass organisations has been accompanied by a decline in links between workers of different factories and between workers and other social groups. The main exception has been the maintenance of the worker propaganda teams in the educational system, as discussed by Chan, and other links with schools such as school workshops and 'open-door' schooling. In most other aspects of political, social and cultural life, the factory has once again come to play the key role. The Changchun No.1 Automobile Plant is not just a factory employing some 40,000 people. It is the centre of a community of up to 200,000 people and provides educational, welfare, entertainment, housing, medical and many of the other services that community requires. Thus the territorial division of economic and political organisation still plays a fundamental part in other social activities as it did before the Cultural Revolution.

In terms of enterprise management, worker participation was at first interpreted in terms of participation at all levels. Although this principle has not been abandoned, the main centre of participation has steadily shifted downwards to the workshop and the production team. The actual managerial personnel at upper levels has not changed considerably[83] and, since 1971, many of the technical and administrative staff have been brought back to their original roles. Nevertheless, worker involvement in management, at least in a consultative role and at some lower levels in an authoritative role, appears to have been maintained, and there has been considerable emphasis on the fact that all rules and regulations are drawn up as part of a consultative process between leaders and led, even if ultimate authority is with the Party and management. Furthermore, as the periods of unrest in Hangchow and other places after 1974 demonstrated, the work force is now much more willing to express its dissatisfactions through wall-posters, demonstrations and other activities.

Finally, the Cultural Revolution has produced little change in the workers' economic position. The eight grade wage system still operates and various forms of individual and collective material incentives have for some periods, at least, been re-instituted. But, little is known about the current distribution of workers between the grades on the wage scale. Joan Robinson reports that, as a result of the wage reform of 1971, workers on the third grade or below who had started working before 1957 were raised to the fourth grade, those on the second grade who had started working before 1960 were raised to the third grade, and those on the first grade who had started working before 1966 were raised to the second.[84] The wage grades themselves were not changed. Howe surmises that this reform may have raised the average wage by 10 per cent.[85] Nevertheless, since the previous wage reform had been in 1963, and assuming a steady increase in the size of the work force through recruitment at the lower end, together with a reduction in the number of higher paid workers through retirement, the average wage may have become weighted towards the lower end of the scale by 1970. Thus, the wage reform of 1971 may have done little more than restore the average wage level to that of the pre-Cultural Revolution situation. For the same reasons, this may also have been true of the distribution of workers across the wage scale. The last official figures for this distribution were quoted in the mid-1950s when from 40 to 60 per cent of the work force was on grades three and four, varying with the industrial sector in which they were employed.[86] An additional point is that the eight grades do not include the rates paid to apprentices which are usually only around one-half of the grade one wage. In the Changchun No.1 Automobile Plant, for example, the grade one worker's wage was 39 *yuan* and apprentices started on 17, 19 or 22 *yuan*.[87] The factory also reported that, after two years, apprentices are appointed to grade one and then, after a further year, to grade two. Thereafter, promotions are decided by the State Council in block cases as in the 1971 reform. Since promotion up through the scale is based on age and seniority, there are no allowances for technical skills or quality of work, a problem that was obviated by the use of bonuses before the Cultural Revolution. After the Cultural Revolution, this appears to have created some problems of motivation among young workers and *Red Flag* reported that some of them considered that 'whether you work hard or not, you still belong to grade one'.[88] They were criticised for the wrong attitude but their remarks underline the fact that this aspect of the wage system has not been affected by the Cultural Revolution. Finally, little is known about the social and political differences between workers at different levels on the scale. Recent criticism of the 'Gang of Four' which claimed that they regarded veteran workers as an 'upper strata' with 'vested interests' and therefore potentially supporters of the line the 'Gang' was opposing imply that such differences may exist.[89] Nevertheless, the Cultural Revolution has not changed the economic aspect of such differences.

In sum, therefore, while the changes in factory management since 1967 have to some extent given slightly more status to the average worker and made workshop management at the lower level more open, much of the daily routine and the economic and social parameters of a worker's life remain the same as before 1966. Furthermore, this similarity is one that has grown stronger as time has elapsed since the Cultural Revolution.

Conclusion

At the outset of this survey of developments in enterprise management since the Cultural Revolution, I briefly outlined the analytical model developed by Schurmann which posited the two types of leadership, the modern manager and the 'cadre'. I further noted the parallels that are often drawn between this model and the Chinese analysis of the 'two-line struggle' since 1949. I also questioned whether the polarisation implied in the 'two-line struggle' helps us to understand developments in enterprise management in China over the past 28 years. I suggested that further consideration of such things as the technological structure of Chinese industry and more detailed information on the structure of Chinese society, as reflected in such things as income levels, patterns of consumption, places of residence, awareness of distinctions between social groups and so forth, might give us a clearer picture of the underlying nature of the struggle taking place in China and the pressures on industrial management.

In some ways, the course of events since 1966 in industrial management has borne out these caveats. Although it is clear that the analytical model put forwarded by Schurmann and others is of great importance in distinguishing the two opposing poles in industrial management and of those aspects of Chinese practice that lean towards either of them, it is also clear that, in practice, Chinese industry has not been entirely subject to one or the other of the two extremes but to an amalgam of them. On the one hand, the technological pressures of modern industry, perhaps heightened by the generally simpler technical levels outside of industry, have placed a premium on the role of trained technicians, managerial skills, and labour discipline. Thus, attempts during the Great Leap Forward and the Cultural Revolution to downgrade the importance of technicians, simplify management and reduce the rules for labour discipline have been short-lived and created problems in production. Conversely, excessive status for managers and technicians and oppressive rules for workers created social divisions that contributed to the demands of those two movements. On the other hand, it is clear that Chinese society is sufficiently divided over these issues to prevent either pole from gaining complete dominance. The divisions within the central leadership which are subsumed under the analysis of the 'two-line struggle' must to some extent reflect divisions – actual or potential – within society as a whole. The fate of Teng Hsiao-p'ing's report, 'Several Questions concerning the Acceleration of Industrial Development', is a case in point.[90] Following on the emphasis given to economic modernisation at the Fourth National People's Congress in January 1975 and in the face of what he saw as continued disruption in industry, misuse of technicians, sloppy management, poor labour discipline and stagnating production, Teng put forward a programme which stressed the importance of ensuring production, the need for capable, strong management, the need to make good use of and raise the level of technicians, the role of comprehensive rules and regulations which must be adhered to, the importance of relating the workers' material well-being to increases in productivity, the need for greater centralised control and planning, and finally the need to import some foreign technology.[91] In criticising this programme, Teng's opponents pointed to the similarities between it and the policies denounced during the Cultural Revolution. Once again, they stressed the importance of management by the masses and of political consciousness above technical rules. More recently, the critics themselves have been accused of causing anarchy, caring little for production or for the material welfare of the workers and of neglecting those aspects of management which are determined by the material conditions of production and by technology. Nevertheless, this recent counterattack has also underlined the fact that it does not discount the importance of such things as political consciousness and management by the masses. Thus the social groups on either side have been constrained to recognise the aspirations of their opponents. Seen in these terms, the problem becomes one of balancing policy and resources. Policy demands political work and innovations which lead towards socialism. Resources influence the speed of change and themselves make demands which cannot be ignored. The struggle between the 'two lines' thus becomes not a struggle between two extremes but a struggle to find the correct balance between them. Policies are 'correct' if they are in line with the prevailing consensus of ultimate goals and 'balanced' if they go no further than the current social realities will permit. Within the sphere of industrial management, the question as to which social forces are deciding the correctness of the balance requires us to look beyond the theoretical model and more closely at the actual division of economic, technical and political power, as suggested by the questions raised during the course of the above survey of developments since the Cultural Revolution.

Notes

1. Schurmann 1966.
2. In terms of function, staff management is concerned with aspects of the production process such as accounting, engineering, inspection, etc. and line management is concerned with overall decision making. Structurally, the two forms may be closely linked, separate or overlapping.
3. Schurmann 1966, pp.166-7 and 225-38.
4. Brugger 1976.
5. Andors 1977.
6. Thus, Brugger (1976) argues that Soviet style 'one man management' was very incompletely implemented in China and was less developed South of the Great Wall than in the North East (pp.189-90), that the organisation of the iron and steel industry might be expected to differ from that of the construction industry (pp.294-5, note 10), and that there is some uncertainty over the extent to which the position of Mao and Liu differed at the time of the Tientsin Talks in 1949 (pp.67-8).
7. Richman 1969, pp.46-57.
8. Gray 1973.
9. Selden 1971.
10. Thus, as Brugger (1976 p.270) points out, it is difficult to reconcile Liu's alleged support for trade union independence and 'economism' with his demand that all organisations should be 'docile tools' of the Party.
11. As has happened since the Cultural Revolution with the fall of Lin Piao, the dismissal of Teng Hsiao-p'ing and the arrest of the 'Gang of Four'.
12. See the wall poster 'Concerning the Socialist Democracy and Legal System' by a group of three students in Kwangchow writing under the name of Li I-che. Ting Wang (ed.) 1976, pp.1-38.
13. Bettelheim 1974.
14. Ibid., pp.73-5. Note that Taylor's own position is not the issue here, merely those aspects attributed to him by others.
15. Ibid, p.10.
16. *PR* 14, 1 April 1977, pp.23-6.
17. Two recent articles have raised questions of this kind on a number of issues. Starr 1976 and Nathan 1976.
18. Mao Tsetung, 25 April, 1956, in *SW,* Chinese edition, Vol.5, pp.267-88, (trans. *PR* 1, 1 January 1977, pp.10-25). December 1976 was the first time an official version was released. For an earlier version see *Wansui* 1969, pp.40-59,

(trans. Schram 1974, pp.61-83).

19. As a result, factories could be encouraged to produce goods which gave a lower rate of profit but which benefited the economy as a whole; e.g. goods for rural consumption.
20. See Andors 1977, pp.98-104 and Richman 1967.
21. A discussion of this constitution may be found in *PR* 14, 3 April 1970, pp.11-15.
22. See Andors 1977, pp.74-85. In 1958, 'two participations and one reform' meant that 'cadres should participate in labour and workers in management and rules and regulations should be reformed'. Triple combination referred to a combination of leaders and led, labour and technique and theory and practice.
23. This is amply demonstrated in Hunter 1969. See also A. Watson reports on the Cultural revolution in Sian; *FEER,* 20 April 1967, pp.123-6; 27 April 1967, pp.231-3; 4 May 1967, pp.266-9; 18 May 1967, pp.403-6; 25 May 1967, pp.449-52 and 24 August 1967, pp.373-6.
24. For an excellent discussion of this issue as it appeared in the first phase of the Cultural Revolution, see Schram (in Schram [ed.] 1973) especially pp.85-101.
25. This was cited as a most recent instruction by Yao Wen-yuan, (*Hongqi* 2, 1968, p.6).
26. See e.g. Ko Hsin-chun, *Hongqi* 6-7, 1969, pp.21-3.
27. Details of this process, given by Andors 1977, pp.173-87.
28. Problems of factionalism in this period were widely discussed. See e.g. *Hongqi* 6-7, 1969, pp.21-3 and pp.68-72; 8, 1969, pp.46-8 and pp.59-64; 9, 1969, pp.34-8. An outline of the problems facing soldiers stationed in factories is given in *Hongqi* 5, 1969, pp.77-82.
29. *Hongqi* 8, 1969, pp.28-31.
30. *Hongqi* 1, 1970, pp.61-7 and 7, 1970, pp.19-23.
31. As Young notes, the model for factory Party building was the Peking Hsinhua Printing Works, See *RMRB,* 16 December 1969, p.1.
32. See e.g. *Hongqi* 2, 1972, pp.73-8.
33. *Hongqi* 3, 1970, pp.38-41.
34. Lin Piao's attempt to undermine Mao's line in factories by 'ultra-left' tactics were examined at length during 1972. See e.g. *RMRB* article and Sian radio broadcast quoted in *CQ* 53, Jan/March 1973, pp.192-4.
35. See Kung Hsiao-wen *et al.*(Shanghai 1974) in *Chinese Economic Studies,* Fall 1975, Vol.9, No.1, especially pp.7-8, 15 and 37-8.
36. This aspect of Lin's role is now being reaffirmed. See *PR* 14, 1 April 1977, pp.23.
37. The factories were the Peking General Knitwear Mill, the Peking Hsinhua Printing Works, the Peking No.3 Chemical Plant, the Peking Peich'iao Timber Mill, the Peking February Seventh Locomotive and Rolling Stock Plant and the Peking Nank'ou Locomotive and Rolling Stock Plant. The two schools were Tsinghua and Peking Universities.
38. *RMRB,* 2 March 1972.
39. *Hongqi* 8, 1969, pp.32-5.
40. *Hongqi* 9, 1969, pp.34-38; *RMRB,* 11 January 1970, p.1 etc. By the end of 1970, these criticisms had merged into the 'one strike and three oppositions' movement, i.e. 'strike at counter-revolutionaries; oppose corruption and theft, oppose speculation and extravagance and oppose waste'. See pp. 161-62.
41. An interesting discussion of the problems faced in getting veteran factory cadres back to work is in *Hongqi* 8, 1969, pp.59-64.
42. *Hongqi* 12, 1970, pp.57-62.
43. Lin Piao was not redesignated 'ultra-right' until the beginning of 1973.
44. *RMRB* 2 March 1972.

45. *SWB*, FE/4016/B11/9
46. *The Times*, 26 June 1972, p.4, quoting *RMRB* on 'rational rewards'. See also Sian radio quoted in *CQ*, No.53 (1973) pp.193-4.
47. See *SWB*, FE/4534/B11/17, FE/4538/B11/1-2, FE/4545/B11/2-14 and FE/4554/B11/5-13.
48. *PR* 24, 14 June 1974, pp.5-6.
49. *Hongqi* 4, 1977, pp.25-31.
50. Not all revolutionary committees in fact had military representatives. Small factories like the Sian Art and Handicraft Factory did not (personal notes, 14 April 1971); nor did revolutionary committees at grass roots level, such as the Shanghai Docks, Fifth District (personal notes, 11 April 1971). In such cases, the role of the military might be filled by the unit's own militia.
51. *RMRB*, 16 December 1969 p.1 and *Hongqi* 1, 1970, pp.10-15.
52. *Hongqi* 7, 1970, pp.19-23 especially p.23.
53. This might, of course, have been mitigated by the fact that many mass representatives on the revolutionary committee were also absorbed into the Party committee: though it is important to note that as, Party members, their relationship to the rank and file workers had then changed.
54. See the examples of October and November 1971 in *SWB*, FE/3819/B11/4-8, FE/3820/B11/8-13 and FE/3825/B11/3-6. It is highly likely that reports of this kind were intended at that time to illustrate Lin Piao's own failings as much as those of personnel at lower levels; nevertheless, examples from individual lower level institutions were cited.
55. *SWB*, FE/3840/B11/3.
56. *SWB*, FE/4657/B11/6.
57. Ibid.
58. Most factories I visited in 1971 had four departments.
59. Thus Richman (1969, pp.753-60) reports on a larger proportion of administrative cadres in Chinese factories visited in 1965/6 than in factories in the Soviet Union. He also charts some very complex administrative structures (pp.767-89). Howe (1973, pp.64-5) quotes an example of a Shanghai enterprise that had 30 special departments before the Cultural Revolution and 5 after it.
60. See note 47.
61. Brugger 1976, pp.212-13 and pp.224-77.
62. See e.g. *Hongqi* 7, 1972, pp.63-7 and the call from the First Ministry of Machine Building to improve the quality of work, strengthen the system of rules and make full use of experienced managers. *SWB*, FE/3962/B11/7.
63. Andors 1977, p.231.
64. Andors 1977, p.128 ff; Brugger 1976, pp.204-6.
65. This was the situation described at the Changchun No.1 Automobile Plant, May 1976 (personal notes).
66. This contrasts with the situation in the Soviet Union. There, an enterprise usually consists of several factories. In China, whatever subdivisions there might be, each factory is usually a separate enterprise.
67. While local variations on this pattern can be quite significant, this was the general pattern of formal structure in the four factories I visited in North East China in May 1976.
68. *Hongqi* 12, 1970, pp.57-62, trans. in *Chinese Economic Studies*, Winter 1971/2, Vol.5, No.2, pp.162-72. This system is much the same as that in the model Peking General Knitwear Mill described in Bettelheim 1974, pp.21-32.
69. See note 45.

70. *SWB* FE/3905/B11/15.
71. *SWB*, FE/3930/B11/11.
72. *SWB*, FE/3961/B11/10.
73. See the discussion in Guangdongsheng Geming Weiyuanhui, Gong Jiao Bangongshi, Zhengzhibu 1973. The slogan receives prominent stress in articles in *Hongqi* 4, 1977. In a parallel way the Tachai model, as published in late 1972 and 1973, placed more emphasis on mechanisation and technique than previously.
74. *RMRB*, 2 March, 1972.
75. Andors 1977, pp.234-5. Disturbances in Sian during 1976 also seem to support that conclusion (personal communication).
76. *PR* 14, 1 April 1977, pp.23-6.
77. Personal notes, May 1976.
78. For a further discussion of these issues see Watson in Schram (ed.) 1973, pp.291-330.
79. *Hongqi* 2, 1968, pp.3-7.
80. The trade unions were rebuilt after April 1973. A report on trade union congresses in Peking and Shanghai, in *RMRB*, 24 April 1973, pp.1-2, outlined the differences between the rebuilt unions and pre-Cultural Revolution structure.
81. Thus, in April 1971, most factories reported having set up a congress. The Shanghai No.1 Machine Factory and the Shanghai Docks, Fifth District, however, were still preparing to set up theirs. Personal notes.
82. Bettelheim (1974, pp.32-5) uses the term 'Red Guard' but most Chinese accounts refer to the system of 'Red Sentinels'.
83. Howe 1973, pp.249-50.
84. Robinson 1972, pp.2-3.
85. Howe 1973, p.251.
86. Howe 1973, *Wage Patterns* . . ., p.66.
87. Personal notes, May 1976.
88. *Hongqi* 6-7, 1969, p.28 ff.
89. *RMRB*, 19 April 1977, pp.1-2; *SWB*, FE/5493/B11/1.
90. This document has not been published officially but its content has been outlined in criticisms of it, such as those of *RMRB*, 21 May 1976, pp.1-3; *Xuexi yu Pipan* 4, 1976, pp.28-35; *Hongqi* 3, 1976, pp.64-70; 4, 1976, pp.21-6 and 8, 1976, pp.21-5 and pp.45-50; *Beijing Daxue Xuebao* 3, 1976, pp.60-71 and 4, 1976, pp.48-52.
91. Most of these points are closely parallel to those embraced by the current Chinese leadership. See e.g. *Hongqi* 2, 1977, pp.50-53, 58-63; 3, 1977, pp.66-81 and 4, 1977, pp.3-31.

7 CHINESE FOREIGN POLICY — FROM 'ANTI-IMPERIALISM' TO 'ANTI-HEGEMONISM'

Greg O'Leary

Previous chapters have demonstrated that significant developments took place in Chinese political, military and economic policies in the period under review. These developments were complemented in the realm of foreign policy by dramatic changes, of which burgeoning diplomatic activity was but the most obvious. The improved relations with the United States, diplomatic recognition of Japan and most other capitalist countries and membership of the United Nations were the symptoms of profound developments in the way Chinese foreign policy theorists came to view the world. It is these latter developments which form the subject of this chapter.

No attempt is made here to compile a detailed diplomatic chronology of China's behaviour during the period nor is there any comprehensive discussion of the way in which China's foreign policy is implemented. Such painstaking — and largely descriptive — tasks have been undertaken elsewhere, with considerable industry, and reference is made to them where appropriate. The focus here is an analysis of why China's foreign policy changed in the way it did. To what forces was it responding? In what way was the new policy formulated? What arguments were used by those responsible for the new formulation in successfully urging its adoption? By focusing the enquiry in this way, it is hoped that light may be shed not simply on the foreign policy developments during the period but also on the way in which the Chinese Communist Party formulates foreign policy generally.

China's Foreign Policy as a Reaction to the Soviet Threat

The most widely accepted interpretation of China's post Cultural Revolution foreign policy considers that policy initiatives, since the end of the 1960s, have been a response to Soviet military pressure — primarily that along the common border. This pressure, combined with the Brezhnev Doctrine of 'limited sovereignty' enunciated after the Soviet-led invasion of Czechoslovakia, is considered so fundamental to the policy initiatives undertaken during the period that all Chinese external relations are seen as a reaction to it. Thus, Chinese policy, whether it be in Bangladesh, the Middle East, South-East

Asia or Angola is best understood, according to this view, as an unprincipled opposition to any policy which the Soviet Union adopts in any one of these regions.

Anti-Soviet concerns too, it is claimed, are responsible for China's turn to the West. The United States has been deliberately sought out as an ally in a power game so that the possibility of a Soviet attack might be forestalled by China's association with the American nuclear umbrella. This alliance, it is also claimed, necessitates compromises with respect to China's support for revolutionary movements, its opposition to other capitalist powers and reactionary Third World states.

Although this position has been widely adopted,[1] there have been few attempts to demonstrate its validity, and those that are available leave much to be desired. In one of the better argued cases for this interpretation, Allen S. Whiting shows that there was a major reassessment, by the Chinese leadership, of Soviet military intentions after the invasion of Czechoslovakia, and, more particularly, after Brezhnev's subsequent enunciation of the doctrine of 'limited sovereignty'.[2] Indications of this reassessment are perceived in the Chinese Ministry of Foreign Affairs statement of 16 September 1968, which 'suddenly' protested about Soviet overflights during the preceding year, and in Chou En-lai's National Day address on 1 October, which enjoined the Chinese people to 'smash any invasion launched by US imperialism, Soviet 'revisionism', and their lackeys whether individually or collectively'. Whiting claims (incorrectly) that this was the first time that the possibility of invasion had been explicitly linked to Soviet 'revisionism'. In fact, the then PLA Chief or Staff, Huang Yung-sheng, speaking at an Army Day reception on 1 August 1968,[3] three weeks prior to the invasion of Czechoslovakia, had warned of the possibility of a Soviet invasion in terms almost identical to those he used two weeks after the invasion and which are cited by Whiting as an indication of a reassessment of Soviet strategic intentions.

Huang Yung-sheng's statement, moreover, was scarcely novel. Mao Tsetung had noted with obvious disapproval, in 1964, that there were Soviet troop concentrations on|China's borders[4] and the Foreign Minister, Ch'en Yi had warned, in September 1965, of Soviet military aggression in China.[5] Since that time, the position was developed in the Chinese press that Soviet 'revisionism' was increasingly concerned to collaborate with the United States in its strategic attempts to contain China. That there was in Peking, in the winter of 1968-9, serious concern about Soviet military pressure is not in question, but such concern had presumably accompanied and grown with the military build-up along the common border, since the collapse of the border negotiations in 1964, to the point where Soviet military concentrations were even greater than those arrayed along the Soviet Union's European borders.

A Ministry of Foreign Affairs statement of 26 November 1968, proposing the following 20 February as a date for resuming the Sino-American ambassadorial talks, is seen by Whiting as indication of the fact that the concern with Soviet military intentions was directly responsible for a decision, by at least one section of the Chinese leadership, to foster *détente* with the United States. The aspect of the statement which is considered indicative of a new posture towards the United States is the mention of the 'five principles of peaceful coexistence'. While it must be conceded that emphasis on the 'five principles' had not been great during the Cultural Revolution, no other basis had ever been put forward for relations with the United States or any other country having a 'different social system'. To assert, moreover, as does Whiting, that the Chinese statement is not only an analytical development of some novelty but is also hypocritical, is quite misleading. Whiting suggests that China had come to accept a position on relations with the United States, which the Chinese press had spent years denouncing in relation to the Soviet Union. In doing so, he ignores the stated differences in content of the Chinese and Soviet notions of 'peaceful coexistence' and the different situations to which they were applicable. In the Sino-Soviet polemics of 1963-4, the Chinese had argued that it was the duty of socialist countries at all times to work for relations of 'peaceful coexistence' even with the imperialist countries. The latter countries, they claimed, would only accept relations on such a basis at times when they were forced on to the defensive, and that acceptance would be a considerable victory for socialist countries.

Even if Whiting's view of developments up to this point were to be accepted, events subsequent to those immediately following the invasion of Czechoslovakia do not bear out his interpretation. Both the Sino-Soviet border clashes in March 1969, and the as yet vague, but to Chinese ears still menacing, proposal by Brezhnev in June 1969 for an Asian system of 'collective security', with all its anti-Chinese implications, could only have served to exacerbate Chinese fears of Soviet intentions. Whiting is unable to demonstrate that the injection of these new 'threats' into the already apprehensive Chinese state of mind produced any more 'feelers' or 'signals' towards an accommodation with the United States.

The implications of accepting the 'Whiting thesis' are considerable. China is said to have taken the initiative in reducing Sino-American diplomatic hostilities as a result of an increasing fear of Soviet military attack. It is not argued that China developed a consciousness, at this time, of a global ideological and strategic threat which it called 'Soviet social-imperialism' and which it saw as emanating from a new constellation of class forces within the Soviet Union. Nor is it claimed that China's reduced hostility towards the United States was the result, in part or in whole, of any perception that the United States was less able to exert its imperial dominance than in a previous era. Nor indeed, is it simply being claimed that the Chinese leadership feared the likelihood and consequences of a Soviet military attack. The argument is formulated in far broader terms. It is claimed that fear of the Soviet Union came to be of decisive significance in the formulation and implementation of China's foreign policy. The stated foreign policy platforms of the Chinese government with its attention to the class composition of national leadership groups, the different forms of relationship appropriate to states, parties and peoples and the relationships between states are thus seen as a smokescreen for the protection of China's 'real' foreign policy interests; these are identified with a pragmatic concern for China's strategic survival against its most likely source of military threat. In this way, China's foreign policy is denuded of revolutionary initiative and intent.

Underlying the interpretation adopted by Whiting and others are a number of contentious assumptions which are nowhere explored. Foremost among these, and most contentious of all, is the apparent willingness, ascribed to the Chinese leadership, to seek a *rapprochement* with the United States as a defensive ally against the Soviet Union. The credibility of such an assumption must be judged, at least in part, by the historical context of Chinese perceptions of United States policy towards China for the preceeding twenty years. The Chinese leadership had consistently considered United States foreign policy to be the international arm of the United States ruling class which sought, as its primary objective, the extension of that class's power as widely as possible. Furthermore, China had, for at least ten years, considered that one of the prime ideological functions of United States foreign policy was to pose Chinese communism as the principle threat to world peace. Over and above these perceptions, on the part of the Chinese, was the physical presence of the United States army, navy and air force along sections of China's perimeter. To the constant threat they presented, was added the hostility of America's client states in Asia.

It could be assumed, in the light of these widely known facts, that a major point of the thesis put forward by Whiting and others would explain why and how the Chinese came to perceive the possibility of the United States being prepared to form an alliance, which in undefined ways shielded China from possible Soviet aggression. Such, however, is not the case. That the United States had reasons of its own for proceeding along the path of diplomatic relations with China is not here being questioned. Nor is the fact that Chinese spokesmen had frequently alluded to such a possibility. What is implied in the thesis is much more than this. We are asked to assume that the Chinese leadership consciously sought out the United States, believing it would put its diplomatic and military influence behind China in its dispute with the Soviet Union. It is sufficient to elaborate this major assumption of the Whiting thesis to expose its contentiousness, if not its absurdity.

Another major unexplored factor, in the Whiting analysis, is the apparent pliability of American foreign policy in such a crucial area. Once the Chinese have reconsidered their position in the face of a potential Soviet threat, it is assumed that the United States is automatically prepared to accede to Chinese demands for improved relations. Liberal scholars, such as Whiting, have generally applauded the dismantling of containment policies in favour of a form of 'peaceful coexistence' as a sane, if overdue, reaction to the non-aggressive character of Chinese international behaviour. But the timing of the American decision, given the long-standing commitment of that country to either a 'roll back' or 'containment' policy, cries out for explanation. In the years immediately prior to 1969, there was little, in developments which had taken place within China, which could have encouraged the United States to reconsider its determined opposition towards China. If China had changed at all during the Cultural Revolution, it had become more decisively socialist and more stridently opposed to capitalism in its various forms. It is not possible, therefore, that a conciliatory change in United States policy towards China originated from changes within China amenable to United States policy. Moreover, the Vietnam war in which China had consistently supported the liberation forces to the point where Sino-American war was imminent, had served to exacerbate tensions up to and subsequent to Nixon's visit to China.

Suffice it to say that the argument is based on assumptions so novel and apparently false that they would require extensive justification to attain credibility and that, at each step of the argument, there is a reliance upon evidence which is, at the very least, misleading. Most important, however, the position ignores the fundamental changes which were taking place in the Chinese view of the world at the time and from which a coherent analysis of China's foreign policy may be made.

Foreign Policy as a Result of Internal 'Revisionism'

There is a quite separate analysis of the changes which took place in China's relations with the United States which does not rely on the geopolitical/*realpolitik* assumptions involved in the previous position. It is argued that the opening to the United States is essentially the result of an emerging technocratically-based group gaining dominance or re-emerging after the Cultural Revolution. The interests of such a group — if not class — in the international arena, it is suggested, are more divorced from those of the proletariat of the capitalist countries and liberation movements of the Third World than were the interests of those who held power during the Cultural Revolution.

As advanced in this way, the argument is primarily concerned with domestic policy. The link with foreign policy, it is argued, arises out of the development programme of the newly dominant group which deems advanced technology as essential to its technocratically-oriented policy. It is mandatory, therefore, that bonds be forged with the major capitalist industrial powers, especially the United States, Japan and Western Europe — at least to the extent that advanced technology can be imported from them. Considerable emphasis in this regard has been given to the importation of complete plants (or 'turnkey plants') which, Cheng has noted in an earlier chapter, was a major element in post-Cultural Revolution trade policy. These, it is claimed, only serve to consolidate further the productive foundations of a technocratically oriented élite by creating divisions among Chinese workers in terms of productivity, work style, conditions of work, participation in management and the like. Machinery, it is argued, is not socially neutral but embodies the relations of production of the society which brought it forth. Given the origins of the turnkey plants imported after the Cultural Revolution, they will, according to this view, tend to produce capitalist productive relations.

The argument is frequently supported by domestic events other than the incorporation of foreign technology. Changed attitudes towards the 'red *v.* expert debate' and the role of expertise generally, the position to be adopted towards private plots in the countryside and the rehabilitation of cadres after the Cultural Revolution, have all been taken as indicative of the revival of a 'revisionist' group within the leadership. The apparent loss in terms of self-reliance involved in the incorporation of such large amounts of foreign technology is taken as proof, in this view, that what was distinctive about Mao Tsetung's perspective on economic development has been abandoned.

The resolution of the 'red *v.* expert' debate, which had placed such emphasis on 'redness' that the importance of expertise was no longer acknowledged, came under severe criticism after Lin Piao's fall. The criticism was accompanied by the return to political respectability of a large number of experts dismissed during the Cultural Revolution. In the majority of cases, their return would seem to have signalled no more than the end of their period of re-education in the May Seventh Cadre Schools — not, as implied in the argument outlined above, the mass return of unreconstructed technocrats about to resume their functions in the same manner as prior to the Cultural Revolution. The degree of endorsement given to the retention of private plots in agriculture and material incentives in industry was justified by attacks on idealist attitudes in those areas. 'Short-cuts' to socialism, which ignored the level of mass consciousness and by-passed objective laws of social development, were criticised as 'ultra-leftist' deviations which opened the way to new divisions between leaders and led, to élitism, and ultimately to class antagonism.

As many of the contributions to this book have shown in far greater detail, the argument that China's economic policy and economic management were restored after the Ninth Congress to their pre-Cultural Revolution status is open to serious challenge. In fact, a plausible case may be made out that idealist elements generally associated with the 'ultra-left' in the Cultural Revolution period were being redressed — a development which, it may be argued, could only enhance the transition to socialism in China.

With respect to the proposition that the import of capital equipment may harm China's policy of self-reliance, a number of points can be made. First, China's policy of self-reliance does not imply a complete disavowal of capital imports; it merely states that they be adapted to Chinese usage with socialist initiative and that they should not become the vehicle of economic dependence on other countries. If these qualifications can be observed, it is argued, advantage should be taken of technological developments elsewhere. Mao Tsetung himself is quoted in a press communiqué of 1969, announcing the explosion of a Chinese H-bomb, in terms which will now be quite familiar:

> We cannot just take the beaten track traversed by other countries in the development of technology and trail behind them at a snail's pace. We must break away from convention and do our utmost to adopt advanced technique in order to build our country into a powerful modern socialist state in a not too long historical period.[6]

As Cheng suggests, the importation and selective incorporation of advanced technological equipment in the Chinese economy can actually advance rather than retard a policy of self-reliance. One area in which this would seem to be the case is in relation to the import of complete fertiliser plants, designed to boost production in the vicinity of some of the larger cities without the need for recurrent fertiliser and/or grain imports with the attendant drain on foreign reserves. In one analysis of the data available on China's complete plant and heavy equipment orders for 1972-4, it was concluded that:

> The policy behind the complete plant purchases is in line with a long-term policy of self-reliance in that it aims at diminishing China's dependence on imported raw materials (notably fertilisers, cotton, industrial chemicals, rubber, steel) and imported grain. Also the programme would make China's economy less subject to fluctuations of its own harvests by substituting synthetic raw materials for those of agricultural origin; and through greater use of chemical fertilisers, it would make yields more stable as well as higher.[7]

It is far from clear, therefore, that the policy of importing 'turnkey plants' supports the position that a 'revisionist' élite emerged after the Cultural Revolution, let alone one which was prepared to make compromises, at an international level, with the major capitalist powers for the sake of acquiring such plants. Such developments would seem to be more logically grounded in a socialist consciousness which had been sufficiently developed to adapt inbuilt capitalist relations of production in imported technology to the needs of socialism, and to continue the long term advantages of the policy of self-reliance with the short term advantage of a rapid technological advance.

Apart from these considerations, however, the argument is open to criticism from outside the terms within which it is framed. The major limitations of such an argument – which is exclusively based on domestic developments – result from the lack of attention given to the profound impact made on the formulation of China's foreign policy by the international developments at the time. It is shown below that Chinese theorists took careful cognisance of what they considered were the major international developments of the period and in response, made sweeping changes to the tactics and strategy underpinning their international behaviour.

An Alternative Analysis

A more adequate explanation of the changes which occurred in China's foreign policy can, I believe, be constructed by contrasting the dominant view of the world adopted by the Chinese Communist Party during the period when Lin Piao exercised most influence and the international environment to which it was a response with the major international developments towards the end of the 1960s. This was to lead to an extensive debate and a new formulation of foreign policy.

Many of the assumptions underpinning the foreign policy formulation, which prevailed when Lin Piao's influence was strongest, were grounded in the belief that the United States had embarked on a course of imperialist expansion by all means at its disposal. In the Chinese view of the time, this gave rise to the world's 'principal contradiction', defined by Lin as that 'between the revolutionary people of Asia, Africa and Latin America and the imperialists headed by the United States'.[8] The centrality of this contradiction in the formulation of China's foreign policy was such that it defined China's attitude towards other powers.

The Soviet Union was thus regarded as the accomplice of imperialism – any contradiction between the Soviet Union and the United States being subordinated, in the Chinese analysis, to their collusion in attacking the revolutionary people of the Third World and the Chinese people in particular. By early 1967, in fact, the Chinese had elevated the Soviet Union to the position of 'accomplice number one of United States imperialism' in a 'counter-revolutionary "holy alliance" and an anti-China ring in Asia'. Insofar as 'domination of the world' was mentioned in connection with the Soviet Union, it was regarded as the 'fond dream' of the Soviet 'revisionists' who envisaged it as the outcome of Soviet-United States collaboration rather

than competition. In general terms, the foreign policy of the Soviet
Union was seen as one of 'capitulation' (to imperialism), 'betrayal'
(of revolutionary movements) and 'splitting' (Marxist-Leninist parties).
So far was the Soviet Union from being considered the rival of United
States imperialism that it was regarded as a 'social prop of imperialism,
a force serving imperialism'.

The Chinese argued, during the period of the Cultural Revolution,
that there had been a shift in the focus of United States imperialist
strategy from Europe to Asia in this period, and they concluded that it
would not have been achieved without the tacit approval of the Soviet
Union, which had made it possible for the United States to withdraw
some of its troops from Europe and re-position them in Asia. In sharp
contrast to the policy which emerged after the Cultural Revolution,
where the Soviet Union was regarded as making 'a feint to the East
while attacking the West', Europe was regarded as a major element in the
global collaboration being effected between the United States and the
Soviet Union. The Soviet interest in policies of European *détente*
and nuclear non-proliferation were taken as supporting American
troop deployments in Asia and stemming from the Soviet Union's
anti-China posture as well as its desire to keep national liberation
struggles from escalating into nuclear conflicts.

The primary focus on United States imperialism during this
period, however, was the linchpin of Chinese foreign policy. While
Soviet 'revisionism' submitted to imperialist nuclear blackmail and
betrayed people's wars, it was not seen as an imperialist power in its
own right, nor was it seen as particularly interested in creating
spheres of influence outside Eastern Europe. 'US imperialism', on
the other hand, was according to Lin Piao, 'like a mad bull dashing
from place to place'.[9] A considerable optimism was entertained about
the global destruction of imperialism as a result of its over-extension
in Third World insurrectionary wars, for which it was improperly
equipped and in which people's wars, based on guerilla tactics, would
prove invincible. The world's 'countryside' would overrun its 'cities'
in the global extension, by Lin Piao, of the image developed in the
Chinese Communist Party's own revolutionary struggles.

If the Third World was ripe for revolution, China's role was to be
a 'bastion of socialism' and 'centre of world revolution' — a touchstone
by which liberation movements could test the correctness of their
ideology and a backstop on which to depend for moral and, to a lesser
extent, material support. While concessions were made to the
particularities of local conditions and contradictions, little hope was

expressed for movements which did not expressly apply the 'genius' of Mao Tsetung Thought. People's war could only be fought by the people concerned but, without the concrete application of Mao's tactical and strategic guidelines under the leadership of a local Marxist-Leninist party committed to protracted guerilla war on the Chinese model, its success was unlikely or impossible.

At a time when the world's revolutionary forces were so sorely pressed and imperialism had been so successful in acquiring the complicity and collusion of most other forces, there was little room in the Chinese view for the tactical perspectives associated with the concept of 'the intermediate zone', of which Third World countries had originally constituted the primary members. The 'five principles of peaceful coexistence' and the possibility of forming a united front with those Third World countries professing non-alignment were also given little or no attention.

Scant mention also was made of Western Europe, whether in terms of the proletarian struggles being waged there, the inter-imperialist contradictions, or even within the 'Linist' perspectives of the time, where Western Europe was treated as a metropolitan adjunct of the United States surrounded by the 'rural areas of the world' – Asia, Africa and Latin America. The upsurge of the anti-Vietnam war movement in the West received extensive coverage in the Chinese press as did the student movement, but the heightened awareness of the importance of correct ideology, which was so prevalent in China's attitude towards the Third World, did not seem to spill over to its understanding of western radicalism. The reasons for this anomaly were not totally obscure. In the view of the world which obtained in China at the time, the objective revolutionary potential of the proletariat in advanced capitalist countries received relatively little stress. Revolution, for the present at least, was to be conducted by the 'countryside of the world' which was 'directly' engaged in the struggle against metropolitan imperialism. Any struggle of workers, students or blacks in the metropoles was deemed 'revolutionary', less it would seem, because of its likelihood of bringing the proletariat to a position of state power within those countries, but because of its ability to weaken the will of metropolitan countries in pursuing their imperialist policies in the Third World. While the expression of the Chinese view of the world at this time was frequently in terms which occasioned ridicule in the West, the basic tenets of the view were non-controversial for a Marxist party.

Post World War II history had been shaped to a remarkable extent by the expansion of American economic and strategic power. This phenomenon was nowhere more evident than in China's vicinity. The United States had largely replaced the collection of colonial powers which had dominated the area. While China, North Korea and North Vietnam escaped the neo-colonial net, the United States was prepared to lend its qualified support to other anti-colonial movements in the area prior to establishing trade, aid and military agreements which ensured that the rich resources of the area would not escape from American domination. By 1954, the Korean War had been fought to a stalemate but the price which Asian nations would have to pay for genuine independence was revealed in the devastation of the Korean peninsula.

By 1965, this accelerated expansion of the United States had reached extraordinary proportions. Direct American investment abroad, which had been less than $25 billion in 1955, had more than doubled by 1965 and was increasing at a rate of $10 million a day.[10] More than half of United States corporations' profits from direct investments overseas came from Third World countries and some 70 per cent of these profits were repatriated to the United States.[11] The Third World had proved to be a far richer source of profit than Europe and Canada which had received more in direct investment from the United States but had returned less than half the amount returned by the Third World between 1950 and 1965. Countries of the Third World returned more than $25 billion in the fifteen-year period; or in net terms, the United States had an inflow from Third World countries of over one billion dollars annually.[12] In fact, 'US foreign investment, on balance, supplied capital to developed countries and took capital from underdeveloped countries'.[13] The much vaunted American and multilateral (but American dominated) foreign aid programmes were equally beneficial to the United States and detrimental to the Third World countries.[14]

The price paid by Third World countries for their incorporation into the American empire is accountable not simply in economic terms. The cost in terms of political independence has been severe whether it involved direct US military intervention as in Greece at the end of World War II, in Iran in 1953, in Guatemala in 1954, in Lebanon in 1958, in the Dominican Republic in 1965 or numerous other instances where American 'advisors' or the CIA have assisted in the overthrow of non-compliant governments. The United States was less successful in the Bay of Pigs assault on Cuba in 1961 and the attempt to support the Sumatran separatist revolt in 1957-8.

But in the mid-sixties, the US seemed to be stepping up its global commitments and intervention. Coups which produced results favourable to the United States in Brazil (1964), Indonesia (1965) Algeria (1965), Ghana (1966) and Greece (1967) underlined the extent of American power. The Untung coup in Indonesia[15] was a particularly severe blow for Chinese diplomacy at the time, as was the overthrow of Ben Bella which ensured that the Second Bandung Conference was not held. Apart from these events, the escalation and Americanisation of the war in Vietnam, to the point where China's security was in doubt, could not but lend weight to the arguments of those within China who promoted the 'bastion of socialism' concept. Though the diplomatic forms in which the Cultural Revolution dictated the expression of this policy were not to be found in the best protocol manuals, the fundamental principles of the policy were based on evidence which was incontrovertible. Lin's estimation of the primary contradiction in the world as that between imperialism headed by the United States and the peoples of the Asian, African and Latin American countries was, therefore, scarcely the product of 'aprioristic dogmatism'.

There was another aspect of Lin Piao's foreign policy which received confirmation from United States policy makers themselves. The United States, in the early 1960s, downgraded the 'massive retaliation' approach to warfare which had been dominant under Eisenhower in favour of counter-insurgency theory. The change represented a recognition by the United States that the Soviet Union was no longer a source of imminent nuclear conflict, or indeed of any *direct* military conflict at all. As George Ball, at the time Under Secretary of State, was to put it a few years later:

A main focus of the [East-West] struggle was shifted recently from Europe to Asia because the Soviet Union, having grown too powerful, has begun to have a stake in the *status quo*.[16]

In Chinese terms, the Americans had realised that the Soviet Union had come to accept the nuclear blackmail which the United States imposed upon them. The change in American strategic policy was also a recognition that wars in which the United States was likely to be involved were guerilla wars, and these almost certainly in Third World countries. Vietnam has been likened to a 'counter-insurgency test tube', and with some justification, given General Westmoreland's infamous comment that 'we are fighting in Vietnam to show that

guerilla warfare doesn't work'.[17] The American empire was no longer
under attack from the Soviet Union but from sporadic and contagious
liberation movements. As did the proponents of 'people's war',
counter-insurgency theorists recognised that force of arms may not be
enough to win in guerilla warfare. The discovery was a startling one for
American leaders. Hubert Humphrey considered that guerilla techniques
were so ingenious as to 'rank with the discovery of gunpowder' and
so ominous as to constitute a 'major challenge to our security'.[18]

Thus, on the major planks of his foreign policy, Lin Piao's view of
the world reflected a keen appreciation of imperialist practice at the
time as well as the Chinese conviction that the Soviet Union had
abandoned its socialist responsibility to support the people's wars
which United States aggression fostered.

The world, to which this Chinese view was a response, underwent
a series of major changes towards the end of the 1960s. These changes
precipitated revised world views and foreign policies on the part of the
United States and the Soviet Union, as well as China. Between 1968
and 1971, most of the major assumptions underpinning the 'Linist'
view of the world were abandoned and replaced by another equally
coherent set.

In 1968, the international financial crisis in the capitalist world, the
Tet offensive and the Soviet-led invasion of Czechoslovakia initiated
many of the strands of the new analysis. For the Chinese, the
financial and trade superiority with which the United States had
emerged from the Second World War was reflected in, among other
things, the direct convertibility of the dollar into gold. In the Chinese
analysis, this had facilitated a massive export of American capital.
In concert with economic and military 'aid' programmes, the
establishment of military bases and recurrent military engagements, this
capital export had produced regular deficits of enormous proportions
in the United States balance of payments, had run down American
gold reserves to less than half that of the immediate post war years, and
had given rise to a massive accumulation of dollars overseas,
especially in Europe.

Even by 1968, these trends had, according to the Chinese, reached
crisis point. United States gold reserves were less than a third of the
dollar claims held against them in foreign hands and the pegged price
for gold was unable to cope with the consequent rush to exchange
dollar holdings in the European bullion markets. President Johnson's
initial moves to strengthen the position of the dollar co-incided with
the beginning of the Tet offensive in Vietnam.

Causal links were drawn by the Chinese as both the dollar crisis and the guerilla offensive escalated. Continued increases in American military spending, particularly in Vietnam, in recent years were said to have intensified the contemporary dollar crisis by adding to the deficits in the United States financial budgets and international balance of payments. The war had been escalated by the United States in 1965, it was claimed, to 'give a shot in the arm to the weakening US economy and thus delay the arrival of a crisis of over-production', but all that had been achieved was 'a sharp rise in budget deficits'.[19] Since the Tet Offensive had shown America that even greater expenditure was needed in order to maintain an offensive posture in Vietnam, it was now clear that the dollar crisis would become more acute. But while the Vietnam war and other Third World encounters were assigned causal significance, the effect of the currency and financial crisis, like that of the trade war which the Chinese judged they were precipitating, was primarily in the 'capitalist world'. And, when the Chinese talked of this latter world, the terminology which was to become so familiar in the articulation of 'Chairman Mao's revolutionary line in foreign affairs' was employed.

The economic crises which had developed were to do with 'hegemony' within the imperialist world. The 'position of strength' of United States imperialism, which had been 'lording it over' European countries and 'bullying' them had meaning within the context of inter-imperialist contradictions, but in 1968 it was in stark contrast to the pro and anti-imperialist contradictions which had generated a quite alternative terminology.

One important distinction between the Chinese view of this time and that which it was later to adopt was in the alignment of European powers. France's attempts to oppose United States 'hegemony' in Europe were still regarded as under pressure from within Europe from United States 'accomplices'. The United Kingdom was considered the primary economic accomplice of the United States, its 'junior partner' in fact; consequently China took the position that British entry into the Common Market should be strongly opposed.[20] West Germany was in a more complex position. Still regarded as intent upon swallowing the German Democratic Republic and afforded ample encouragement by the United States to do so, it was generally considered the prime military accomplice of the United States in Europe — apart, of course, from the military 'hegemony' which the United States was able to exert through the collective forces of NATO. But the West German ruling class was also beginning to realise that there were advantages to be had in adopting the French posture and were beginning to suffer their American alliance with increasing reluctance.

The major point being made here is that a strong and consistent emphasis on inter-imperialist contradictions entered the Chinese analysis of the world after late 1967. Such an emphasis clearly ran a distant second to the stress still placed on the 'raging flames' of guerilla war which were considered to be engulfing United States imperialism, but the schematic outline of the world's major contradictions at the Ninth Congress which included that among the imperialist countries themselves was not, in this sense, an innovation. The assertion of contradictions among imperialist powers, as among the major ones in the world, was simply formalising part of the analysis of the international order which the Chinese had been making for well over a year.

The Tet Offensive stimulated major developments in Chinese attitudes towards imperialist – Third World relations. In their reportage of the war, the Chinese concluded, from this point onwards, that there was no longer any doubt that the Vietnamese people would win. 'A new situation had been opened up' and victory was considered to be 'already in sight', despite accurate warnings of further American escalation.[21] Richard Nixon, it is now known, privately concurred with the Chinese assessment.[22] The war had reached a turning point. The United States had been tried in the 'test case' of its own construction in Vietnam and had been found wanting. While still at the head of the imperialist countries – and even this was under challenge – the United States was still capable of aggression on a prodigious scale and was still the implacable enemy of liberation movements but, to the Chinese, it was now seen as defending its present position rather then enhancing it.

The third major influence on the Chinese view of the world in 1968 was the invasion of Czechoslovakia. This initiated the characterisation of the Soviet Union as 'imperialist' and, for the first time, elements of contention rather than collusion were seen as prominent in Soviet-American relations.

The Soviet Union had now acquired independent imperialist status and Eastern Europe was specified as an area of Soviet-American contention. 'Collusion', however, was still regarded as the dominant element in Soviet – US relations. The Soviets, it was claimed, still wished to preserve direct rights of collaboration to themselves, while the Dubcek regime – equally 'revisionist' in Chinese eyes but less of a

Soviet puppet than the Novotny regime it replaced — wished to pursue direct relations with United States imperialism. But, after the invasion of Czechoslovakia, while the collusive aspect of Soviet-American relations was still afforded priority, it was no longer possible to assert an anti-China motive as its mainstay.

To the Chinese analysts, the events of 1968 indicated primarily a significant decline in the relative strength of US imperialism and also the development of Soviet 'social-imperialism'.

Formulations of the New Foreign Policy

The approach adopted below derives from the seemingly little recognised fact that Chinese foreign policy has consistently been based on consciously held and carefully articulated theoretical propositions derived from an analysis of the international order. China's perception of its international environment is constantly distilled, through its version of Marxist-Leninist principles, to provide what one of the few authors to take such an approach seriously has called a set of 'authoritative conceptualisations as a basis for . . . foreign policy making'.[23]

Articulating the new foreign policy formulation was a protracted affair which began in 1968 when a 'new era of anti-imperialist struggle' was hailed.[24] A 'broad united front' was proposed as the best method by which imperialism could now be opposed. The prominence given within the Lin Piao perspectives to 'oppressed peoples', primarily those of the Third World, was modified by the re-introduction of 'oppressed nations' into the anti-imperialist struggle. For some considerable time, it would appear that the two perspectives were in contention. The joint New Year's Day editorial for 1969, for instance, spoke of 'oppressed nations' and quoted Mao Tsetung to the effect that, in the current era, China would have to engage in 'great struggles' with 'many features different in form from those of the past'.[25] At the same time, however, an article was published which is a quite thorough-going re-statement of Lin Piao's position. 'The main storm centre of the world revolution', it was claimed, 'lies in Africa, Asian and Latin America. In the year gone by, the people's armed struggle made advances in this vast region.'[26] Although the new 'broad united front' was mentioned, there was no hint that 'nations' were to play their part in it. Rather:

> All peoples oppressed by U.S. imperialism and Soviet revisionism
> and their lackeys will further unite, form a broad united front
> and launch a violent, sustained attack on their common enemy.[27]

Reports of Nixon's trip to Europe in early 1969 revealed a new analytical perspective. De Gaulle was given considerable publicity for his attempt to co-opt the British into a decisive reduction of American influence in Europe. In the words of the *Peking Review* commentator, he advocated the establishment of a 'truly independent Europe' and the liquidation of NATO and US domination over it.[28] Nixon was portrayed as exercising caution lest he offend either Britain or France — 'a far cry', it was said, 'from the overweening arrogance with which his predecessors, Eisenhower, Kennedy and Johnson — treated the rulers of France and Britain'.[29] While the 'total collapse' of the imperialist system was still envisaged, a nationalist element had been introduced into its probable causes. Inter-imperialist rivalries, or 'the struggle to shift the burden of the crisis on to one another' was seen as a major factor accelerating the impending doom of capitalist countries. The changed assumptions implicit in the above statements increasingly became reflected in a change in strategy on the part of the Chinese. In this instance, vocal encouragement of de Gaulle's independent tendencies was backed up by renewed interest in Sino-French state-to-state relations.

It was at this time that Peking increased diplomatic and trade contacts with members of the Eastern European bloc, particularly Yugoslavia, Czechoslovakia and Romania which were least integrated into the Soviet bloc and most open to penetration by capitalist countries. There is no evidence to suggest, however, that the Chinese regarded policy changes in these countries with renewed interest, nor is there evidence of more harmonious party-to-party relations which would imply such an ideological confluence. Rather, the Chinese would seem to have followed the logic of their position with tenacity. If the Soviet Union had become an imperialist country, then state-to-state relations with its satellites could be developed in order to exacerbate their tensions with the Soviet Union just as they could in the capitalist world.

In Chou En-lai's report to the Tenth Party Congress, he claimed that the report prepared by Lin Piao and Ch'en Po-ta in March 1969, for the Ninth Party Congress was rejected by the Central Committee and had to be rewritten 'under Chairman Mao's personal guidance'.[30] It is not clear the extent to which foreign policy issues were involved here, although it is unlikely that they were central to the disagreement, but the Report eventually delivered by Lin does make significant departures from the position which he had previously espoused. Although the people/nations dichotomy was left in an ambiguous state, nations were elevated to a new level of importance in the anti-imperialist struggle.

While there are scattered references to the 'people of the world', 'the revolutionary struggles of the people of various countries', 'the proletariat and revolutionary people of all countries' and the like, the world's major contradictions, listed for the first time since 1965, excluded all mention of 'the people'. The four major contradictions were considered to be:

> the contradiction between the oppressed nations on the one hand and imperialism and 'social-imperialism' on the other; the contradiction between the proletariat and the bourgeoisie in the capitalist and revisionist countries; the contradictions between imperialists and 'social-imperialist' countries and among the imperialist countries; and the contradiction between socialist countries on the one hand and imperialism and social-imperialism on the other.[31]

It was the development of all these contradictions which would 'give rise to revolution'. The 'broad united front' strategy was reiterated in its newest form:

> All countries and people subject to aggression, control, intervention or bullying by US imperialism and Soviet revisionism, let us unite and form the broadest possible united front and overthrow our common enemies.[32]

The 'oppressed people and nations' were guaranteed China's support; this policy being presented as a 'consistent' element of the 'foreign policy of our Party and Government'. The changes which had taken place in the theoretical assumptions underpinning Chinese foreign policy at this stage, can be seen by comparing the list of contradictions presented at the Ninth Congress with those presented by P'eng Chen in 1965.[33] In P'eng's version, Marxist-Leninists and contemporary 'revisionists' were seen as two poles of one contradiction, while socialism and imperialism were considered to constitute the poles of another. 'Revisionism', therefore, in spite of the deleterious effects on those subjected to it, was not regarded as being imperialist. In 1965 the principal contradiction had been presented by Lin Piao as that between the oppressed nations of Asia, Africa and Latin America and imperialism headed by the United States.[34]

Another feature of the document presented by Lin was the renewed stress given to the 'five principles of peaceful co-existence' as the basis for relations between China and 'countries with different social systems'.[35] While no other basis for relations had ever been suggested by China, little emphasis had been given to the 'five principles' during the Cultural Revolution.

The Ninth Congress also marks the formal deletion of the more cataclysmic elements of the Lin Piao thesis. While specific revolutionary struggles in the Third World were guaranteed China's support, there was no hint that one or all of these was about to escalate on to a global plane and precipitate capitalism's prompt demise. There was certainly no equivocation at this time, or in fact at any time since, about the certainty of capitalism's demise, but its life-span seems to have been granted an extension. Remarks, such as that made only a few months previously when the 'whole imperialist system' was see as *fast* heading for total collapse',[36] are not found in the Ninth Congress Report. Rather, in keeping with the four major contradictions outlined, struggles on all four fronts were acknowledged as the catalysts of imperial decay.

It would seem that the group surrounding Lin Piao resisted the adoption and implementation of the foreign policy formulation of the Ninth Congress. In one of the first public statements about Lin's disappearance, Chinese embassy officials in Algiers later claimed that Lin had opposed the 'revolutionary foreign policy worked out by . . . [Mao] especially after the Ninth Congress.'[37] In the National Day speeches of October 1969, Lin Piao and Chou En-lai gave *pro forma* speeches, identical in most respects. Chou, however, stressed that 'the peace we uphold is one based on the 'five principles of peaceful coexistence',[38] while Lin omitted any mention of 'peaceful coexistence'. The joint editorial, published at the same time, reflected the position of Lin rather than Chou.[39]

Acceptance of the Ninth Congress position would seem to have been resisted for some time. The New Year's Day joint editorial for 1970 claimed that 'it has long been our consistent policy to develop diplomatic relations with all countries on the basis of the five principles of peaceful coexistence'.[40] But in 'Leninism or Social-imperialism?'[41] the lengthy statement published in honour of the centenary of Lenin's birth in April, all reference to the 'five principles' was deleted. The statement concludes that 'the broadest united front' is being formed by 'all countries and peoples subjected to aggression, control, intervention or bullying by US imperialism and Soviet revisionism'. Since 'countries' had not been mentioned previously in this statement, this was a surprising conclusion.

In another statement published in honour of the Lenin centenary, the position put forward deviated even further from that of the Ninth Congress. It was claimed that 'the broadest united front' was being formed, not with oppressed nations and peoples but with 'the people of the world', and not on the basis of the 'five principles', but 'proletarian internationalism' which had previously, as well as subsequently, been reserved for relations with genuinely socialist countries.[42] It is also noticeable that only three of the four major contradictions of the Ninth Congress received adequate attention; that between imperialist countries was nowhere mentioned. A week later, a series of articles was published under the general heading of 'Chairman Mao's Military Thinking Is the Magic Weapon in Defeating the Enemy' — indicative of an apparent fear of a combined US — Soviet attack on China but also one of the last such reference to Mao Tsetung Thought as the locus of preternatural powers.[43] In June, Huang Yung-sheng, Chief of the General Staff, speaking at a rally in Pyongyang, attended by leaders of liberation movements in Indochina, specifically raised the question of Sino-US relations. He reiterated China's long-standing position that they could possibly be concluded on the basis of the 'five principles', but, since the US was considered to be interfering in internal Chinese affairs by maintaining armed forces in Taiwan and the Taiwan Straits, relations on this basis were 'out of the question'.[44] These remarks are significant when it is realised the Huang Yung-sheng was a member of the Lin Piao, Ch'en Po-ta group. At this time, the lines were being more and more clearly and publicly drawn in the struggle to oppose the Lin-Ch'en group. Huang Yung-sheng's statement was presumably intended to counter the suggestion that Sino-American relations might be normalised which was, no doubt, abroad in Peking at this time. Huang seems to have become something of a spokesman for the Lin group. On Army Day, 1 August 1970, he described the PLA as 'personally founded and led by our great leader Chairman Mao and directly commanded by Vice Chairman Lin'.[45] Mao later claimed this was an attempt to diminish his authority over the Army and, after the Lushan Plenum, the formulation was altered. In the 1 October celebrations, Mao was referred to as 'the great leader of the people of all nationalities of our country, and the supreme commander of the whole notion and the entire Army'.[46]

As Woodward points out, the Second Plenum of the Ninth Central Committee, which met at Lushan from 23 August to 6 September, has generally been judged as a turning point in Lin Piao's political fortunes as well as the policy |he had come to represent.[47] It was at this point that the dispute became public. The communiqué released after the Second Plenum naturally concentrated on domestic issues which had been the bone of most contention, but the section on foreign policy was noteworthy for its revival of the slogan, 'we have friends all over the world'.[48] An obvious reference to the upsurge in Chinese diplomatic activity, the phrase directly followed a reference to China's 'foreign relations which are daily developing' on the basis of the 'five principles', as opposed to the United States and the Soviet Union which were considered to be 'increasingly isolated'. The latter statement, along with the new slogan, was repeated verbatim by Lin Piao at the National Day rally, but Lin omitted all reference to opposing the Soviet Union. A united front was seen as 'constantly expanding and growing in strength', but it was only understood to be in opposition to US imperialism.[49] One of the more mysterious charges against Lin, after his death, was his alleged desire to 'capitulate to Soviet revisionism'.[50] While this seems unlikely, except in the broadest possible sense of policies which he espoused ultimately imparting a direction to Chinese society which would lead to 'revisionism', the above statements of Lin suggest he was unwilling to accept the categorisation of the Soviet Union as co-equal imperialist enemy of the nations (or peoples) of the world along with United States imperialism.

The joint editorial published on the same day as Lin's statements was more in line with the alternative position which was developing on the basis of the Ninth Congress statement:

We must further strengthen our militant unity with the proletariat, the oppressed people and oppressed nations throughout the world and carry the great struggle against imperialism, revisionism and the reactionaries through to the end.[51]

That the position adopted only a few months previously by Huang Yung-sheng was not in line with the position of Chairman Mao himself would seem to be the implication of the latter's remarks to Edgar Snow in December 1970:

In the meantime, he said, the foreign ministry was studying the matter of admitting Americans from the left, middle and right to visit China. Should rightists like Nixon, who represented the monopoly capitalists, be permitted to come? He should be welcomed because, Mao explained, at present the problems between China and the USA would have to be solved by Nixon. Mao would be happy to talk to him, either as a tourist or as President.[52]

From this point onwards, although the new policy was still very much open for discussion, reversal was made extremely difficult by Mao's public endorsement. Domestic opposition to the new foreign policy orientation had presumably been countered if not silenced, at the Lushan Plenum.

The New Year's Day editorial of 1971, reflected the new determination. 'Many medium-sized and small nations', it was claimed, 'have risen against the power politics of the two superpowers, US imperialism and "social imperialism"'; this has become an irresistible trend of history.'[53] It is upon this 'trend of history', which receives wide publicity after this time, that one prong of China's foreign policy strategy was based. The formulation is not in conflict with that of the Ninth Congress, for medium and small powers may be seen as synonyms for 'oppressed nations'. The newly named 'superpowers' form the target of a united front, no longer based exclusively on common exploitation by class opponents. Rather governmental, or state-to-state, opposition to 'hegemonic' control is the basis of the new 'irresistible trend'. It is the 'power politics', or the ability and willingness of the two superpowers to exercise the international muscle, accruing to them by their sheer size and global interests, which is perceived as the issue capable of creating a united front out of all other countries. Against the superpowers, 'proceeding from the position of strength' and wanting to 'lord it over others', China began its promotion of an international egalitarianism 'among all nations, big or small'.[54] This did not imply that movements or fraternal parties would lose China's ideological or physical support or, in fact, that they were no longer the main force fighting imperialism directly, but merely that a new weapon had been added to the strategic armoury of Chinese foreign policy. It is presumably with possible objections of this kind in mind that the editorial continued:

> We will persistently fulfil our proletarian internationalist obligations, firmly support the revolutionary struggles of the people of all countries and learn from them, and together with them we will fight to the finish to defeat the US aggressors and all their running dogs and oppose modern revisionism, with Soviet revisionism at its centre, and the reactionaries of all countries'.[55]

Beginning in May 1971, a quite distinctive position appeared. This was a different version of the united front in which the United States is the only target. The May Day editorial claimed that 'the international united front against US imperialism is constantly expanding'.[56] Although

the new conventional wisdom of medium-sized and small nations uniting
in opposition to superpower 'hegemony' received brief mention, it was
greatly overshadowed by the stress on the former version. Later in the
month 'A Programme for Anti-Imperialist Struggle' was issued by the
editorial departments of *People's Daily*, *Red Flag* and *Liberation Army
Daily* in which the same theme was taken up. It claimed that:

> The international united front against US imperialism is an important
> magic weapon for the world's people to defeat US imperialism and
> all its running dogs.[57]

In an even more explicit revision of the Ninth Congress strategic
orthodoxy, it was proclaimed, in unmistakeable fashion, that the US
was the principal enemy of the world's people:

> In order to completely defeat US imperialism, the common enemy
> of the world's people, we should further expand and strengthen the
> international united front against US imperialism, unite to the
> greatest extent with all forces that can be united, mobilise to the
> fullest extent all the positive factors favourable to the struggle
> against US imperialism, and isolate and strike at the chief enemy
> to the utmost, so as to push to a new high the struggle of the world's
> people against US imperialism and all its running dogs.[58]

Even in this statement, however, cursory reference was made to the
thesis that, 'more and more small and medium-sized *countries* have
risen to oppose the power politics of the superpowers'.[59] It will be
remembered that, only a month prior to these statements. American
table tennis players had been invited and admitted to China,
apparently at Mao's behest,[60] making opposition to the emerging
Sino-American normalisation of relations even more urgent for those
who considered it undesirable.[61] The period from February to
September was generally marked by increasingly desperate
manoeuvres by both parties to the dispute, prior to the final
confrontation, and it is likely that the above statements were part of the
Lin group's campaign. The United States-backed South Vietnamese
invasion of Laos in February was seized upon by them as further
evidence of US unwillingness to vacate South-East Asia.

By July, in the joint editorial commemorating the Chinese
Communist Party's fiftieth anniversary, the two conflicting versions
of the united front were given equal emphasis and placed side by side.[62]

But, by this time, Henry Kissinger was in Peking, presumably
pre-empting further discussion about the advisability of normalising
relations with the US which Mao had publicly aired the previous
December.[63] In August, only six weeks before Lin's death in Mongolia,
the fullest statement yet of the new position was published and
referred to as 'Chairman Mao's revolutionary diplomatic line'.[64]
Variations on this title such as 'Chairman Mao's great strategic plan',[65]
and 'Chairman Mao's revolutionary line in foreign affairs'[66] were
also used, apparently with the deliberate intention of setting the
new foreign policy quite apart from its predecessor and to identify the
latter with Lin Piao.[67] For the first time, the rapid increase in China's
diplomatic relations was acknowledged as well as approved:

> We have established diplomatic relations with more and more
> countries. The U.S. imperialist policy of blockading and isolating
> China has failed completely. Chairman Mao's revolutionary
> diplomatic line has won great victories. China's international
> prestige is increasing. We have friends all over the world.[68]

Somewhat ironically this Army Day editorial which amounts to a
thorough-going reversal of Lin Piao's policy still refers to him, although
in terms of which he would scarcely have approved.[69] The article
amounts to a 'defence' of China's flourishing diplomatic relations
along the lines that they signify the decreased 'hegemonic' capacity
of the United States to prevail upon other countries to refrain from
recognising China. It is within this context — the collapse of the
US-imposed diplomatic blockade of China being symptomatic of the
decline of US imperialism — that subsequent explanations of China's
diplomatic activity, especially in relation to the US, were formulated.
  Chinese statements on the subject still contain no hint that they
consider imperialist leaders to have changed either their subjective
orientation or their objective need to exploit others in an aggressive
manner. The sole basis alluded to for any change in United States
behaviour is its decreased objective capacity to implement policies of
aggressive exploitation which stem from its basic structure.[70]
  The editorial article under consideration foreshadows a defence
of Chinese relations with the United States along such lines as these:

> Imperialism will never change its aggressive nature because it is
> defeated. Sometimes it has to change its tactics and play every
> kind of insidious trick, but in the final analysis it does so only to

serve its policies of aggression and war . . . Imperialism means war.
So long as imperialism exists, the world will have no peace.[71]

The 'whole Party, the whole Army and the people throughout the country'
were enjoined to 'conscientiously study' the 'historical experience of
our Party in carrying out tit-for-tat struggles against the class enemies
at home and abroad, so as to follow Chairman Mao's great strategic plan
closely and advance victoriously'.[72]

Historical Precedents for the New Policy

One such historical experience recommended for study was the
Chungking Negotiations with the Kuomintang at the end of the war
with the Japanese in 1945. Mao's article on the subject received regular
commentary in the Chinese press particularly in connection with the
normalisation of relations with the United States.[73] The aim of such
commentaries was similar to that of the original article — to reassure
cadres, hardened in the struggle, that negotiations were not tantamount
to unity but may, in fact, constitute a new form of struggle:

> How to give 'tit for tat' depends on the situation. Sometimes not
> going to negotiations is tit-for-tat; and sometimes, going to
> negotiations is also tit-for-tat. We were right not to go before and
> also right to go this time; in both cases we have given tit-for-tat.[74]

A further aim may well have been to assure the Chinese people that,
as well as having no illusions as to the continued imperialist character
of the United States, they also had no illusions as to what was
achievable in such negotiations. The article states for instance:

> The Kuomintang and the Communist Party are sure to fail in
> their negotiations, sure to start fighting and sure to break with each
> other, but that is only one aspect of the matter. Another aspect is
> that many other factors are bound to make Chiang Kai-shek have
> misgivings.[75]

'On Policy', another article chosen to illustrate the historical
precedents for the changes occuring in Chinese foreign policy at this
time, contains even more obvious lessons. The article written in 1940,
begins with an admonition against 'ultra-left policies' which had been
current in the former period of the Agrarian Revolution, but which, it
is claimed, were wrong then and even less appropriate now. 'This tendency',

Mao claims, 'has been corrected to some extent but not altogether, and it still finds expression in concrete policies in many places. It is, therefore, most necessary for us to examine and define our concrete policies now'.[76] The article continues to delineate policies suitable to the present and to distinguish them from those of an 'ultra-left' character. Mao wrote 'On Policy' at a time when the Communist Party was under severe pressure from both the Japanese and the Kuomintang and when, within the Party, 'the ultra-left viewpoint . . . [was] . . . creating trouble and . . . [was] . . . still the main danger.'[77]

The general point made is that the present 'policy is neither all alliance and no struggle nor all struggle and no alliance, but combines alliance and struggle'.[78]

'On Policy''s most direct implications for Chinese policy in the 1970s are in Mao's discussion of imperialism. The principle governing his analysis is the same — how to 'win over the many, oppose the few and crush our enemies one by one'.[79] The contradictions in question at the time were outlined:

First, between the Soviet Union and the capitalist countries, second, between Britain and the United States on the one hand and Germany and Italy on the other, third between the people of Britain and the United States and their imperialist governments, and fourth, between the policy of Britain and the United States during their Far Eastern Munich period and their policy today.[80]

On the basis of these distinctions, all foreign assistance possible was sought, subject only to the basic principle of 'independent prosecution of the war and reliance on our own efforts, and not, as the Kuomintang does, to abandon this principle by relying on foreign help or hanging on to one imperialist bloc or another.'[81]

The 'ultra-leftist' alternative to this policy outline is sketched only briefly, but some indication of its different emphasis is apparent. The 'ultra-left' viewpoint, it is said, cannot accept 'the policy of having well-selected cadres working underground for a long period, of accumulating strength and biding our time, because they underestimate the Kuomintang's anti-Communist policy'. Further, such a viewpoint tends to 'oversimplify matters and consider the entire Kuomintang to be quite hopeless'. As a result, those espousing such a viewpoint are not prepared to engage in the expansion of the united front.[82]

Lest there be any doubt as to the contemporary implications of this text, the commentaries of the time made clear what lessons were to be drawn from them. It was pointed out, in the most notable of these commentaries, that for every historical period there is not only an appropriate general line but also 'tactical principles and various concrete policies for struggle'.[83] These tactical principles and policies, it was argued, are formulated on the basis of a rigorous analysis of both the domestic and international situations. It was claimed that:

> ... correct observations and a concrete analysis of the situation in class struggle internationally and domestically, the relations between the various classes and the changes and developments in them . . .[84]

are the basis for a Marxist set of tactical principles and policies. The point clearly being made here is that there had been developments which made it incumbent on the Marxist to formulate a new set of 'tactical principles and policies'.

The developments indicated centred around the exacerbation of contradictions in the imperialist camp. The contemporary opposition indicated was clearly the remains of Lin Piao's foreign policy, which, with slight exaggeration, was viewed as regarding all enemies as the same, 'completely affirming or negating complicated matters' and not recognising the changes which had taken place in their tactics.[85] This lack of recognition was said to have considerable consequences for the possibility of forming a broad united front and isolating the principal enemy. The central passage dealing with the application of 'On Policy' to the contemporary situation needs to be quoted at length:

> To preserve their reactionary force and exploit and oppress the people, the imperialist countries and the various classes, strata, cliques and factions in all enemy camps are bound to collude and work hand in glove. But, as determined by their class nature, they are bound to have many contradictions and contentions. That these contradictions are an objective reality means they are independent of the subjective wishes of any reactionary. The view that all enemies are the same, that they are one monolithic bloc, is not in accord with objective reality. Moreover, with the development of the situation and with the people's revolutionary forces daily expanding, the enemies' contradictions will become more and more acute. The proletariat and its party must learn to concretely analyse the situation in the international and domestic spheres at different historical periods and be good at seizing the opportunity to 'turn to good account all such fights, rifts and contradictions

in the enemy camp and turn them against our present main enemy.' ('On
Tactics Against Japanese Imperialism', *Selected Works,* Vol.1). . . On our
part we must seize and make use of all enemy contradictions and
difficulties, wage a tit-for-tat struggle against him, strive to gain as much
as possible for the people's fundamental interests and seize victory in the
struggle against him. To smash the enemy's counter-revolutionary dual
policy, we must adopt a revolutionary dual policy. While
persisting in armed struggle as the main form of struggle, we must
also engage in various forms of struggle with the enemy on many
fronts. The different forms of flexible tactics in struggle are
required by the proletariat in the fight against the enemy.[86]

The above passage shows clearly how little the momentous changes
taking place in Chinese foreign policy at this time had to do with the
rationale commonly ascribed to them by western observers. The
Chinese, whether at the time of Lin's dominance or in mid-1971, were
basing their foreign policy, not on a defensive nationalism reawakened
by the sound of Soviet battledrums on their borders, but by a
thoroughgoing class analysis — preferably one which took account of the
subtlest differences in the international balance of class forces and their
relationship to the domestic situation. Lin is not accused of succumbing
to an international viewpoint which denied the relevance of class
differences but rather of not noticing their complicated nature or the
manner in which they were developing.

In 'On the Chungking Negotiations', Mao had suggested that
'complicated' brains were necessary to understand China's complicated
situation.[87] To those without such an asset, the Chinese press of the
time was something of a mystery — but it did express the new
determination in foreign policy with considerable validity. In the
same issue of *Peking Review* which bore the translation of the
Red Flag article discussing the relevance of 'On Policy', there appeared
an article on the armed struggle of the Thai People's Liberation Army
against the 'US-Thanom clique', a *People's Daily* editorial greeting
the establishment of diplomatic relations with the Iran government
and stressing the latter's struggle against imperialism 'in order to
uphold national independence', articles on Yugoslavia and Romania
stressing their determination to resist domination from the Soviet
Union, warnings against Japanese militarism and a lengthy rebuttal of
the American sponsored 'two Chinas' policy which was being debated
before the United Nations.[88] Such a collection of articles, although
markedly dissimilar from a typical collection during the Cultural

Revolution, nevertheless reflected a foreign policy which took seriously the 'four major contradictions' in the world and sought to exacerbate them 'to the benefit of the people'.

The 'Intermediate Zone'

The Army Day editorial of August 1971 marks the revival of the 'intermediate zone' category which had formerly been used to describe a range of countries sandwiched politically, and usually geographically, between the socialist and imperialist blocs – i.e. capitalist countries which are both exploiters and exploited as well as Third World countries. The revival of the category marks a shift in its meaning to take account of the changed international situation – especially the collapse of the 'socialist camp'. Now this 'vast intermediate zone' was seen as uniting against the superpowers and would seem to include all non-superpower countries (notably Eastern European countries).

For some time prior to this use of the 'intermediate zone', there had been an element of theoretical indecision surrounding the issue. The vacillation centred on the way in which eastern European countries ought to be categorised, both in respect of their domestic social formation and their role in the international arena. The vacillation is scarcely surprising, given the complex character of the issue which involves the nature of the Soviet Union and its international relations – both with respect to the world at large as well as in eastern Europe, the way in which the 'five principles of peaceful coexistence' ought to be applied to the Eastern European countries and a number of other issues which the Chinese consider to be mutually interdependent within their foreign policy structure.

To indicate something of the considerations which were involved in this issue, two of the related topics which appear to have come under scrutiny were the types of countries with whom diplomatic relations should be entered into on the basis of the 'five principles', and the existence of the 'socialist camp'. The New Year's Day editorial for 1970 had (misleadingly) claimed:

> It has long been our consistent policy to develop diplomatic relations with *all countries* on the basis of the Five Principles of Peaceful Coexistence.[89]

China's 'consistent policy' had in fact been 'to strive for peaceful co-existence on the basis of the five principles with countries having different social systems'. Between socialist countries, relations were

meant to develop 'in accordance with proletarian internationalism' and
China's role towards the oppressed people and nations was one of
support and assistance. Such was the policy decided and defended in the
ideological dispute with the Soviet Union in the early 1960s, and
repeated almost verbatim at the Ninth Congress in 1969.[90]

In the months following the New Year's Day editorial — a time when
the 'five principles' were receiving considerable attention in the
Chinese press as an explanatory mechanism for the increased diplomatic
activity in which China was engaging — the more orthodox version of
the way in which the principles were applied, and to whom, was
mentioned frequently. The communiqué of the Lushan Plenum
claimed, for instance, that 'we strive for peaceful co-existence with
countries having different social systems . . . on the basis of adhering
to the five principles.'[91] But Ch'iao Kuan-hua, at the time vice
foreign minister, at celebrations for the Yugoslavia national day
proclaimed that:

> The Chinese government has always held that the relations
> between states should be guided by the Five Principles of mutual
> respect for sovereignty . . . [etc.] . . . These principles should
> apply to *all countries, whether they have the same or different
> social systems.* We note with pleasure that it is precisely on the
> basis of these principles that the relations between China and
> Yugoslavia have developed in recent years.[92]

As noted earlier, there was a tendency associated with 'ultra-left'
spokesmen to omit references to the 'five principles' in the period
after the Ninth Congress when other spokesmen were giving them
emphasis. Such a reaction is intelligible given the small role
which 'peaceful co-existence' had to play within the 'ultra-left'
foreign policy perspective. But the above differences as to how far
'peaceful co-existence' should extend would not seem to be
connected with this basic dispute. At least two explanations are
possible. First, given the reluctance of the Soviet Union or any
Eastern European country to accept a form of relation with China
which directly implied that the country involved was not a socialist
one (as a relationship on the basis of the 'five principles' does), then
Ch'iao Kuan-hua was saving the Yugoslav leaders any embarrassment
on this score by leaving ambiguous his assessment of the character of
the social formation over which they presided. If this is the correct
interpretation, then the concession involved in terms of theoretical

classification is slight or non-existent, particularly with respect to the possible gains to be had by the incorporation of the Eastern European bloc into a united front against the superpowers.[93]

A more likely explanation, however, leads to the second topic which was discussed in the Chinese press in relation to the 'intermediate zone' — the existence of the 'socialist camp'. If the Chinese no longer regarded any other countries as socialist, then clearly relations with all other countries were 'with countries having different social systems'. There were, nevertheless, countries whom China definitely did regard as socialist at this time — notably Albania, North Korea and North Vietnam.[94] But the 'socialist camp' which China had in mind, in formulating the relations which one socialist country should have with another in the dispute with the Soviet Union, was at this time being written out of the Chinese view of the world. At the Ninth Congress, the role of the 'socialist camp' had been minimised in the four major contradictions in the world — only one of which involved the socialist countries, viz. that between imperialism and social imperialism on the one hand and the socialist countries on the other. By 1972, it was reported that:

> In East Europe there are countries, for instance Albania, which are socialist. Apart from these, countries in East Europe in general belong to the second intermediate zone.[95]

The logical extension of these propositions did not come until 1974 when it was stated that, 'as a result of the emergence of social-imperialism, the socialist camp which existed for a time after World War II is no longer in existence'.[96] Thus, the former 'socialist camp' had been collapsed as a category. The few remaining countries which were classified as socialist did not, presumably, exercise such a centrally-organised, Comintern-style leadership over the broad united front as was envisaged in 1963, when it was stated:

> In all this we have but one objective in view, that is with the socialist camp and the international proletariat as the nucleus, to unite all the forces that can be united in order to form a broad united front against imperialism and its lackeys.[97]

That the new foreign policy formulation which was emerging had come a considerable way from the period when only genuine Marxist-Leninist parties, adhering to Mao Tsetung Thought and engaging in protracted guerilla warfare, received Chinese endorsement, can be gauged from two statements in the Army Day editorial to which reference has already been made. 'Whoever opposes imperialism or makes revolution', it was claimed, 'has our support', and 'we firmly support the just struggles of all the countries and people subjected to aggression, control, intervention or bullying by the two superpowers'.[98] The manner in which imperialism is opposed or revolution made seemed no longer to require the dogmatic conformity of a few years previously and there was a recognition of the fact that non-revolutionary groups, acting in accordance with their non-revolutionary class interests, could objectively obstruct imperialist development or propel its demise.

With Nixon's visit to Peking in February 1972, the distinctiveness of the new policy formulation was fully evident. No longer was Nixon to be referred to as the 'god of plague', 'imperialist chieftain', or 'fanatic advocate of counter-revolutionary war' – but as 'President Nixon'. Criticism of US policy, both domestically and internationally did not noticeably alter, but invective, particularly of a personal kind, was dropped. Chou En-lai's toast to Nixon made patently clear the limited store set by China on the achievements made possible by such diplomacy. In a rather pointed remark he reminded those present that 'the people and the people alone are the motive force of world history'.[99] Kuo Mo-jo had been even more frank in an interview with an Australian delegation just before Nixon's visit. 'The Chinese', he claimed, 'do not think the trip will change anything'; it was better, however, to talk than fight with nuclear weapons. Kuo made a point of dispelling illusions that China was unappreciative of Nixon's motives in visiting China or his basic philosophy. 'Nixon', he said, 'makes this trip because of pressure. The pressure has come both from the US domestic and international situation'.

The Chinese [he also claimed] have studied Nixon's way of working and think that Nixon's way will not change. For example, on January 20th of this year in his State of the Union message, Nixon increased military expenditure from $76.1 billion to $83.1 billion, showing that he hasn't changed . . . Nixon has dual tactics, namely negotiation and at the same time military preparedness. The Chinese are prepared for Nixon's dual tactics. The Chinese . . . will not change for Nixon and if there is any result from his visit and negotiations it will have to be by compromises from Nixon and not by the Chinese.[100]

Chinese spokesmen went to considerable lengths to explain that *détente* diplomacy could neither mask nor replace international divisions based on exploitation. To cite but one example, the former Chairman of the Chinese delegation to the United Nations, Ch'iao Kuan-hua, (later foreign minister) claimed:

> The Chinese Delegation holds that the people of all countries must not be deluded by certain temporary and superficial phenomena of *détente* at the present time and develop a false sense of security. While striving for world peace and the progress of mankind, we must maintain sufficient vigilance and make necessary preparations against the danger of new wars of aggression any imperialism may launch.[101]

The 'irresistible historical trend' of 'intermediate zone' countries opposing the superpowers was set in historical perspective at this time and endorsed as the distinguishing characteristic of the 1970s:

> In the 1950s, US imperialism was swashbuckling as the sole world overlord, claiming wildly that the whole world must be put under US 'leadership'. In the 60s, the United States and the Soviet Union contended for world hegemony and domination . . . Today in the 70s, the medium-sized and small countries are uniting against hegemony and this situation is developing . . . A vast number of medium-sized and small countries have come to the fore on the stage of history. They are further closing their ranks and waging a resolute struggle against the hegemony and power politics practised by the two superpowers.[102]

From about this period onwards, changes which took place in the Chinese analysis of the international situation and their responses to it were of a marginal kind — clarifications, elaborations and changes of emphasis. Some of these, however, are interesting.

The National Day editorial of 1972 pointed out that the 'five principles of peaceful coexistence' were 'not only conducive to the easing of international tensions' (the position expressed by the United States but not endorsed by China in the joint communiqué) 'but are in the interests of the revolutionary struggles of the people of various countries'.[103] The point is worth noting. It is essential to distinguish the Chinese position on 'peaceful co-existence' from that of the Soviet Union which regards such a relationship as much more passive and defensive. The Chinese had made it clear, as early as 1963, that their 'five principles' were more properly seen as embodying active and revolutionary attitudes and policies, in spite of the accomodating, diplomatic ring of the terminology involved. 'We have always held', it was claimed:

> that the correct application of Lenin's policy of peaceful co-existence by the socialist countries helps to develop their power, to expose the imperialist policies of aggression and war and to unite all the anti-imperialist peoples and countries, and it therefore helps the people's struggles against imperialism and its lackeys.[104]

The editorial mentioned above stated very briefly the position that has been argued in this chapter, — that the developments which had come to be subsumed under the title of 'Chairman Mao's revolutionary diplomatic line' flow quite logically from the analysis of the world's major contradictions made at the Ninth Congress. 'The new achievements on the diplomatic front', it was claimed, 'are victories for Chairman Mao's proletarian revolutionary line, victories for the line of the Ninth Congress'.[105] 'Diplomatic achievemnts' continued to be given great stress — one *People's Daily* editorial even elevating the 'establishment of diplomatic relations with all countries, which are willing to live peacefully with us' on the basis of peaceful co-existence, to the level of 'principle'.[106] The new perspective on the Soviet Union was also clarified at this time. 'The Soviet revisionist renegade clique', it was claimed:

> has further revealed [the]. . . true colours of social-imperialism. With a growing appetite, it has further reached out its hands everywhere. It is even more deceitful than old-line imperialist countries, and therefore more dangerous.[107]

The Tenth Congress

At the Tenth Congress, both Chou En-lai and the newly elected Vice-Chairman, Wang Hung-wen read reports. The report delivered by Chou — at least in its foreign policy sections — was not marked by the crisp theoretical distinctions which characterised the report delivered by Lin at the Ninth Congress. The four major contradictions, for instance, which were set out with such precision in Lin's report, were not explicitly mentioned at the Tenth Congress although they were clearly implied.

Chou claimed that 'the Party and Government had firmly implemented the foreign policy laid down by the Ninth Congress.'[108] The proof he immediately offers for this statement is somewhat less than convincing. He states:

> Our revolutionary friendship with fraternal socialist countries and with genuine Marxist-Leninist Parties and organisations of various countries and our co-operation with friendly countries have been further strengthened. Our country has established diplomatic relations with an increasing number of countries on the basis of the Five Principles of Peaceful Co-existence. The legitimate status of our country in the United Nations has been restored. The policy of isolating China has gone bankrupt: Sino-US relations have been improved to some extent. China and Japan have normalised their relations. Friendly contacts between our people and the people of other countries are more extensive than ever; we assist and support each other, impelling the world situation to continue to develop in the direction favourable to the people of all countries.[109]

Notable in this passage, which is aimed to link the prevailing foreign policy to the Ninth Congress, are: first, the omission from such a general policy summary of a statement of support and assistance for the oppressed people and nations and secondly, the inclusion (or intrusion) into such a general statement of such practical achievements as entry into the United Nations, the developments in Sino-American and Sino-Japanese relations and the increasing number of diplomatic relations generally. This section of Chou's report is admittedly brief — but as a summary of the Ninth Congress it is scarcely accurate.

The next session of Chou's report deals with 'Smashing the Lin Piao Anti-Party Clique'. The most significant point made with respect to foreign policy is that,

> Today, in both international and domestic struggles, tendencies may still occur similar to those of the past, namely, where there was an alliance with the bourgeoisie, necessary struggles were forgotten and when there was a split with the bourgeoisie, the possibility of an alliance under given conditions was forgotten.[110]

The context of the passage makes it reasonably clear that the former error was associated with Liu Shao-ch'i and the latter with Lin Piao. Chou's catalogue of Lin's deviations in relation to domestic policy is quite extensive and it is, therefore, surprising to see such little attention devoted to Lin's foreign policy. Given the theoretical material which had been assembled over the previous two years and more as a critique of Lin's foreign policy, it is also surprising that Chou did not draw on it more heavily.

The major section of Chou's report and the section most concerned with foreign policy is entitled 'On the Situation and Our Tasks.' As mentioned above, the four major contradictions which had been outlined in the Report delivered by Lin, were implicit in Chou's analysis, but they certainly did not receive the same emphasis as given them by Lin. The changes can best be illustrated by setting the appropriate passages from the two reports alongside each other.

Lin:

On the one hand, the revolutionary movement of the proletariat of the world and of the people of various countries is vigorously surging forward. The armed struggles of the people of southern Vietnam, . Malaya, Indonesia, India, Palestine and other countries and regions in Asia, Africa and Latin America are steadily growing in strength. The truth that 'political power grows out of the barrel of a gun' is being grasped by ever broader masses of the oppressed people and nations.[111] The US imperialists . . . have dispatched aggressor troops to many countries and have also set up hundreds upon hundreds of military bases and military installations in different parts of the world . . . By doing so they make themselves the enemy of the people everywhere, and find themselves besieged and battered by the broad masses of the proletariat and people all over the world, and this will definitely lead to revolutions throughout the world on a still larger scale.[112]

Chou:

The Third World has strengthened its unity in the struggle against hegemonism and power politics of the superpowers and is playing an ever more significant role in international affairs. The Great victories won by the people of Vietnam, Laos and Cambodia in their war against US aggression and for national salvation have strongly encouraged the people of the world in their struggles against imperialism and colonialism. A new situation has arisen in the Korean people's struggle for the independent and peaceful reunification of their fatherland. The struggles of the Palestinian and other Arab peoples against aggression by Israeli Zionism, the African peoples' struggles for maintaining 200 nautical mile territorial waters or economic zones, all continue to forge ahead. The struggles of the Asian, African and Latin American peoples to win and defend national independence and safeguard state sovereignty and national resources have further deepened and broadened. The just struggles of the Third World as well as of the people of Europe, North America and Oceania support and encourage each other. Countries want independence, nations want liberation and people want revolution – this has become an irresistible historical trend.[113]

The difference in theoretical perspective is marked. For Lin Piao, there is no question of Third World *governments* playing an 'anti-hegemonic' role — let alone an anti-imperialist one. Nor did Lin envisage support for the defence of 'state sovereignty', for the unity of Third World countries generally or for their increased role on the international stage. While the report delivered by Lin laid the groundwork for very significant changes, as has been shown — it was still very much a product of its time in its discussion of the Third World. 'Armed struggle' was the secret which would free the peoples of the Third World and more and more of them were coming to know it. The United States, on the other hand, was persisting in its counter-revolutionary aggression and thereby continued to encourage wide-scale revolution.

For Chou En-Lai, in 1973, the Third World was discussed almost entirely within the bounds of opposition to superpower 'hegemony'. The tactic to be adopted in this struggle was no longer simply 'armed struggle', but unity on a country to country, government to government basis. This passage is characteristic of Chou's report in which direct anti-imperialist struggle is hardly mentioned while the 'anti-hegemonic' struggle against the superpowers receives great attention.

The differences between the two reports is also very clear in their respective approach to proletarian struggles within capitalist countries.

Lin:

The revolutionary movement of the proletariat of the world and of the people of various countries is vigorously surging forward . . . An unprecedentedly gigantic revolutionary mass movement has broken out in Japan, Western Europe and North America, the 'heartlands' of capitalism. More and more people are awakening.[114] . . . we firmly support the proletariat, the students and youth and the masses of the Black people of the United States in their just struggle against the US ruling clique; we firmly support the proletariat and the labouring people of the Soviet Union in their just struggle to overthrow the Soviet revisionist renegade clique . . . we firmly support the revolutionary struggles of the

Chou:

On the international front, our Party must uphold proletarian internationalism, uphold the Party's consistent policies, strengthen our unity with the proletariat and the oppressed people and nations of the whole world.[116]

people of Japan and the West
European and Oceanian countries.[115]

Thus, Lin in 1969 was prepared specifically to endorse the working class struggles in both capitalist and 'revisionist' countries and to speak of mass 'revolutionary' movements in the capitalist countries. Chou En-lai, on the other hand, was not prepared to state that the proletarian struggle was 'vigorously surging forward' or to endorse any specific proletarian struggles.

Another interesting development, over the period of four and half years, is the change in attitude towards other Marxist Leninist parties. The respective statements read:

Lin

The genuine fraternal Marxist-Leninist Parties and organisations are growing steadily in the course of integrating Marxism-Leninism with the concrete practice of revolution in their own countries.[117] The genuine Marxist-Leninist Parties and organisations of various countries, which are composed of the advanced elements of the proletariat, are a new rising force with infinitely broad prospects. The Communist Party of China is determined to unite and fight together with them.[119]

Chou:

We must unite with all genuine Marxist-Leninist Parties and organisations the world over, and carry the struggle against modern revisionism through to the end.[118]

The different bases for unity between China and the Marxist-Leninist parties expounded by Chou and Lin, suggest the parties had been downgraded by Peking. Lin talked of uniting 'to fight together with them', in their capacity as 'advanced elements of the proletariat' while Chou merely sought unity with them in the context of carrying on 'the struggle against modern revisionism'. Whether they were still considered forces capable of carrying on the struggle against the local bourgeoisie was not mentioned in 1973.

Perhaps the most noticeable of all the differences between the two reports is the great emphasis placed by Chou En-lai on exploiting the 'anti-hegemonic' struggle and in defence of the particular type of compromise which is involved in such tactics. The basis for Chou En-lai's emphasis was the assumption that there was a 'broad united front' against the 'hegemonism' of the superpowers as well as a number of united fronts on specific issues and that these united fronts were at least as important, in the contemporary situation, as the more direct anti-imperialist struggle. A few selected passages will illustrate the different perspectives involved.

Lin:

They collude and at the same time contend with each other in a vain attempt to redivide the world . . . They scheme against each other and get locked in strife for raw materials, markets, dependencies, important strategic points and spheres of influence. They are both stepping up arms expansion and war preparations, each trying to realise its own ambitions. Lenin pointed out: Imperialism means war . . . 'imperialist wars are absolutely inevitable under *such* an economic system, *as long as* private property in the means of production exists'.[120]

Chou:

Lenin said that 'an essential feature of imperialism is the rivalry between Great Powers in the striving for hegemony.' Today, it is mainly the two nuclear superpowers – the US and the USSR – that are contending for hegemony . . . . They contend as well as collude with each other . . . At present, the Soviet revisionists are 'making a feint to the east while attacking in the west', and stepping up their contention in Europe and their expansion in the Mediterranean, the Indian Ocean and every place their hands can reach. The US-Soviet hegemony is the cause of world intranquillity [*sic*]. It cannot be covered up by any false appearances they create and is already perceived by an increasing number of people and countries. It has met with strong resistance from the Third World and has caused resentment on the part of Japan and West European countries.[121]

Thus, while Lin, in 1969, quoted Lenin to show that imperialism meant war, Chou, in 1973, quoted him to prove that imperialism meant rivalry.[122] Both are, of course, correct, depending on whether the strictly exploitative aspect of imperialism is being considered or its coercive, 'hegemonic' aspect. In a passage, the like of which was certainly not to be found in Lin's report, Chou En-lai talked about the type of compromises necessary:

We should point out here that necessary compromises between revolutionary countries and imperialist countries must be distinguished from collusion and compromise between Soviet revisionism and US imperialism. Lenin put it well: 'There are compromises and compromises. One must be able to analyse the situation and the concrete conditions of each compromise, or of each variety of compromise. One must learn to distinguish between a man who gave bandits money and firearms in order to lessen the damage they can do and a man who gives bandits money and firearms in order to share in the loot.' ('Left-Wing Communism, an Infantile Disorder').The Brest-Litovsk Treaty, concluded by Lenin with German imperialism, comes under the former category; and the doings of Khrushchov and Brezhnev, both betrayers of Lenin, fall under the latter.[123]

Chou could as well have quoted Mao on the subject of compromise in order to point out the continuity of tactical compromise within the Chinese Communist Party. After the Second World War, Mao had argued that 'the capitalist and the socialist countries will yet reach compromises on a number of international matters, because compromise will be advantageous.'[124] Explaining this policy in some detail a few months later, Mao made it clear that compromise on 'all international issues' was impossible as long as 'the United States, Britain and France continue to be ruled by reactionaries.' He also made clear that such international compromises do not entail similar compromises on the part of domestic revolutionaries themselves. 'The people in those countries', he claimed, 'will continue to wage different struggles in accordance with their different conditions.'[125]

Wang Hung-wen, in his Report on the revision of the Party Constitution given at the Tenth Congress, made some brief comments about foreign policy.[126] He carefully drew the distinction between China's permanent policy of always standing 'together with the proletariat and the revolutionary people of the world to oppose imperialism, modern revisionism and all reaction' and China's current and temporary policy which aims 'to oppose especially the "hegemonism" of the two superpowers – the US and the USSR'.[127] The remainder of his comments were confined to reiterating China's own position – that it seeks to become 'prosperous and strong' but not to seek 'hegemony' or become a superpower.

The Basis of the New Policy

The foregoing textual analysis shows that, after extensive debate over a period of some years, the Chinese Communist Party radically altered a number of key assumptions underpinning its foreign policy. The primary focus of China's concern was shifted from United States imperialist aggression in the Third World to the 'hegemony' of the two superpowers in the 'intermediate zone'. The most critical basis for this reassessment was that the United States, always subject to the economic problems and long term decline inherent in the very nature of capitalism, had entered a period where these characteristics of capitalism were being actualised at an accelerated rate. Although Chinese spokesmen had continually remarked on the inevitability of United States imperialism's downfall even prior to the Cultural Revolution, a tone of immediacy was injected into their predictions at the time of Nixon's election as President in 1968. The Chinese media concentrated, in its coverage of the election, on those sections of his campaign which recognised the necessity of reducing America's overseas commitments, its lone-handed policing of the capitalist empire and its military over-extension. They had, in fact, extracted from the mass of campaign propaganda the seeds of the 'Nixon Doctrine', which they clearly regarded as the logical military consequence of United States imperialism's decline. Underlying the new policy formulation, therefore, was the assumption that an era had begun in which US imperialism was no longer capable of the rampant aggression which characterised its previous behaviour, particularly in the Third World, but where it was on the defensive — as much from rivals with similar imperial ambitions as from Third World peoples themselves. The other critical assumption, involved in this aspect of the reassessment, was the reappraisal of the Soviet Union as imperialist — a judgement which entered the formulation of China's foreign policy at the time of the Ninth Congress and was thoroughly integrated into its web of principles and policies over the ensuing years. The Soviet Union had become an imperialist power in its own right. As such, it was subject to the same general tendency to self-destruct, under the weight of its own internal contradictions as any other imperialist power, but at this particular stage of history it was becoming strong at a time when United States imperialism was in serious decline and, moreover, was doing so under the banner of socialism. From its modest beginnings in exploiting the Eastern European bloc countries, Soviet 'social-imperialism' was regarded as having set its sights on the world. This relative improvement in the fortunes of Soviet 'social-imperialism', however, was only one of the perceived assaults on the dominance of United States imperialism. The domestic proletariat as well as the people of the Third World were still considered to be directly countering imperialist power while the states of the Third World, in league with those of the 'second intermediate zone', had begun an assault on the 'hegemony' of both the United States and the Soviet Union. By 1972, this assault by the 'intermediate zone' countries had been established as the distinguishing feature of the 1970s.[128] With the change in perspective on such fundamental aspects of China's foreign policy, it was not surprising that changes in emphasis occurred in almost every other aspect of China's policy. Under the Lin Piao formulation of foreign policy, the world's contradictions frequently tended to be reduced to one – that between United States imperialism and the peoples of the Third World. In the new formulation the four major contradictions, outlined at the Ninth Congress, all received attention.

One consequence of the alteration of the key elements mentioned above was a shift in, or at least a diversification of, the *locus* of contemporary contradictions. While the United States was perceived as being no less anxious to retain its dominance over Third World countries, it was also seen as being increasingly unwilling and unable to do so directly and, therefore, in need of assistance from the other major capitalist powers as well as Third World governments themselves; the former to assume their capitalist 'responsibilities' in this regard and the latter to bolster their own counter-insurgency capabilities in order to cope with their recurrent insurrectionary problems. In this sense, the *locus* of contemporary contradictions was judged to have shifted from Third World countries to imperialist countries themselves. While the contradictions between oppressed nations and imperialism still receives considerable attention from Chinese commentators, as John Gittings argued,

> the potential for revolution in this area is now very closely linked to and inspired by the 'imperialism versus social-imperialism' contradiction. The implication follows that developments in the latter contradiction dictate the shape of the former contradiction, whereas in the mid-1960s the relationship was seen to be the other way around.[129]

It should be noted that the above statement of the position, while perceptive, is not strictly accurate in that 'social-imperialism' did not exist as a description for the Soviet Union in the mid-1960s and other imperialist powers, as well as the 'social-imperialist' Soviet Union are said to be in opposition to United States imperialism, and, therefore, contribute to the 'shape' of the contradiction between oppressed nations and imperialism.

Whereas in the Lin Piao phase the Indo-China war had been the archetypal example of the world's major contradictions, in the new policy it became the exception. Vietnam embodied not only the major contradictions but showed also how imperialism should be fought –

by armed struggle and guerilla war. As Vietnam came to be considered as less of a stereotype of imperialist practice and more as an example of abandoned policy, there was also a marked change in the tactics to which China gave emphasis. As has been pointed out previously, one of the major texts presented in the Chinese press to explain the new policy argued that every historical period, as well as having a correct general line, must also have appropriate 'tactical principles and various concrete policies for struggle.'[130] In accordance with the newly identified contradictions, a variety of new tactics were culled from the historical experience of the Chinese Communist Party and developed for use in the contemporary circumstances. If the enemy uses counter-revolutionary peaceful tactics as well as counter-revolutionary war to oppress people and nations, then the enemy must be fought with its own weapons and its own 'dual tactics'. If there were opportunities to win advantages from negotiation and compromise without sacrificing principle, then such would be the order of the day. If there were opportunities for the Leninist tactic of exploiting inter-imperialist rivalries then these too should be used. Limited tactical alliances with one imperialist power or group of powers against others, so long as China did not come to rely 'on foreign help or [hang] on to one imperialist bloc or another', were in order.[131] If advantage could be taken of the 'dual character' of many capitalist or 'revisionist' governments (i.e. their different positions when viewed from the perspective of different contradictions) then such advantages should be taken.

Conclusion

Although the contradiction between United States imperialism Soviet social-imperialism and the 'oppressed nations of the world' was not officially designated as the world's 'principal contradiction' it clearly fulfilled that function within the new Chinese foreign policy. As a result, it was this very broad contradiction which generated most propagandistic and strategic energy in China's conduct of its foreign policy. The 'broad united front' pole of the principal contradiction was discussed and promoted in its various aspects — as 'small and medium countries', as 'Second and Third World countries' or as 'oppressed nations', while at the other pole of the contradiction the United States and the Soviet Union were regarded in their 'imperialist/social-imperialist' aspect and in their 'hegemonic' aspect as superpowers.

In this new situation, liberation movements were considered to be under less direct imperialist pressure and, in general, imperialism had been forced to make a number of concessions — a development which was epitomised for the Chinese in the willingness of the United States to abandon its policy of 'containing' China. The governments of Second and Third world countries were considered, however, to have come under increased pressure from imperialist contention. Many of these states were dominated by ruling classes which were particularly reactionary. Nevertheless they found it in their interest to oppose the 'hegemony' of one or both of the superpowers and were, therefore, capable of contributing to the latters' demise. In fostering such developments, the Chinese did not, thereby, indicate any support for the domestic policies of the governments concerned. On the contrary, in weakening the bonds between such governments and imperialism, the Chinese appeared to be conscious that the internal position of the local ruling classes would be weakened vis-a-vis progressive and revolutionary forces. But, in the meantime, the possibilities of regional cooperation between Third World states and between Second World and Third World states were promoted as a central strategic feature of the new policy. Co-operation, on a regional basis or on a global basis, in political, military or economic terms, particularly where these involved energy or raw materials, was vigorously promoted by China as a desirable direction in which Second and Third World states were moving and should continue to move.

The new policy which emerged between the Ninth and Tenth Party Congresses had as its *leitmotiv* the slogan, 'countries want independence, nations want liberation and the people want revolution'. The commitment of the Chinese Communist Party to the second and third elements of this slogan, i.e., to the struggles of national liberation movements and the international working class movement has been a consistent feature of its foreign policy. The stress given, in the new policy, to the independence of 'countries' is far more novel and is the direct result of the new formulation of the world's major contradictions.

For China, a vigorous diplomacy was called for. By the Tenth Congress and in the months following, it had moved to take advantage of the changed situation by forming government-to-government and people-to-people relations with most countries. The strategy and tactics demanded by the new situation, as perceived by the Chinese leadership, meant that China's international behaviour was more sharply differentiated from that of the immediately preceeding phase of foreign policy than from any other phase in its history. This most visible aspect of the new policy, especially in its sharp contrast with the isolationist diplomatic tendencies of the Cultural Revolution period, formed the basis for a number of assessments of China's foreign policy which argued that its revolutionary direction has been lost. Such arguments cannot be less superficial than the basis from which they begin.[132] The analysis undertaken in this chapter shows that far from being an extravagant retreat to *realpolitik*, the new policy was formulated in response to anti-imperialist and revolutionary principles and tactics no less firmly held than in the past, but married to a new assessment of the international balance of class forces. It has also been demonstrated that the lengthy and profound debate which took place was not basically concerned with whether or not China ought to continue its revolutionary course but with the dominant features of the international order and consequently the tactics which should be adopted to implement its revolutionary principles.

The resistance to the new policy from the group surrounding Lin Piao was founded in the belief that the international disposition of class forces had not substantively altered since the mid sixties. It was thus not until the leaders of that group had become politically 'inoperative' (or even physically so) that the full dimensions of the new policy were clarified. By the time of the Tenth Congress, the implications and practical repercussions of the new policy were still being clarified, but the basic view of the world which informed the new policy was no longer debated.

The change which had taken place was considerably more than the victory of one leadership faction over another, in apparent isolation from the major domestic or international issues of the period, as some élite theorists would have us believe.[133] It is clear that 'factions' or ideological tendencies of different varieties were involved in the debate discussed in this chapter, but to assume that personal, non-ideological, disputes which are primarily concerned with status, prestige and private power formed the very basis of the debate would seem to be a gross violation of the available evidence.

Notes

1. For examples of this interpretation, see Adie 1972; Michael 1972; Scalapino 1974; Barnett 1972; Feuerwerker 1972; Rice 1973; Whiting 1973; Hinton H. 1972; Rhee 1970.
2. Whiting 1973.
3. *PR* 32, 9 August 1968, p.13.
4. Schurmann and Schell 1968, p.370.
5. Ibid, p.542.
6. *PR* 1, 3 January 1969, p.5.

7. Donnithorne 1975, p.6.
8. Lin Piao 1965, p.54.
9. Lin Piao 1965, p.58.
10. Barber 1966.
11. Lederer and Cutler, quoted in Committee of Concerned Asian Scholars 1970, p.270.
12. Magdoff 1969, p.198.
13. Committee of Concerned Asian Scholars 1970, p.272.
14. See e.g. Payer 1974 (on the IMF); de Camp 1974 (on the Asian Development Bank); Nissen 1971 (on the World Bank) and Hayter 1971.
15. For a discussion of Sukarno's downfall and possible CIA complicity, see e.g. Ransom 1970; Griswold 1969; Wertheim 1971.
16. *New York Times,* 1 February 1966, quoted in Oglesby and Schaull 1967, p.28.
17. Committee of Concerned Asian Scholars 1970, p.74.
18. Ibid.
19. *PR* 13, 29 March 1968, p.25.
20. *PR* 10, 8 March 1968, p.27.
21. *PR* 7, 16 February 1968, p.8; *PR* 10, 8 March 1968, p.21; *PR* 13, 29 March 1968, p.21.
22. Stone 1972, p.11, quoting Whalen 1972.
23. Yahuda 1974, p.13.
24. *CB* 865, 30 September 1968, p.14.
25. *PR* 1, 3 January 1969, p.10 (emphasis added).
26. *PR* 1, 3 January 1969, p.17.
27. Ibid., p.19.
28. *PR* 14, 4 April 1969, p.28.
29. Ibid., p.29.
30. PFLP 1973, p.5.
31. Lin Piao, 1 April 1969, *PR* 18, 30 April 1969, p.31.
32. Ibid., p.34.
33. *PR* 24, 11 June 1965, pp.10-20. Despite his subsequent condemnation as a leading 'revisionist' in the Cultural Revolution, P'eng's formulation reflected the policies pursued by China (and Lin Piao) at the time.
34. Lin Piao 1965, p.53.
35. The five principles are 'mutual respect for territorial integrity and sovereignty, mutual non-aggression, non-interference in each other's internal affairs, equality and mutual benefit, and peaceful co-existence.' *PR* 18, 30 April 1969, p.33.
36. *PR* 1, 3 January 1969, p.18.
37. To the newspaper *El Moudjahid,* Reuters, 28 July 1972, quoted in *CQ* 52, October-December 1972, p.768.
38. *PR* 40, 3 October 1969, p.16.
39. Ibid.
40. *PR* 1, 2 January 1970, p.7. In fact, this is a bastardisation of the 'consistent policy' which had reserved the 'five principles' as the basis for relations with countries naving 'different social systems'.
41. *PR* 17, 24 April 1970, pp.5-15.
42. *PR* 18, 30 April 1970, p.17.
43. *PR* 2, 9 January 1970, pp.15-17. As is now known, Mao was highly critical of this conception of his thinking, which he claimed was promoted by Lin Piao; cf. *Zhongfa* 1972/12, in *Issues and Studies,* Vol. 8, No.12, September 1972 pp.67-68.

44. Huang Yung-sheng, *PR* 27, 3 July 1970, pp.36-8.
45. *PR* 32, 7 August 1970, p.9.
46. *PR* 41, 9 October 1970, p.9.
47. The basis for this judgement is Mao Tsetung's statements in *Zhongfa* 1972/12, in *Issues and Studies,* Vol.8, No.12, September 1972, pp.18-24.
48. CCP CC, 6 September 1970, *PR* 37, 11 September 1970, p.6.
49. Lin Piao, *PR* 41, 9 October 1970, p.15.
50. See e.g. Chou En-lai, 24 August 1973, *PR* 35-6, 7 September 1973, p.20.
51. *PR* 41, 9 October 1970, p.19.
52. Snow 1971, p.146.
53. *PR* 1, 1 January 1971, p.8.
54. Ibid., p.9. The basis for unity expounded here was clearly likely to maximise widespread opposition to the 'superpowers' in international organisations, including the United Nations, to which China was on the verge of gaining entry.
55. Ibid.
56. *PR* 19, 7 May 1971 p.10.
57. 20 May, in *PR* 21, 21 May 1971, p.5. This article was a commentary on Mao's statement issued a year earlier. 'People of the world, unite and defeat the US aggressors and all their running dogs!' *PR* Special Issue, 23 May 1970, pp.8-9.
58. Ibid., p.5. Robert Guillain has claimed that 'Lin Piao still had control of the information media' at this stage. Milton and Schurmann 1974, p.384.
59. *PR* 21, 21 May 1971, p.5.
60. Cf. Chou En-lai's insistence that this was the case, in an interview with Harrison E. Salisbury. Salisbury 1973, p.256.
61. In February, Lin had allegedly written 'B-52 [the code name for Mao used by Lin and his group] cannot enjoy good sense for long; within a few years he must hurriedly arrange for things after his death. He is wary of us. It is better to burn our bridges behind us rather than to sit and wait to be captured. If we act first militarily and then politically . . . will be greatly threatened.' CCP CC, *Zhongfa* 1972/4 in *Chinese Law and Government,* Vol.5, No.3-4, Fall-Winter 1972-3, p.48.
62. 'The task of the Chinese Communist Party is . . . to exert our greatest efforts to struggle together with the people of all countries to defeat the US aggressors and all their running dogs, oppose the politics of hegemony pushed by the two superpowers', *PR* 27, 2 July 1971, p.21.
63. One exception to this was the determined Huang Yung-sheng, whose Army Day speech (1 August 1971) seemingly remained opposed to the prevailing position on normalisation with the US, Cf. *Current Scene,* Vol.14, No.12, 7 December 1971, pp.13-19. See also his speech to a Korean military delegation on 18 August, *PR* 35, 27 August 1971, p.29.
64. *PR* 32, 6 August 1971, p.8.
65. *New China News,* 25 October 1972.
66. *PR* 9, 3 March 1972, p.10.
67. Chang Wen-chin, interview with delegation from the Australian National University, Peking, 14 June 1973.
68. *PR* 32, 6 August 1971, p.8.
69. The Chinese people were exhorted to 'strengthen Army-government and Army-civilian unity . . ., under the leadership of the Party Central Committee, with Chairman Mao as its leader and Vice Chairman Mao as its deputy leader'. Ibid., p.9.
70. Contrast this with the position of Whiting outlined above.
71. *PR* 32, 6 August 1971, p.8.
72. Ibid.

73. Mao Tsetung, 17 October 1945, *SW* English edition, Vol.4, pp.53-63.
74. Ibid., p.56.
75. Ibid., p.54.
76. Mao Tsetung, 25 December 1940, *SW* English edition, Vol.2, pp.441-5.
77. Ibid., p.444.
78. Ibid., p.442.
79. Ibid., p.444.
80. Ibid.
81. Ibid.
82. Ibid.
83. *Hongqi* 9, 1971, in *SCMM* 711, 7 September 1971, pp.1-9. Abridged trans. *PR* 35, 27 August 1971. This is taken from the latter, p.10.
84. Ibid., pp.11-12.
85. Ibid., pp.12-13.
86. Ibid., p.12.
87. Mao Tsetung, 17 October 1945, *SW*, Vol.4, p.56.
88. *PR* 35, 27 August 1971.
89. *PR* 1, 2 January 1970, p.7 (emphasis added).
90. PFLP 1965, pp.259-301 and Lin Piao, 1 April 1969, *PR* 18, 30 April 1969 p.33.
91. *PR* 37, 11 September 1970, p.6.
92. *PR* 49, 4 December 1970, p.23 (emphasis added).
93. The theoretical concession involved is, in fact, minimal. The most complete statement of the Chinese position is: 'Of course, socialist countries too must abide by the Five Principles in their mutual relations. It is absolutely impermissible for any one of them to undermine the territorial integrity of another fraternal country, to impair its independence and sovereignty, interfere in its internal affairs, carry out subversive activities inside it, or violate the principle of equality and mutual benefit in its relations with another fraternal country.' PFLP 1965, p.283. The article went on to say that such relations, while necessary, were not sufficient for fraternal socialist countries.
94. In late 1972, in an uncharacteristic confusion of class and 'anti-hegemonic' alliances, China was said to have 'sustained, consolidated and strengthened fraternal and revolutionary unity with *such socialist countries* as Albania, Korea, Vietnam and *Romania.' GMRB,* 12 October 1972, in *SCMP* 5244 30 October 1972, p.1 (emphasis added).
95. *Wenhuibao* (Hong Kong) 19 November 1972, cited in *CQ* 53 January/March 1973, p.200.
96. Teng Hsiao-p'ing, 10 April 1974, *PR* 16, 19 April 1974, p.6.
97. PFLP 1975 p.274.
98. *PR* 32, 6 August 1971, p.9.
99. *PR* 7-8, 25 February 1972, p.8.
100. From a transcript by Bill Synnot, an agronomist who was a member of the delegation. Chou En-lai expressed similar views in an interview with Neville Maxwell, *Sunday Times,* 5 December 1971.
101. *PR* 41, 13 October 1972, p.5.
102. *PR* 4, 28 January 1972, p.16.
103. *PR* 40, 6 October 1972, p.10.
104. PFLP 1965, p.285.
105. *PR* 40, 6 October 1972, p.11.
106. *RMRB,* 30 September 1972, in *PR* 40, 6 October 1972, p.14.
107. *PR* 40, 6 October 1972, p.10.
108. *PR* 35-6, 7 September, 1973, p.19.
109. Ibid.

110. Ibid. p.21.
111. Lin Piao, 1 April 1969, *PR* 18, 30 April 1969, p.31.
112. Ibid., p.32.
113. Chou En-lai, (*loc cit*), p.22.
114. Lin Piao, (*loc cit*), p.31.
115. Ibid., p.34.
116. Chou En-lai, (*loc cit*), p.22.
117. Lin Piao, (*loc cit*), p.31.
118. Chou En-lai, (*loc cit*), p.24.
119. Lin Piao, (*loc cit*), p.34.
120. Ibid., p.31.
121. Chou En-lai, (*loc cit*), p.22.
122. Chou also stated that Lenin 'pointed out repeatedly that imperialism means aggression and war' but he went on to point out that it would be possible to prevent a new world war. Ibid., p.23. Lin, on the other hand, did not quote Lenin to the effect that imperialism means rivalry.
123. Chou En-lai *loc cit.,* p.23.
124. Mao Tsetung, 17 October 1945, *SW* English edition, Vol.4, p.59.
125. Mao Tsetung, April 1946, *SW* English edition, Vol.4, p.87.
126. For the background to Wang Hung-wen's sudden prominence and its probable significance, see Wich 1974 and Chang 1974.
127. *PR*, 35-6, 7 September 1974, p.33.
128. See note 102.
129. Gittings 1972, p.32.
130. *PR* 35, 27 August 1971, p.10.
131. Ibid.
132. For a 'left' argument of this kind, see 'A Progressive Labor Party Member' 1973, p.13.
133. See e.g. Bridgham 1973; Joffe 1973; Kau and Perolle 1974; Parish 1973. The ability of many sinologists to carry out extended debates without reference to policy issues is considerable — as exemplified in the above articles where it would seem that the intrigue and hypocrisy of the Watergate Affair, particularly in its non-class aspects, would make it a universal archetype of all political struggle.

CONCLUSION

Bill Brugger

The Case of Lin Piao

The contributors to this book have focused on the period 1969-73, with the aim of evaluating the achievements of the Cultural Revolution. Perhaps the single most important event in that period was the attempted coup which Lin Piao, one of the most important figures in that revolution, was said to have organised. The various charges levelled against Lin, both from within China and without, have been discussed in every chapter and there is general agreement that they are contradictory. There is agreement too that, whatever else the Cultural Revolution might have been, it did not constitute a military take-over. As Woodward has argued, military personnel were not just appointed to important Party and state posts on the basis of their military function but also according to their standing in the old Party structure which was about to be reorganised and rebuilt. Secondly, the bulk of these military personnel, from regional military commands, did not form part of Lin Piao's alternative Party structure and were peacefully removed from civilian administration once Lin Piao's faction was no more. Nevertheless, the threat posed by Lin Piao was such that the phasing out of the Army was by no means a simple operation. Nor is it at all clear, now that many military personnel have been removed from civilian administration, whether one is still not confronted with the problem with which Lin Piao began work in 1959 — a growing division of labour between soliders and civilians.

Describing the demise of Lin, Woodward concentrates on the relationship between politics and military affairs and touches on one of the major concerns of Young — the extent to which Lin's policies hindered the process of Party reconstruction. Lin was accused first of 'ultra-leftism' which can be seen as an idealist view of socialism based on the vision of the guerilla base. This defined the priority of politics in such a way that objective economic and social limits were disregarded and production suffered. A belief in individualistic heroism prevented the rehabilitation of old cadres necessary for the reformed Party and book-waving and slogan chanting was no substitute for the ideological reconstruction of the Party. As Chan points out, however, the criticism of Lin's excessively narrow interpretation of 'politics in command' gave rise to a number of conservative policies which, in the field of education, occasioned a new bout of radical criticism in which Lin Piao was designated an 'ultra-rightist'. Certainly there are good theoretical grounds for pointing out the similarity between an 'ultra-left' and an 'ultra-right' position. Both tendencies tend to under-rate mass initiative. Whilst the former tends to coerce the masses into an acceptance of what it believes to be socialism and the latter into an acceptance of order and discipline, the methods of leadership are much the same and condition the ends for which both strive. In all due honesty, however, one does not see in Chinese discussions of that time a great degree of sophistication in the development of this argument. On the contrary, the shift in the designation of Lin Piao led to his being accused of many of the opposite policies to those with which he had been associated in the earlier period. Observing that Lin Piao, once charged with pushing politics at the expense of production, was now accused of being concerned only with production and that the advocate of individualistic heroism was held to be tailing after mass demands, Young can only conclude that Lin Piao was being used as a scapegoat. Yet others have suggested an alternative (or perhaps a complementary) explanation. Just as some of the earlier criticism of Lin Piao was in fact directed against Liu Shao-ch'i (and his ilk) who had pursued diametrically opposite policies, so the new criticisms of Lin Piao were, in fact, directed against Chou En-lai. Such an explanation would be consistent with current revelations that the major critics (the 'Gang of Four') had singled out Chou En-lai as the major obstacle to the development of their conception of Mao Tsetung's theory of 'continuous revolution'.[1]

The above explanation might also help us to evaluate the suggestion that Lin Piao, the supposed advocate of an autarchic fortress China, should have been interested in technological assistance from overseas. It is said that Lin's concern for the development of nuclear and missile technology necessitated some reliance on overseas countries for the development of the electronics industry. Such a view contradicted the more 'self reliant' policy of concentrating first on the development of iron and steel.[2] It has never been satisfactorily demonstrated that Lin was ever involved in such a debate[3] and Cheng goes so far as to suggest that 'electronics versus steel' was a non issue. The

importation of foreign technology, however, was certainly a very live
issue and it could well be that some of the criticism of Lin Piao on
this score was, in fact, directed at Chou En-lai and Teng Hsiao-p'ing.
The 'Gang of Four' have also been charged with attempting to
restrict foreign trade and the importation of technology,[4] the
spectacular growth of which post-dates Lin Piao's demise.

Just as it is often maintained that the Lin Piao issue had no
substantial effect on development policy, so, it is argued, was there
no effect on foreign policy. Charges to the effect that Lin Piao pursued a
'revisionist' foreign policy[5] do not refer to any particular period and
are difficult to pin down. In his contribution to this book, however,
O'Leary, following Peck,[6] argues that there was a particular view of
world affairs which may be directly associating with Lin Piao. It
consisted of a generalised version of Lin's 1965 essay 'Long Live
the Victory of People's War'[7] whereby the world's countryside
surrounds the world's cities and where the focus of world tension
is found in Asia. This view had some validity in the mid 1960s, but,
with the beginnings of the decline in United States global power in
the late 1960s, it was replaced by one which saw the super-powers
vying for 'hegemony' over a Third World and a 'second intermediate
zone' which together had begun to realise their common interest.
In such a situation, China was required to do more than await the
victory of national liberation struggles, and diplomatic relations
were entered into with an increasing number of states. It is possible,
therefore, that this view contradicted what remained of the earlier
view and was a factor in the Lin Piao episode. O'Leary's essay is a
healthy corrective to those accounts which see the foreign policy
line of 1971 as a simple reaction to growing Soviet strength or as a
reflection of internal 'revisionism'.

O'Leary's analysis is based mainly on the documents of the time
but most other chapters have drawn selectively on material released
after 1973, particularly in the major campaign launched in 1973 to
Criticise Lin Piao and Confucius. That campaign was, in 1975, to
yield place to another major campaign to Study the Theory of the
Dictatorship of the Proletariat which, in turn, developed into a
movement to criticise the newly rehabilitated Vice Premier and
Party Vice Chairman, Teng Hsiao-p'ing. An attempt must be made,
therefore, in this concluding chapter to relate the arguments of
preceding chapters to these three major movements.

The Movement to Criticise Lin Piao and Confucius

The academic criticism of Confucius after the Cultural Revolution
began with the publication of an article by Yang Jung-kuo of
Chungshan University in Kwangchow in December 1972.[8] The
movement proper, however, did not begin until after the Tenth Congress
when the criticism of Confucius was linked directly with Lin Piao.[9]
The central issue was the extent to which Confucian ideas might
facilitate 'retrogression'. Thus, the movement turned on an evaluation
of the Cultural Revolution and the need for a new upsurge in the
process of 'continuous revolution'. In case any one should have any
doubt on that score, one only has to recall a similar (though less
widespread) movement in the early 1960s which turned on the
evaluation of the Great Leap Forward.

The parallel with the early 1960s is striking. The Anti-Confucius
movement and the Socialist Education Movement were alike not
only in general orientation but also in the confusion attending their
operation. Both movements saw groups articulate very different aims
whilst using the same slogans and both movements gave rise to
considerable confusion in interpreting 'the struggle between the two
lines'.[10]

As in the Socialist Education Movement, there was probably general
agreement among all groups on the explicit aim of the movement – to
eradicate the Confucian values of reverence for the past, filial piety,
'righteousness' (transcending classes), particularistic loyalty, and
ritualism.[11] But, like the Socalist Education Movement of 1963-6,
where there was similar agreement on general goals (which at that time
meant the need to combat corruption and the degeneration of cadres),
there was clearly profound disagreement in the field of operations.

At one pole stood the persistent 'rebels' (*zaofanpai*). These would
include the most extreme of the 'reds' which Chan identifies in the
field of higher education. It might include the 'ultra-leftists' who
opposed all rural sideline production and advocated the premature
adoption of the Tachai system of remuneration and the widespread
transfer of the agricultural unit of account to brigade level, though
Woodward's chapter indicates that this was probably not a persistent
problem in 1974. It might include what was left of the proponents
of the more 'anarchistic' policies which Watson identifies in industry.
It might also embrace those who did not like the kind of Party
which emerged following the reconstruction of the early 1970s,
as outlined by Young, and who still had fond dreams of a
Paris Commune-type organisation. For these groups, 'retrogression'

meant a return to the pre-Cultural Revolution situation. The 'socialist new things' of that revolution had to be defended at all costs and the ground prepared for a new upsurge in the process of 'continuous revolution'. If history was any guide, such preparation had to be in the field of culture. Such was the repeated theme of Chiang Ch'ing (soon to be identified as one of the 'Gang of Four') and it might be traced to the 'superstructural-push' interpretation of Mao's position in the early 1960s which I discussed in the Introduction.

Though there is nothing inherently 'ultra-leftist' in the notion of superstructural-push, the catalogue of 'ultra-left' policies indicated above would suggest that it could easily lead to idealism and that hallmark of 'ultra-leftist' behaviour in the Cultural Revolution – the concentration on the person as opposed to the line.[12] Not to put too fine a point on it, this group was, as Chan mentions, out to discredit Premier Chou En-lai, his newly rehabilitated protegé Teng Hsiao-p'ing, and the host of old cadres retrained in May Seventh Cadre schools. All too frequently, when they spoke of Lin Piao they meant Chou En-lai,[13] sometimes referred to as the Duke of Chou (*Zhou gong*), that paragon of Confucian virtues who was said to have symbolised Confucius' golden age of minority cultural excellence and general slavery. During the Cultural Revolution in Hunan, the antecedents of this group had spoken of Chou En-lai as the 'representative of China's "red bourgeoisie" '[14] and had been defeated by the Chairman of that province's revolutionary committee – Hua Kuo-feng.

The notion of a 'red bourgeoisie' was clearly linked with a generative notion of class, and may be seen as a corruption of Mao's position in the early 1960s. It was a contentious notion which was to be worked up to the level of general theory in the period which followed the launching of the Anti-Confucius campaign.

At the opposite pole stood those who were concerned that radicalism might harm production. When they criticised Lin Piao, they meant precisely what they said – idealism was potentially very dangerous. Those who were aware, however, that the movement had been interpreted by some as a weapon with which to attack Chou En-lai, probably attempted to select those aspects of Anti-Confucian thought which supported Chou's leadership. Indeed, one writer has gone so far as to suggest that what started as an attack on Chou's policies finished up as an attack on those of his opponents.[15]

Since we are only now beginning to be able to identify the various contributors to the debate, it is premature to advance even a tentative hypothesis. One may illustrate the problem, however, by describing one salient feature of the polemics and suggest divergent interpretations. Much of the discussion in 1973-4 focused on the Ch'in dynasty which, in the third century BC unified China and from which our term 'China' is derived. The First Emperor of Ch'in, had long been denounced as a tyrant by Chinese scholars and the Lin Piao group had likened him to Mao Tsetung.[16] The conventional wisdom had it that the Ch'in Emperor maintained his harsh rule by supporting a 'legalist' code of punishment and had ruthlessly put down an attempt at rebellion by his frustrated first minister Lu Pu-wei who sought to restore feudal states and the Confucian virtues. A later first minister, Li Ssu, persuaded the First Emperor to burn the Confucian books and bury Confucian scholars alive and such harsh action eventually occasioned the downfall of the empire.

A new interpretation maintained that 'legalism' was older than Confucianism and Confucius himself had brought about the murder of Shao Cheng-mao his contemporary 'legalist' opponent. 'Legalism' was held to be an ideology appropriate to the progressive feudal system as opposed to the old slave system to which the Confucians wished to return.[17] The First Emperor of Ch'in, therefore, who lived three centuries after Confucius, was a progressive monarch who aimed at consolidating the feudal system and eradicating old ideas. Thus, Lü Pu-wei was a reactionary conspirator who organised a faction with the aid of forces outside Ch'in and launched an abortive coup.[18] The First Emperor's endorsement of Li Ssu's advice to burn the books and bury the scholars was indeed the appropriate response to conspiracy and his aim was merely to eradicate sedition and not creative thought. The Emperor was not opposed to literature; he loved it.[19] Li Ssu's advocacy of 'legalism' was a plea for the rule of law and the promotion of modernisation and economic development. Finally the Ch'in Empire was brought to an end by the conspiracy of another Confucian, Chao Kao, who thereby negated many of the progressive measures undertaken in the short dynasty.[20]

There can be no doubt that Lü Pu-wei was an analogue of Lin Piao and the First Emperor of Ch'in was Mao but one may interpret the other characters in vastly different ways. If Li Ssu's most notable contribution was his policy towards recalcitrants, then he could be taken as the analogue of someone who supported a harsh interpretation of the exercise of the dictatorship of the proletariat — perhaps Chang Ch'un-ch'iao or Yao Wen-yuan. If, however, his most notable contribution was, in fact, technical modernisation, the

promotion of centralisation and the abolition of independent
military power, then he was Chou En-lai or perhaps his putative
successor Teng Hsiao-p'ing. These men were just as eager to get rid
of conspirators only they had a very different view as to who they
were. Occasionally Li Ssu was portrayed as a grey vacillating
character[21] which might support either interpretation. The same
confusion attends the identification of Chao Kao, who flattered the
First Emperor whilst he was alive and plotted for the overthrow of
his system once he was dead in the same manner as Lü Pu-wei.[22]
One wonders who was being likened to Lin Piao. Was it Chou En-lai
or one of the 'Gang of Four'?

The above should not be taken just as an imaginative exercise in
Pekingology. The policy implications of the Ch'in dynasty (and
many other) analogues were of crucial importance. It is surely the
case that most people fell somewhere between the two extreme groups
outlined above but sufficient argument has been presented to show
that support for the Anti-Confucius campaign might come from very
different sources with very different consequences – and this was
precisely what had happened in the Socialist Education Movement
a decade before. Just as, in the Socialist Education Movement, a
number of discrete movements eventually came together, so the
separate movements to criticise 'The Lin-Ch'en Anti-Party clique'
and to Criticise Confucius came together as a movement to
Criticise Lin Piao and Confucius in the autumn of 1973. Once this was
done, those who were worried about production attempted to keep
the movement focused on Lin Piao's idealism and to prevent the
target shifting to the new 'Duke of Chou'. By March 1974, they
had succeeded and the intense poster campaign of the previous
month receded. Perhaps with confidence, Teng Hsiao-p'ing, as
Chou's choice for the next premier, could attend in April the United
Nations General Assembly conference on raw materials and development.[23] From the time Chou En-lai entered hospital in May 1974
until his death in 1976, Teng remained as effective acting premier
symbolising a policy in which politics should not be interpreted in
such a way that production was harmed.

The movement to Criticise Lin Piao and Confucius continued
into the autumn of 1974 and did sometimes give rise to renewed
fears about the effect on production.[24] It was clear, however, that it
was not going to develop into a new round of the Cultural Revolution.
As the movement went on, the journal and newspaper articles became
more and more obscure to the point that I am sure the masses didn't

understand them. It had been feared that the Cultural Revolution in early 1966 might degenerate into an academic discussion on how to interpret history; the Anti-Confucius movement did just that.

This is not to say, however, that the Anti-Confucius movement had no impact. It may be that, amid the verbiage, there was a lot of very sound historiography. But that cannot be the main point. It would be a strange movement indeed if the results of months of poster campaigns and mass criticism was just an improvement in historiography. Undoubtedly, a movement which took as a main target the continuing influence of a gerontocratic, male-dominated Confucian ideology would have an impact on the field of social relations. It is not surprising then that, in a manner much more thorough-going than the Cultural Revolution, issues such as the subordination of women[25] and the danger of particularistic loyalties were examined in depth.

We are now in a position to examine the movement of 1974 in terms of the conclusions reached by preceding chapters. Young maintains that a Cultural Revolution of the 1960s-type might not be seen as the best way to invigorate the Party. The failure of the 'rebels' to inaugurate a new round of that revolution would suggest that many in China took this view. Describing Party rebuilding in the early 1970s, Young claims considerable success in overcoming factionalism. The fact that, although criticism in the Anti-Confucius campaign came from all quarters, the Party was able to maintain a high degree of unity, would support such a claim. In Chapter 2, Woodward argues that, in the Army, the divisive legacies of the Cultural Revolution had been overcome by the time the Anti-Confucius movement got under way. Such a conclusion is borne out by the reorganisation of regional military commands in late 1973, in line with the policy of unity promoted by Chou En-lai and actually proposed, it is rumoured, by his deputy – Teng Hsiao-p'ing.[26] In Chapter 3, Chan asserts that, whereas, at a policy level, the Anti-Confucius campaign resulted in stalemate, one might anticipate that the beneficiaries of the revolution in education would continue it. Indeed, within two years, there was to be a new upsurge in that revolution, fuelled no doubt by the attitudes and behaviour engendered in the Anti-Confucius campaign. In Chapter 4, Cheng maintains that the Anti-Confucius campaign had little impact on development strategy. Bearing in mind Woodward's objections in Chapter 5, it would seem that he is on much firmer ground here than in his similar assertion concerning the demise of

Lin Piao. In Chapter 7, O'Leary argues that China's changed foreign policy stance in the early 1970s was not the result of internal 'revisionism' or merely a response to the Soviet threat but was arrived at after an examination of the objective world situation. The view, in 1974, that the ability of the state of Ch'in to unite the six states of that time lay in a similar examination and on playing one state off against another[27] suggests the continuity of this view.

Though the criticism of Confucius continued through 1975 to 1976, it is fair to say that the movement was concluded in November 1974. At that time, its achievements were officially summed up[28] and a renewed stress on unity was in evidence. Such was the theme of the Fourth National People's Congress which met in January 1975 in which both Teng Hsiao-p'ing and Chang Ch'un-ch'iao were most prominent. The same balance was achieved later in January, for when Teng was appointed Chief of Staff of the Army, Chang was appointed to head its General Political Department. There has been much speculation as to the significance of this balance and the fact that Mao did not attend either the Congress or the plenary sessions (which could have been held at his residence some ninety minutes flight away),[29] but a concluding chapter is not the place to involve the reader in new complexities. Suffice it to say that unity was taken extremely seriously and the major speeches of Chou En-lai and Chang Ch'un-ch'iao were both moderate in tone. Whilst stressing the importance of making China into a modern socialist state by the year 2000, Chou also paid attention to the political tasks with which China was confronted.[30] For his part Chang, whilst stressing the continuance of class struggle, gave a speech entirely in keeping with the new Constitution which he introduced.[31]

The Campaign to Study the Theory of the Dictatorship of the Proletariat

Some three weeks after the end of the Fourth National People's Congress, a movement was launched which was to shatter that unity.[32] At first sight, however, the Campaign to Study the Theory of the Dictatorship of the Proletariat seemed to be more than a necessary corrective to the historical obscurantism engendered in the Anti-Confucius Campaign. As in the case of the Anti-Confucius campaign, there was probably substantial agreement on the need for such a movement. Those who were more concerned with maintaining production were eager to encourage the criticism of Lin Piao's idealism and the use of a book of Mao's quotations as the sole source of theory. If 'legalism' was the order of the day, then there was a need to examine the basis for the laws which would govern conduct and to articulate the centralised administration of the First Emperor of Ch'in to a more acceptable theory of dictatorship. Yet, as we now know, the influence that this group had over the media was not, by 1975, as great as their opponents and the movement was interpreted in a way which went far beyond their concerns.

The 'rebel' interpretation of the movement was articulated most clearly in two major articles by Yao Wen-yuan and Chang Ch'un-ch'iao (two other members of the 'Gang of Four') in March and April 1975.[33] These amounted to a full-blown explication of the generative theory of class. The most important item to be studied in the campaign was Marx's description in *The Critique of the Gotha Programme* of inequalities arising from the fact that workers are paid according to the time they spend at work irrespective of productive capacity.[34] Thus, according to Lenin, 'bourgeois right . . . gives to unequal individuals, in return for unequal (really unequal) amounts of labour, equal amounts of products.'[35] The generation of new classes in socialist society, therefore, stems from a failure sufficiently to restrict this 'bourgeois right' by the dictatorship of the proletariat.[36] The implications were clear; a new major struggle was to be launched against the 'new bourgeoisie'.

Coming at a time when strikes (guaranteed under the new Constitution approved by the Fourth National People's Congress), had taken place in Hangchow,[37] such an interpretation was very unwelcome to those who wished to prevent major social upheavals. Our analysis of the impact of Yao's and Chang's articles is hindered by the fact that it has never been satisfactorily explained just exactly what the causes of the Hangchow strikes were. It is rumoured that they were settled by Teng Hsiao-p'ing who thereafter felt compelled to issue a set of documents putting forward a highly provocative defence of the position that industrial production should in no way suffer for the sake of wider political goals.

It is very difficult to reconstruct Teng's position at this point (July 1977) since his second rehabilitation has only just taken place[38] and the fragments of his documents available to us have been edited by his staunchest opponents. It would seem, however, that Teng promoted those aspects of Chou En-lai's January 1975 Report which stressed the importance of unity and the maintenance of production. Allegedly, he insisted that Mao's "three directives' (on studying the theory of the dictatorship of the proletariat, on

promoting unity and on furthering the national economy) should
equally constitute the 'key link' for at least the next twenty-five years.[39]
Here, he took a line diametrically opposed to the 'Gang of Four' who
argued that the stress on unity and maintaining production should be
subordinated to class struggle. Impatient with those who sought to
bring about turmoil under the rubric of restricting 'bourgeois right',
Teng branded his critics as 'ultra-leftist':

> They talk only of politics and not of the economy; only of
> revolution and not production. When they hear about taking a
> grip on production and fostering economic construction, they
> cap people as advocates of the 'theory of productive forces'
> and say they are practising revisionism.[40]

Allegedly, Teng saw his opponents as sham Marxists, for the acid test
for deciding whether a policy was correct or not was whether it
'liberated the productive forces'.[41] This was the essence of what the
'Gang of Four' criticised as 'the sinister theory of productive forces'.
Put at its crudest, it held that changes in the productive forces
determined the whole field of social relations and ideology not just in
the last instance (an unobjectionable Marxist position) but in all
instances. There can be few Marxists who were that crude and
certainly, amongst those who were familiar with Mao's ideas
outlined in the early 1960s, there were even fewer.[42] The portrayal
of Teng is clearly an exaggeration but the polemic does indicate
very different emphases in development policy.

Though the position ascribed to Teng concerning productive
forces is hardly credible, the assertion that he saw the three major
struggles (class struggle, the struggle for production and scientific
experiment) as being governed by different laws[43] is quite
believable. Thus, he could affirm class struggle whilst advocating the
more rigid implementation of the various programmes of industrial
regularisation outlined by Cheng and Watson — the responsibility
system,[44] the strengthening of central (as opposed to provincial)
control,[45] and the de-emphasis on political activity.[46] He could
affirm China's relatively autarchic stand on development in world
forums[47] whilst asserting positively the importation of technology[48]
and concluding credit agreements with foreign powers.[49]

Development strategy, I would argue, was a major feature of the
polemics of 1975 and the documents attributed to Teng reveal a far
less revolutionary position than those of Chou En-lai. This is not,

however, to dismiss the charge that the 'Gang of Four' were guilty of 'ultra-leftism' (or 'ultra-rightism' as it has been called since the case of Lin Piao). Nor do I wish to be categorical at this point. The number of alleged forged documents to have surfaced in recent months would suggest extreme caution.

Teng's counter attack, which was to be referred to in 1976 as 'the right deviationist wind to reverse previously correct verdicts', lasted from July to October 1975[50] and was to be bitterly attacked by the 'Gang of Four' through their journal *Study and Criticism*. It was to give rise to a heated poster campaign in universities concerning academic and technical standards and a new upsurge in the revolution in education. As Chan points out, Teng was associated with the 'expert' group headed by Minister of Education Chou Jung-hsin who came under increasing attack for his professional orientation.[51] The crucial point was how to apply the dictatorship of the proletariat to the field of education and Teng is reported to have implied that in some fields (particularly science and technology which he designated 'a productive force') it could have no relevance at all.[52] Thus, one might assess positively some of the scientific achievements made before the Cultural Revolution regardless of the 'line' then currently in force. Most contentious of all was Teng's alleged support of those who criticised the 'open door' principle of education which sacrificed theory to practice. Indeed Chou Jung-hsin appeared to criticise the notion of taking 'society as a school' and 'learning by doing' as the 'bourgeois' education theories of Dewey.[53]

By the autumn of 1975, the stage was set for a major confrontation and Mao Tsetung was called upon to mediate in a particularly acute debate at Tsinghua University. He apparently refused and, in November, sent a series of contentious documents back to Tsinghua University 'for the comment of the masses'. The result was predictable. Chou Jung-hsin was openly attacked,[54] the polemic intensified and a new round in the revolution in education began. By the New Year, the new climate was reflected in a statement from Mao published in a joint editorial: 'Stability and unity do not mean writing off the class struggle. Class struggle is the key link and everything else hinges upon it.'[55] The implications for Teng Hsiao-p'ing, who had maintained that Mao's 'three directives' constituted the 'key link', were profound.

The events of 1975 raise a number of important questions relating to the various contributions to this book. In Chapter 1, Young describes the call for Party members to 'study Marxism

seriously' as an accompaniment to a period of consolidation. Called
upon to study the theory of the dictatorship of the proletariat in
1975, many cadres may have made a similar evaluation until it
become clear that the dictatorship of the proletariat was to be linked
with the generative view of class and constituted a call for a new period
of radicalism. In Chapter 2, Woodward describes the phasing out of
Army involvement in civilian life but, in the tense situation of 1975,
it was not at all clear whether promotion to high Army posts of
the arch exponents of the two different approaches to current
developments might create the very factionalism that was brought to
an end in the late 1960s. Woodward describes also the new importance
ascribed to the militia in the early 1970s but what would happen if
part of that militia were mobilised behind the Shanghai-based 'Gang
of Four'[56] in this new attempt to 'drag out the handful'. In Chapter
3, Chan describes the stability imparted to the education sector,
following the involvement of workers, but what would happen if
the industrial strife of 1975 extended into the educational
institutions already torn by the polemic on education? Would this
be the reverse of 1966? What would the 'worker theorists'
employed in the current campaign do in such a situation? As Cheng
maintains in Chapter 4, the impact of the 1975 movement on current
production was limited to its first few months, but there was
sufficient ferment in the factories (as well as the universities) to
suggest new and significant developments in 1976. Woodward, in
Chapter 5, discusses the defeat of 'ultra-leftism' in agriculture in the
early 1970s. Would the new movement see its recrudescence? This
was certainly in the mind of Hua Kuo-feng who addressed a national
conference on 'Learning from Tachai' in September and October. He
conceived the possible appearance of 'new bourgeois elements' in
agriculture but stressed that in most cases, the contradictions were
'among the people' rather than antagonistic.[57] As for the factories,
discussed by Watson in Chapter 4, the battle was especially significant
since workers could hardly ignore the implications of the notion of
'bourgeois right' for the 'eight grade wage scale'.[58]

There were implications too for foreign policy though not
explicitly in the Movement to Study the Theory of the Dictatorship
as such. Here we must turn to a significant, though minor, movement
which began in September 1975. This was the Movement to Criticise
the *Water Margin*. This Ming dynasty novel had long been popular
in China and had been a particular favourite of Mao himself. It
portrayed the Robin Hood-type exploits of a group of worthy bandits

during the Sung dynasty. The names of the leaders of this group had, over the centuries, become household words in China and, when Mao allegedly urged people to criticise the 'capitulationism' of one of the most prominent, he could not fail to strike a chord. This 'capitulationist' was Sung Chiang,[59] who allegedly abandoned the rebels. His action was said to have contemporary relevance for those who were guilty of 'class capitulationism in home affairs and national capitulationism in foreign affairs'.[60] This campaign may be interpreted in a way similar to the earlier campaign to Criticise Lin Piao and Confucius. The 'capitulationist' Sung Chiang expressed loyalty to the bandit leader Chao K'ai but, after the latter's death, sold out to the Imperial Court. Thus Sung Chiang may be identified with Lin Piao. A contrary interpretation is that the target was not Lin Piao but Chou En-lai[61] and the movement was apparently launched without his knowledge.[62] Coming at a time when there was a marginally greater stress on the menace of US imperialism[63] and when conciliatory moves appeared to be made towards the Soviet Union[64], the movement might well have represented an attack by the 'Gang of Four' or other 'rebels' on the new foreign policy. To be sure, the marginally different posture adopted towards the United States in 1975 might represent merely the application of pressure on President Ford, who visited China at that time, to speed up the process of normalisation of diplomatic relations but it is difficult to interpret the charge of 'capitulationism' in foreign affairs in any way other than a Lin Piao-type critique of the new foreign policy position outlined in Chapter 7 by O'Leary. Current re-evaluations of the movement do not help us much here. They agree that Chiang Ch'ing wished to discredit the Premier and cast him as Sung Chiang,[65] whereas Mao had Lin Piao in mind, but they focus on Chiang Ch'ing's portrayal of Sung's flattering Chao K'ai (the analogue of Mao) in order to turn the latter into a mere figurehead. When faced with this interpretation Mao is reported to have uttered an obscenity.[66]

The Campaign to Criticise Teng Hsiao-p'ing

'Take class struggle as the key link' remained the dominant slogan throughout the first three quarters of 1976. One week after it was put forward in the New Year editorial, Premier Chou En-lai died leaving the State Council in the charge of a man who was said to have a very different notion of the 'key link'. In his funeral eulogy on 15 January, Teng called upon people to 'turn their grief into strength' and seemed to call for a movement to emulate the qualities of Chou En-lai,[67] yet on the same day an article in *People's Daily* called for an intensification of the campaign in education and for attacks to be made on those who attempted to restore any part of the pre-Cultural Revolution education system.[68] In the following months, press articles reiterated the Cultural Revolution's theme of 'top persons in authority taking the capitalist road' and indicated that the 'expert' position in education might constitute an attack on the Cultural Revolution itself. Wall posters appeared speaking of 'China's new Khruschev' who erroneously put forward Mao's 'three directives' as the 'key link' and who had declared that 'it did not matter whether a cat was black or white so long as it caught mice'.[69] This famous quotation from Teng, of Cultural Revolution notoriety, made it quite clear that Teng was under considerable pressure and it was in such a climate that Hua Kuo-feng was appointed acting Premier.[70]

There has been much speculation as to the exact position of Hua Kuo-feng on the various debates that had raged over the past six months and to his assessment of the current situation. Suffice it to say that whilst the media, under the control of the 'Gang of Four', declared that a 'life or death struggle' was in progress (and Teng's opinion could not have been much different), Hua assured the visiting ex-President Nixon that this was just an example of 'extensive democracy'.[71] Indeed the moderation of the polemics in March would suggest that Hua had achieved partial success in cooling down frayed tempers. Then, in April, matters came to a head. An attempt to remove wreaths, laid in Peking's T'ien An Men Square in honour of Chou En-lai on the occasion of the traditional Ch'ing Ming Festival, erupted into violence,[72] ushering in one of the least edifying periods in contemporary Chinese history.

An immediate consequence of the 'T'ien An Men Incident' was the dismissal of Teng Hsiao-p'ing from all posts both inside and outside the Party and the elevation of Hua to substantive Premier and First Vice-Chairman of the Party.[73] As a press campaign against Teng began to unfold, Peking (and most other places) was alive with rumours as to what exactly had gone on in early April and who had staged the T'ien An Men Incident.[74] Allegations and counter allegations of perfidious conduct, forgery of documents and all kinds of skullduggery abounded.[75] Such one might expect in the early stages of a mass movement and indeed such had characterised the early Cultural Revolution. Yet the atmosphere could not have been more different. Observing China at first hand in 1966 and 1976 and attempting to compare the two movements, I could not but conclude that the campaign against Teng Hsiao-p'ing was not a mass movement at all. Though the press of 1966 did not always accurately reflect what was going on at the basic levels, the tone of its polemics and that of mass criticism was similar. In 1976, the press campaign against Teng rarely corresponded to mass activity. When I asked factory cadres just what the concrete manifestation of Teng's 'line' had been in their particular unit, I was frequently told that, it had little impact since he had been 'nipped in the bud in time' and that policy would not change. Such a reply might indicate that the cadre concerned did not share in the official condemnation of Teng or that he had not studied Marxist theory sufficiently 'seriously' to see Teng as the manifestation of a particular approach rather than just a 'bad egg'. The former was perhaps the more likely explanation. As Watson indicated in his chapter, the factories that he and I visited at that time did not seem to envisage any operational implications of the re-evaluation of Teng Hsiao-p'ing.

There are two possible explanations for such a state of affairs. First, one might hypothesise that the criticism of Teng was unpopular either because its substantive content did not strike a chord amongst ordinary people or because they were heartily fed up with the 'Gang of Four' who were firmly behind the denunciation. An article in late May in the press which the 'Gang of Four' supposedly controlled, quoted Mao's criticism of those who sought to 'reverse verdicts' but which might easily apply to them:

> The masses are the real heroes, while we are childish and ignorant
> . . . very often people at the lower levels can do better than those
> at the higher and the masses [do better] than the leaders; leaders
> are not as good as ordinary labourers because they are detached
> from the masses and do not have practical experience.[76]

The above explanation is borne out by the apparent joy with which the subsequence ousting of the 'Gang of Four' was greeted. Yet there is another explanation which is much more ominous. The lack of mass enthusiasm in the Anti-Teng movement might be explained by the fact that the movement was blocked by the reconstructed Party which was under no circumstances going to see the development of a new upsurge in Mao's 'continuous revolution'. This is what the Party machine had tried to do in early 1966 and had failed. Had it now succeeded?

Throughout the summer and early autumn of 1976 the Anti-Teng movement continued, though the problems that had to be faced were often completely beyond the scope of the 'struggle between two lines'. The death of Chu Teh in July[77] removed from the central leadership one of the rumoured architects of the compromise leadership formed earlier in the year and a force for unity around which different groups might rally. The massive Tangshan earthquake, later in the month, diverted energies, and *People's Daily* could only make a plaintive appeal that concern for the earthquake relief operations should enhance rather than detract from the Anti-Teng movement.[78] This massive natural disaster absorbed the energies of Hua Kuo-feng[79] and many of the top Chinese leadership throughout August and perhaps removed them from the stresses and strains of the struggle. It was probably a tired Hua Kuo-feng who had to face the greatest crisis in his life following the death of Mao Tsetung on 9 September.

Once again, we may relate the developments in the third movement to the conclusions reached by contributors to this book. In Chapter 1, Young implies that Party leadership and a movement like the Cultural Revolution may be in contradiction. If the lack of vigour in the Anti-Teng campaign was in fact due to Party opposition, then clearly he is not alone in this view. One might conclude from Woodward's arguments in Chapter 2, that all parties to the disputes in China in 1976 would be wary of a renewed bout of Army factionalism and it is significant that, when the chips were down, the military hats worn by the two major protagonists in the struggle did not reflect any serious cleavages in the Army. In Chapter 3, Chan points out that, however much academic standards are stressed, it will be extremely difficult to undo many of the achievements of the revolution in education. Though surprised at the low-key in which the Anti-Teng movement was carried out in 1976. I could not but be impressed at the unprecedented achievements in the integration of schools and society that were the continuing legacy of the Cultural Revolution. Though officials at the Ministry of Education informed me that 'people-run' (*minban*) education was but a temporary expedient in a developing country,[80] this disappointing statement was belied by the successes in the social integration of education observed in the North East. The fact that this area was said later to be a bastion of the soon to be discredited 'Gang of Four'[81] has done nothing to dampen one's optimism. Cheng is probably correct in his view that the Anti-Teng movement had little impact on production but one cannot deny that the developmental significance of what was criticised was of profound importance. The 'Gang of Four' feared that Teng's policies would turn China into another version of the Soviet Union and the fact that their actions were less than admirable should not blind us to that possibility and prevent us evaluating critically the policies pursued now Teng has been rehabilitated. Finally, it should be noted that, for all the subsequent charges that the 'Gang of Four' might have colluded with foreign countries during their period of power,[82] there was no significant change in foreign policy during the period.

The Campaign Against the 'Gang of Four'

Within one month of the death of Mao, Hua Kuo-feng was appointed Chairman of the Party and head of its Military Commission[83] in addition to his post as Premier and, before October was out, a major campaign was under way to denounce the 'Gang of Four' who had taken such an active part in initiating the three major movements of the past three years.

The accusations came thick and fast. They were charged with fabricating Mao's final instructions 'to act according to the principles laid down',[84] of plotting to seize power with the aid of the Shanghai militia,[85] of attempting to overthrow Chou En-lai[86] as well as maintaining illicit relations with foreign countries. They were said to have called for the dismissal of large numbers of rehabilitated cadres who played key roles in the national economy[87] and of pursuing policies which damaged foreign trade[88] and industrial and agricultural production.[89] They were held responsible for throttling artistic creation[90] and of totally dominating the news media.[91] They were even alleged to have sought to disrupt the unity of the armed forces and to have opposed their modernisation.[92] Mao himself, we are told, had warned long ago of their conspiratorial activities and, as early as 17 July 1974, had criticised them.[93] At a Politburo meeting on 3 May 1975, he himself had coined the term 'Gang of Four'.[94]

I shall not discuss the charges here but some reference must be made to these attacks in a final evaluation of this book and, in view of the incompleteness of the information, this is done with some diffidence.

General Conclusions

A major theme of all chapters is the 'struggle between two lines'. Though other works may see this as merely an intra-bureaucratic fight between the forces of Mao Tsetung and opposition groups, all the contributors to this book see it as the result of different approaches

to development. The classic Cultural Revolution form counterposed
the line of Mao Tsetung and Liu Shao-ch'i. Mao represented the
mid 1950s version of the Yenan spirit, chastened by some of the
experiences of the Great Leap Forward. Mao's approach includes the
Mass Line, the economic and social policies laid down in 'On the Ten
Major Relationships', the educational revolution of 1958 and 'cadre'
as opposed to managerial or bureaucratic leadership. Liu Shao-ch'i
on the other hand, represented the 'revisionist' transformation of the
Soviet model in the early 1960s. It includes Libermanist economic
policy,[95] an 'economic' view of rationality, the strengthening of
market relationships, a partial recentralisation of administrative
control, an education system geared to technical expertise, and
managerial/bureaucratic leadership. Though all would agree on this
categorisation, there is disagreement as to its importance. Chan, who
focusses on higher education, where the struggles were most intense,
regards it as crucial to our understanding of the early 1970s.
Woodward, considering the Army and agricultural policy, also thinks it
important. Cheng, on the other hand, in discussing general
economic strategy, whilst acknowledging its theoretical importance,
tends to discount its practical significance after 1969. Watson argues
that, whatever the theoretical validity of the concept of a 'two line
struggle', its real content requires acknowledgement of the dictates
of technology and resources and a clearer definition of the classes in
contemporary Chinese society than is currently available to us. Finally
Young comes to the conclusion that, as far as reconstructing the
Party in 1969-70 was concerned, there was only one practical line.

If Cheng is right in the view that the 'two line struggle' did not
have much impact on economic strategy in the 1970s, despite the
recent condemnation of the 'Gang of Four',[96] it may well be that there
was a desire to avoid a repetition of the adverse effects that a
denunciation of all and sundry produced once the Cultural Revolution
expanded beyond the sphere of education in late 1966. Moreover, if
Woodward is right that the 'two line struggle' in agriculture was of
more significance in the years 1968-70, this may be because the
Cultural Revolution had less impact on the rural areas and there was
consequently less of a fear of repeating earlier mistakes. It was
certainly my impression, visiting factories in mid-1976 and comparing
them with similar factories that I visited in 1966, that the 'two line
struggle' was not having the impact the press might indicate, whereas
in schools and universities it was a lively issue. What does all this tell
us about the impact of the Cultural Revolution?

One thing the above might indicate is that the Cultural Revolution, which began in the superstructure, later achieved a number of revolutionary changes in the economy so that, by the mid-1970s, whilst the economy was consolidated, the preconditions for a new stage were being established once again in the superstructure. It cannot be denied that significant changes had occurred in agriculture and these Woodward notes. Watson, however, discussing industry, is less sanguine. Yet one thing which does not appear to have happened is any significant move towards 'ownership by the whole people'. Though Cheng, Woodward and Watson would testify to marked economic growth, I doubt whether any would agree that the structural changes envisaged by Mao in the early 1960s were coming about.

A different view is that the Cultural Revolution, which started in the field of education, had its major impact in that field and only had a slight impact on the economy. That field in which an idealist view of socialism had been dominant in 1966 had undergone a major transformation without the idealist view yielding place, in any major sense, to a materialist view. The residual view of class had been dominant in 1966 and it remained dominant in the early 1970s. Thus, those early protagonists of the Cultural Revolution in Shanghai — the 'Gang of Four' — were most active in promoting a generative view of class once again in the Campaign to Study the Theory of the Dictatorship of the Proletariat in 1975.[97]

If this is the case, we have a clue not only to why the generative view was eclipsed for more than ten years but why the 'Gang of Four' were attacked with such venom. A major reason why the generative view of class disappeared after 1964 may have been that it was widely held that it would damage production. When it was put forward once again in 1975, after a relatively peaceful period in the economy, it was resisted with such a ferocious intensity that the 'Gang of Four' were ousted and Chairman Hua turned back to a residual view of class. When the new Chairman extolled Chairman Mao's 'theory of continuing the revolution under the dictatorship of the proletariat' he projected it back to the late 1950s and, in fact, talked about the 'uninterrupted revolution' of that time in which the generative view of class and the notion of 'superstructural-push' were both absent. At the same time, Hua Kuo-feng quoted Mao to the effect that: 'The productive forces are the most revolutionary factor. When the productive forces have developed, there is bound to be a revolution'.[98] Adding that this was a Marxist theory applicable to *any* society, Chairman Hua ignored the particular relationship between base and superstructure outlined by Mao in the early 1960s and elaborated in the Introduction above.

I do not wish to deny here that the 'Gang of Four's' insistence on creating the superstructural conditions for a new stage of development may have degenerated into fundamentalist anti-technologism Nor may I refute the charges that they plotted a coup, subverted the Army and were in every respect a thoroughly bad lot. My point is merely to doubt Chairman Hua's suggestion that Mao Tsetung's thinking on socialist transition was fully developed by the late 1950s and to suggest that recent *explicit* denunciations of the generative theory of class[99] may not have met with Mao's approval.

The current official view (ascribed to Mao Tsetung) is that the Cultural Revolution consisted of 70 per cent achievements and 30 per cent mistakes[100] (the reverse of Liu Shao-ch'i's assessment of the Great Leap Forward). Indeed, the argument above would suggest that the Cultural Revolution was much less thorough-going than some of us had thought. Young's picture of Party reconstruction also tends to support this view. Clearly a Party which sets out to lead the proletariat might avoid idealism by testing rather than disregarding social, political and economic limits[101] but, in doing so, it might take the view of itself as social engineer. Moreover, a generative view of class, as an implicit rebuttal of Stalin (or at least his position before 1952), might lead to the kind of thinking manifested by people like Djilas[102] whom most Marxist-Leninists consider to be counter-revolutionary. It is indeed along these lines that the 'Gang of Four's' view of class has been subjected to sharp criticism.[103] In my view, one need come to no such conclusion but one cannot but observe that, if 'top persons in authority taking the capitalist road' will continually be generated, then there are limits to how 'correct' the Party may be in a Leninist sense. If one is frightened by the implications of such an argument, then one is left with the unsatisfactory (and all too current) explanation of 'antagonistic' struggle within the Party in terms of persons 'sneaking in' through conspirational means.[104]

It is understandable, therefore, why, in the Cultural Revolution, some Red Guards and revolutionary rebels abandoned the Party and moved to an idealist view of socialism. Mao Tsetung Thought became for many Red Guards a 'magic wand' and their 'ultra-leftist' disregard of objective social and economic conditions often alienated the masses and violated the Mass Line. In her contribution to this book, Chan sees the idealism of these Red Guards as a consequence of the élitist pre-Cultural Revolution education system. Their anti-élitism was all too often itself élitist and led to sectarian faction fighting. To Chan, therefore, what the Chinese called 'bourgeois' factionalism was 'bourgeois' in *origin*. To Young, on the other hand, adopting a more structuralist perspective, it was 'bourgeois' in *effect*. As Young sees it, there can be no Mass Line without an effective Party organisation. Red Guard élitism, therefore, resulted from the *breakdown* of social structures rather than the *rigidity* of social structures inherited from the past. The logic of Chan's position is that the failure in early 1967 of the attempts by revolutionary rebels in Shanghai to dispense with the Party by forming Paris Commune-type organisations was due to an inadequate ideological basis. Young's analysis, on the other hand, would lead us to the conclusion that no Paris Commune-type organisation could possibly succeed so long as a Party was needed to process mass demands. Both the concerns of Chan (the bourgeois class affiliation of intellectuals) and of Young (the isolation of leaders from masses) required the reconstruction of the Party after the Cultural Revolution but their difference in focus might lead to different conclusions. Young, observing the rebuilding of Party structures, by much the same people in much the same form as before the Cultural Revolution, suggests that, as far as revitalising the Party was concerned, the Cultural Revolution was a failure. Chan, on the other hand observing the criticism both of policies which might resurrect the old education system and those which elevated political opportunism above academic standards, suggests that the preconditions for the growth of a Party élite are no longer so marked.

With these possibilities in mind, can we now reach some conclusions on more recent events? In my view, we should abstain from judgement on the merits of Teng Hsiao-p'ing or the 'Gang of Four' at this stage. We should wait a while until some of the more absurd accusations have been fully tested against their opposites. I suspect we might finish up with the position taken by Cheng that development policy has not, in fact, changed very much or of Chan, who foresees more of the same kind of struggles though within the context of a much more widely educated populace. In the meantime, we can only note the continuing stress on discipline in industry, the strengthening of Party control, the focus on the technical role of the Army — policies which first began to grow in importance during the period studied in this book. If, over the years, these policies remain unchanged then, without a doubt, China will become 'revisionist' in the manner of the Soviet Union. If they give place to opposite policies and these continue unchanged for years, then China will still be far from the goals envisaged by Mao. If, in fact, policies continue to alternate and the changing limits of human action and motivation are sounded, then China's socialist transition will mean something of very great value. In the meantime, we may anticipate further absurdities, further dejection and excitement, and perhaps further enlightenment.

The value of the contributions to this book lie in the extent to which they explicate the contradictions inherent in the current debate. How does one resolve the contradiction between Party leadership and 'continuous revolution'? The ultimate answer is surely by eliminating the need for a Party. In the meantime, a generative view of classes intensifies that need. One cannot resolve the issue by wishing the generative view of classes away, as the present leadership seems to have done, and I suspect that their position is merely the extreme response to the extreme 'ultra-leftist' (or 'ultra-rightist') interpretation of the generative view of class. We will leave open the question as to whether the extreme position was, in fact, explicated by Yao Wen-yuan and Chang Ch'un-ch'iao. How does one prevent the Army insulating itself from society and becoming a technocratic élitist organisation? The ultimate answer is surely by eliminating the need for an Army. But the solution to that problem is not in China's hands. In the meantime, one cannot resolve the issue by relegating the tradition of people's war to the place occupied by the colours in a Western military unit. But is not this the extreme response to the absurdity of a view which consigned much of the Army's time to reconciling faction fights both outside and within its own ranks? How does one resolve the contradiction between the need for high technical standards in education and an 'open door' policy? The ultimate answer is predicated on a high standard of material life which both concerns must jointly bring about. In the meantime the problem may not be solved by separating out an élitist sector of education from the general system. This retreat from an 'open door' system has not yet happened; I doubt whether it will. How does one resolve the contradiction between making workers politically aware participants in matters which affect their daily lives and the need for factory discipline? The ultimate answer lies in \the voluntary imposition of self-discipline and the transformation of industrial processes. In the meantime, the new stress on rules and regulations is but the response to extreme anarchy. How does one maintain the need for balanced sectoral growth in the

economy and policies of imbalance which might release human
creativity? How does one resolve the contradiction between consumption
and investment? How does one profit from foreign trade and not be
subject to the crises of the capitalist world? How does one import
technology and not inbuilt capitalist relations? Since the 1950s, there
has been an unwillingess to push any of these latter contradictions
to the level of 'absurdity' but, would economic development have
been more spectacular if there had? Finally, how does one respond
to a changing international environment without succumbing to what
one writer has called the 'logic of world power'? The ultimate
answer lies in the need to eliminate the contemporary division of the
world which, for a Marxist, means the elimination of capitalism. In
the meantime, China is caught between the dangers inherent in 'great
power' status and the 'absurdity' of the 'mountain-top mentality'
of the Cultural Revolution.

Notes

1. *PR* 3, 14 January 1977, p.13.
2. Goodstadt L, *FEER* 40, 2 October 1971.
3. Sigurdson (1973, pp.227-32) does not establish any link with Lin Piao.
   On the general debate, see Cheng 1973, pp.2-3.
4. Kuo Chi, *PR* 9, 25 February 1977, pp.16-18.
5. Chi Ping, *PR* 13, 31 March 1972, p.6.
6. Peck 1972.
7. Lin Piao 1965.
8. Yang Jung-kuo, *Hongqi* 12, 1972, pp.45-54.
9. See e.g. Shih Lun, *Hongqi* 10, 1973, pp.33-43.
10. For different sets of documents relating to different views on the Socialist
    Education Movement, see Baum and Teiwes 1968. On the different
    perspectives in the Anti-Confucius campaign, see Goldman 1975.
11. See the collection of articles in PFLP 1974.
12. See Esmein 1973, p.159.
13. *PR* 3, 14 January 1977, p.28.
14. Shengwulian 6 January 1968, in Mehnert 1969, p.88.
15. Goldman 1975.
16. CCP CC, *Zhongfa* 1972/4, 13 January 1972, in *Chinese Law and Government*,
    Vol.5, No.3-4, Fall-Winter 1972-3, p.48.
17. Yang Jung-kuo, *GMRB*, 24 August 1974, in *SCMP* 5690, 6 September 1974,
    pp.140-3.
18. Lo Ssu-ting, *Hongqi* 11, 1973, p.36.
19. Ibid., p.38.
20. *RMRB*, 8 September 1974, in *SCMP*, 5700, 20 September 1974, pp.191-203.
21. Ibid., p.193.
22. Ibid.
23. *PR* 16, 19 April 1974, pp.6-11.
24. CCP CC, *Zhongfa* 1972/21, 1 July 1974, in *Issues and Studies*, Vol.11, No.1,

pp.101-104. The explicit message of this document was, in fact, that
production had declined in certain places because of failure to implement the
movement adequately.

25. See Fu Wen, *PR* 10, 8 March 1974, pp.16-18; Li Chen, *PR* 12, 22 March 1974,
pp.17-19 and 21; Liu Chao, *PR* 13, 29 March 1974, pp.15-17; Hsing
Yen-tzu, *PR* 14, 5 April 1974, pp.18-21.
26. Personal information not confirmed in official sources.
27. Li Shih, *Hongqi* 3, 1974, p.16.
28. *RMRB,* 28 November 1974, in *PR* 49, 6 December 1974, pp.5-6. Though this
was a call to continue the movement, as Starr (1976, p.465) points out,
the article reads like an official summary.
29. Discussed in Starr 1976, p.467.
30. Chou En-lai, 13 January 1975, *PR* 4, 24 January 1975, pp.21-5.
31. Chang Ch'un-ch'iao, 13 January 1975, *PR* 4, 24 January 1975, pp.18-20.
32. *RMRB,* 9 February 1975, in *PR* 7, 14 February 1975, pp.4-5; Chih Heng
in ibid., pp.6-9.
33. Yao Wen-yuan, *Hongqi* 3, 1975, *PR* 10, 7 March 1975, pp.5-10. Chang
Ch'un-ch'iao, *Hongqi* 4, 1975, *PR* 14, 4 April 1975, pp.5-11.
34. Marx 1875, pp.18-19.
35. Lenin 1917, p.307. The English term used in this Soviet edition is
'bourgeois law', though the term 'bourgeois right' *(faquan)* is used in all
official English translations from the Chinese.
36. Yao Wen-yuan, *Hongqi* 3, 1975, *PR* 10, 7 March 1975, p.6.
37. Goodstadt L., in *FEER* 31, 1 August 1975, p.30.
38. CCP CC, 21 July 1977, in *PR* 31, 29 July 1977, pp.3-8.
39. Teng Hsiao-p'ing, 7 October 1975, quoted in Chai Ch'ing, *Xuexi yu Pipan* 4,
1976, p.11. For a summary of the criticisms of Teng, see Gittings 1976.
40. Chai Ch'ing, *Xuexi Yu Pipan* 4, 1976, p.14.
41. Ibid., p.15. Teng quotes Lenin and Mao to this effect and is rebutted by
Chai Ch'ing, Ibid., pp.15-17.
42. See pp.20-27.
43. Teng Hsiao-p'ing, 7 October 1975, quoted in Chai Ch'ing, *Xuexi yu Pipan* 4,
1976, pp.16-17.
44. Ibid., p.17 and Teng Hsiao-p'ing (undated) in ibid., p.31.
45. Ibid., p.31.
46. K'ang Li and Yen Feng, *Xuexi yu Pipan* 4, 1976, pp.24-5.
47. Teng Hsiao-p'ing, 10 April 1974, in *PR* 15, 12 April 1974, Supplement, p.iv.
48. Teng Hsiao-p'ing (undated), quoted in *Xuexi yu Pipan* 4, 1976, p.22.
49. Ibid., p.30.
50. Chai Ch'ing (*Xuexi yu Pipan* 4, 1976, p.11) speaks of this trend exhibiting
a 'high tide' from July to September 1975.
51. See pp.111-2.
52. Apparently Teng's authority for this was a supposed statement by Mao in
1963 which the other side denied Mao ever made. K'ang Li and Yen Feng,
Xuexi yu Pipan 4, 1976, p.26 (discussing the Marxist credentials of this
statement).
53. The most contentious article for which Chou was held responsible was
published in *Jiaoyu Geming Tongxun* 10, 1975 and is translated in *Vento
dell'est* (Milan) 42, 1976, pp.124-7. This article purported to *contrast*
'open door' education with Dewey's notion of 'school as society'.
54. Gittings 1976, pp.492-3.
55. *PR* 1, 2 January 1976, p.9.
56. *PR* 6, 4 February 1977, pp.8-9; *PR* 13, 25 March 1977, pp.10-12.

57. Hua Kuo-feng, 15 October 1975, in *PR* 44, 31 October 1975, p.9.
58. Yao Wen-yuan, *Hongqi* 3, 1975, in *PR* 10, 7 March 1975, p.6.
59. *RMRB*, 4 September 1975, in *PR* 37, 12 September 1975, p.7.
60. Ibid.
61. This is the interpretation of Starr (1976, p.474).
62. Ibid., from Taiwan sources.
63. Ibid., p.473, based on evidence from *RMRB*, 20 May 1975, in *PR* 21, 23 May 1975, pp.6-7.
64. *PR* 1, 2 January 1976, p.7.
65. *PR* 23, 3 June 1977, p.18.
66. Ibid., p.22.
67. Teng Hsiao-p'ing, 15 January 1976, in *PR* 4, 23 January 1976, pp.5-8.
68. Liang Hsiao, *RMRB*, 15 January 1976, p.2.
69. Mao had allegedly criticised this statement. K'ang Li and Yen Feng, *Xuexi yu Pipan* 4, 1976, p.26.
70. *PR* 7, 13 February 1976, p.3. Hua's meeting with the Venezuelan ambassador was the first official confirmation that he had been appointed Acting Premier.
71. Hua Kuo-feng, 22 February 1976, *PR* 9, 27 February 1976, p.5.
72. *PR* 15, 9 April 1976, pp.4-7.
73. CCP CC, 7 April 1976, *PR* 15, 9 April 1976, p.3.
74. Personal information gained in Peking.
75. Liang Hsiao, *Hongqi* 5, 1976, p.22.
76. *RMRB*, 29 May 1976, in *PR* 23, 4 June 1976, p.12.
77. CCP CC NPC, Standing Committee and SC, 6 July 1976, in *PR* 28, 9 July 1976, pp.3-4.
78. *RMRB*, 11 August 1976, in *PR* 34, 20 August 1976, pp.5-6.
79. *PR* 32-33, 9 August 1976, p.7.
80. Discussion at Ministry of Education, Peking, 22 May 1976.
81. Mao Yuan-hsin was said to have been the 'top henchman of the Gang of Four in Liaoning'. Apparently he master-minded the publicity given to Chang T'ieh-sheng.
82. Theoretical Study Group, Ministry of Foreign Affairs, *PR* 5, 28 January 1977, p.15.
83. *PR* 44, 29 October 1976, pp.7-11 and 21.
84. *PR* 3, 14 January 1977, p.30.
85. *PR* 6, 4 February 1977, pp.8-9; *PR* 13, 25 March 1977, pp.10-12.
86. *PR* 3, 14 January 1977, p.28.
87. Ibid., p.8.
88. Kuo Chi, *PR* 9, 25 February 1977, pp.16-18.
89. Chi Wei, *PR* 11, 11 March 1977, pp.6-9.
90. *PR* 23, 3 June 1977, pp.14-17.
91. *PR* 3, 14 January 1977, p.29.
92. Hsieh Cheng, *PR* 10, 4 March 1977, pp.9-12.
93. *PR* 3, 14 January 1977, p.28.
94. Ibid. p.29.
95. I.e. the belief in a socialist market.
96. See Chi Wei, *PR* 11, 11 March 1977, pp.6-9; *PR* 6, 4 February 1977, pp.9-10.
97. Yao Wen-yuan, *PR* 10, 7 March 1975, pp.5-10; Chang Ch'un-ch'iao, *PR* 14, 4 April 1975, pp.5-11.
98. Hua Kuo-feng, *PR* 19, 6 May 1977, p.24.
99. Hsiang Chun, *PR* 14, 1 April 1977, pp.6-12.
100. *PR* 19, 6 May 1977, p.37.
101. For a discussion of 'testing limits' see Pfeffer 1976, pp.433-4 and Schwartz

1976, p.465.
102. Djilas 1966.
103. Hsiang Chun, *PR* 14, 1 April 1977, pp.6-12.
104. Ibid and Hua Kuo-feng, *PR* 19, 6 May 1977, pp.15-27.

BIBLIOGRAPHY

Adie, W. 'One World Restored? Sino-American Relations on a New Footing', *Asian Survey,* Vol.12, No.5, 1972

Andors, S. 'Revolution and Modernization: Man and Machine in Industrializing Society, the Chinese Case', in Friedman and Selden (eds.) 1971

—— *China's Industrial Revolution, Politics Planning and Management, 1949 to the Present*. (New York, Pantheon Books, 1977)

Ashbrook, A. 'China: Economic Overview 1975', in US Congress, Joint Economic Committee, 1975

Barber, R. 'Big, Bigger, Biggest: American Business Goes Global', *New Republic,* Vol.154, No.18 (30 April 1966)

Barnett, A. *Cadres Bureaucracy and Political Power in Communist China* (New York, Columbia University Press, 1967)

—— 'The Changing Pattern of U.S.-China Relations', *Current Scene,* Vol.10, No.4 (10 April 1972)

Bastid, M. 'Economic Necessity and Political Ideals in Educational Reform During the Cultural Revolution', *CQ* 42 (April-June 1970)

—— 'Levels of Economic Decision Making', in Schram (ed.) 1973

Baum, R. 'The Cultural Revolution in the Countryside: Anatomy of a Limited Rebellion', in Robinson (ed.) 1971

—— and Teiwes, F. *Ssu-Ch'ing: The Socialist Education Movement of 1962-1966* (Berkeley, University of California, Center for Chinese Studies, 1968)

Bennett, G. 'Military Regions and Provincial Party Secretaries: One Outcome of China's Cultural Revolution', *CQ* 54 (April-June 1973)

—— and Montaperto, R. *Red Guard: The Political Biography of Dai Hsiao-ai* (Garden City, N.Y. Doubleday 1971)

Bettelheim, C. *Cultural Revolution and Industrial Organization in China* (New York, Monthly Review Press, 1974)

Bowie, R. and Fairbank, J. *Communist China 1955-1959: Policy Documents with Analysis* (Cambridge Mass, Harvard University Press, 1965)

Bradsher, H. 'China: The Radical Offensive', *Asian Survey,* Vol.13, No.11 (November 1973)

Bridgham, P. 'The Fall of Lin Piao', *CQ* 55,
　(July-September 1973)
Brugger, W. *Democracy and Organisation in the Chinese Industrial
　Enterprise 1948-1953* (Cambridge University Press, 1976)
—— (B) *Contemporary China* (London, Croom Helm 1977)
Buck, J. 'Food Grain Production in Mainland China before and during
　the Communist Regime', in Buck, Dawson and Wu (eds.) 1966
—— Dawson, O. and Wu Y., *Food and Agriculture in Communist
　China* (New York, Praeger, for the Hoover Institution on War,
　Revolution and Peace, 1966)
Bulletin of the Atomic Scientists *China After the Cultural Revolution*
　(New York, Vintage Books, 1970)
Burchett, W. 'Lin Piao's Plot — The Full Story', *FEER,* 20 August 1973
de Camp, R. 'The Asian Development Bank: An Imperial Thrust into
　the Pacific', in Selden (ed.) 1974
Chang, P. 'Regional Military Power: The Aftermath of the Cultural
　Revolution', *Asian Survey,* Vol.12, No.12 (December 1972)
—— 'Political Profiles: Wang Hung-wen and Li Teh-sheng', *CQ* 57
　(January-March 1974)
Chao Kang 'Policies and Performance in Industry', in Eckstein, Galenson
　and Liu (eds.), 1968
—— 'The Production and Application of Chemical Fertilisers in China',
　CQ 64 (December 1975)
Chen, C. and Ridley, C. *Rural People's Communes in Lien-chiang:
　Documents Concerning Communes in Lien-chiang County, Fukien
　Province 1962-63* (Stanford, Hoover Institution Press, 1969)
Ch'en, J. and Tarling, N. *Studies in the Social History of China and
　South East Asia* (Cambridge University Press, 1970)
Chen Nai-ruenn 'China's Foreign Trade 1950-74' in US Congress,
　Joint Economic Committee, 1975
Cheng Chu-yuan 'China's Machine Building Industry', *Current Scene,*
　Vol.9, No.7 (July 1973)
Cheng, J. (ed.) *The Politics of the Chinese Red Army: A Translation
　of the Bulletin of Activities of the People's Liberation Army*
　(Stanford, Hoover Institution Press, 1966)
Chu Wen-lin, 'Personnel Changes in the PLA Military Regions and
　Districts Before and After the Cultural Revolution', in
　Institute of International Relations, 1971
Collier, J. and E. *China's Socialist Revolution* (London, Stage 1, 1973)
Committee of Concerned Asian Scholars *The Indochina Story* (New
　York, Bantam Books, 1970)

Compton, B. *Mao's China: Party Reform Documents 1942-44* (Seattle and London, University of Washington Press, 1966)

Djilas, M. *The New Class; An Analysis of the Communist System* (London, Unwin Books, 1966)

Domes, J. 'The Role of the Military in the Formation of Revolutionary Committees 1967-68', *CQ* 44 (October-December 1970)

—— (trans. Machetzki, R.) *The Internal Politics of China 1949-1972* (London, Hurst and Co., 1973)

—— 'Transition Towards a New Political System in China: The Role of the Party and The Army', in Wilson (ed.), 1973

Donnithorne, A. 'China's Cellular Economy: Some Economic Trends Since the Cultural Revolution', *CQ* 52 (September-December 1972)

—— 'China's Import of Capital Goods and Policy on Foreign Credit', paper given at seminar on China's foreign trade, Australian National University, Canberra, 7-9 March 1975

Eckstein, A. 'Economic Growth and Change in China: A Twenty-year Perspective', *CQ* 54, (April-June 1973)

—— *China's Economic Development: The Interplay of Scarcity and Ideology* (Ann Arbor, University of Michigan Press, 1975)

—— 'China's Trade Policy and Sino-American Relations', *Foreign Affairs,* Vol.54, No.1 (October 1975)

—— Galenson, W. and Liu Ta-chung (eds.), *Economic Trends in Communist China* (Edinburgh University Press, 1968)

Esmein, J. (trans. Jenner, W.) *The Chinese Cultural Revolution* (New York, Anchor Books, 1973)

FEER Yearbook: Asia, 1970; 1976; 1977

Feuerwerker, A. 'Chinese History and the Foreign Relations of Contemporary China', *The Annals of the American Academy of Political and Social Science,* Vol.402 (July 1972)

Field, R. 'Civilian Industrial Production in the People's Republic of China 1949-74', in US Congress, Joint Economic Committee 1975

—— Lardy, N. and Emerson, J., 'Industrial Output by Province in China, 1949-73', *CQ* 63, (September 1975)

Franke, W. *The Reform and Abolition of the Traditional Chinese Examination System* (Cambridge Mass., Harvard University Press, 1960)

Fraser, S. (ed.) *Chinese Communist Education: Records of the First Decade* (Nashville, Vanderbilt University Press, 1965)

Friedman, E. and Selden, M. (eds.) *America's Asia: Dissenting Essays on Asian-American Relations* (New York, Vintage Books, 1971) van Ginnekan, J. *The Rise and Fall of Lin Piao* (Harmondsworth, Penguin Books, 1976)

Gittings, J. *The Role of the Chinese Army* (London, Oxford University Press 1967)

—— 'China's Foreign Policy' Continuity or Change?', *Journal of Contemporary Asia,* Vol.2, No.1 (1972)

—— 'New Material on Teng Hsiao-p'ing', *CQ* 67 (September 1976)

Goldman, M. 'The Unique "Blooming and Contending" of 1961-62', *CQ* 37 (January-March 1969)

—— 'China's Anti-Confucian Campaign 1973-74', *CQ* 63 (September 1975)

Goodstadt, L. 'Rice vs Rockets', *FEER,* 2 October 1971

—— 'China: Calendar of Conspiracy', *FEER*, 27 November 1971

—— *Mao Tse-tung: The Search for Plenty* (Hong Kong, Longman, 1972)

Gray, J. 'The High Tide of Socialism in the Chinese Countryside', in Ch'en and Tarling (eds.), 1970

—— 'The Economics of Maoism', in Bulletin of the Atomic Scientists 1970

—— 'The Two Roads: Alternative Strategies of Social Change and Economic Growth in China', in Schram (ed.), 1973

Griswold, D. *Indonesia – Second Greatest Crime of the Century* (New York, Youth Against War and Fascism, 1969)

Guangdong sheng Geming Weiyuanhui, Gong Jiao Bangongshi Zhengzhibu *Zou Daqing de Daolu, Ban Daqing shi Qiye* (Guangdong Chubanshe, 1973)

Gurley, J. 'Capitalist and Maoist Economic Development', in Friedman and Selden (eds.), 1971

Hallford, S. 'Mechanization in the PRC', *Current Scene,* Vol.14, No.5 (May 1976)

Hayter, T. *Aid as Imperialism* (Harmondsworth, Penguin Books, 1971)

Heymann, H. 'Acquisition and Diffusion of Technology in China', in US Congress, Joint Economic Committee, 1975

Hinton, H. *The Bear at the Gate: Chinese Policymaking under Soviet Pressure* (Washington DC, American Enterprise Institute for Public Policy Research, 1972)

—— *An Introduction to Chinese Politics* (Melbourne, Wren, 1973)

Hinton, W. *Fanshen: A Documentary of Revolution in a Chinese Village,* (New York, Vintage Books 1966)

—— *Turning Point in China* (New York, Monthly Review Press, 1972)

—— *Hundred Day Way: The Cultural Revolution at Tsinghua*

University (New York, Monthly Review Press, 1972)

Howe, C. 'China', *International Institute for Labour Studies, Bulletin,* No.10 (1972)

—— *Wage Patterns and Wage Policy in Modern China 1919-1972* (Cambridge University Press, 1973)

—— 'Labour Organisation and Incentives in Industry Before and After the Cultural Revolution', in Schram (ed.) 1973

Hsu Ch'ien-sun 'An Analysis of the Personnel Reshuffle in China's Military Regions', *Feiqing Yuebao,* February 1974, trans. *Chinese Law and Government* Vol.7, No.3)

Hsu Tak-ming (Hsü Te-ming) *Wenge hou de Zhong Gong Jingji* (*Communist Chinese Economy after the Cultural Revolution*) (Hong Kong, Union Research Institute, 1974)

Hunter, N. *Shanghai Journal* (New York, Praeger, 1969)

Institute of International Relations *Collected Documents of the First Sino-American Conference on Mainland China* (Taipei, 1971)

Joffe, E. 'The Chinese Army after the Cultural Revolution; the Effects of Intervention', *CQ* 55 (July-September 1973)

Johnson, C. 'China: The Cultural Revolution in Structural Perspective', *Asian Survey,* Vol.8, No.1 (January 1968)

Kau Ying-mao and Perolle, P. 'The Politics of Lin Piao's Abortive Military Coup', *Asian Survey,* Vol.14, No.6 (June 1974)

Klatt, W. 'A Review of China's Economy in 1970', *CQ* 43 (July-September 1970)

Klein, D. and Hager L. 'The Ninth Central Committee', *CQ* 45 (January-March 1971)

Kraus, R. 'Class Conflict and the Vocabulary of Social Analysis in China', *CQ* 69 (March 1977)

Krivitsov, V. and Sidikhmenov, C. (eds.) *A Critique of Mao Tse-tung's Theoretical Conceptions* (Moscow, Progress Publishers, 1972)

Lardy, N. 'Economic Planning and Income Distribution in China', *Current Scene,* Vol.14, No.11 (November 1976)

Lenin, V. 'The State and Revolution' (1917), in *SW,* Vol.2 (1976)

——, *Selected Works,* Vol.2 (Moscow, Progress Publishers, 1976)

Levy, R. 'New Light on Mao: His views on the Soviet Union's "Political Economy" ', *CQ* 61 (March 1975)

Lewis, J. *Leadership in Communist China* (Ithaca, NY, Cornell University Press, 1963) |

Lin Piao, *Long Live the Victory of People's War* (PFLP 1965)

Lindsay, M. *Notes on Educational Problems in Communist China 1941-47* (New York, Institute of Pacific Relations, International

Secretariat, March 1950)

Lippit, V. 'The Great Leap Forward Reconsidered', *Modern China*, Vol.1, No.1 (January 1975)

Liu Ch'ing-po (Simpson C.P. Liu) *Zhonggong Xianfa lun*, (English title: *A Review on the Constitution of the People's Republic of China*) (Taipei, published by author, 1972)

Liu Shao-ch'i *Collected Works* (Hong Kong, Union Research Institute, 1969), Vol.1 (Before 1944); Vol.2 (1945-57); Vol.3 (1958-67)

MacDougall, C. 'Collision in the Countryside', *FEER*, 13 February 1969
—— 'The Cultural Revolution in the Communes: Back to 1958?', *Current Scene*, Vol.7, No.7 (11 April 1969)

Magdoff, H., *The Age of Imperialism*, (New York, Monthly Review Press, 1969)

Mao Tsetung *Selected Works*, English edition, vol.1 (1965); Vol.2 (1965); Vol.3 (1965); Vol.4 (1961); Chinese edition, Vol.1 (1952); Vol.2 (1952); Vol.3 (1953); Vol.4 (1960); Vol.5 (1977). English edition published by PFLP; Chinese edition by Renmin Chubanshe
—— *Quotations from Chairman Mao Tse-tung* (PFLP, 1966) (Chinese edition, *Mao Zhuxi Yulu,* Zhongguo Renmin Jiefangjun Zong Zhengzhibu, 1967)
—— *Mao Zedong Sixiang Wansui* (referred to in notes as *Wansui*), 1967 (1); 1967 (2); 1969
—— *Mao Zhuxi Wenxuan* (no publisher no date — probably 1967)
—— *Selected Writings* (PFLP, 1971)
—— *Miscellany of Mao Tse-tung Thought*, *JPRS* 61269-1 and 2, 20 February 1974 (referred to in notes as *JPRS* 1974)

Marx, K., *Capital*, Vol.1 1867 (Moscow, Foreign Languages Publishing House 1954)
—— 'Marginal Notes to the Programme of the German Workers' Party', 1875, in Marx and Engels 1970
—— and Engels, F., *Selected Works*, Vol.3 (Moscow, Progress Publishers, 1970)

Mehnert, K. *Peking and the New Left; At Home and Abroad* (Berkeley, University of California, Center for Chinese Studies, 1969)

Michael, F. 'The New United States China Policy', *Current History* Vol. 63, No.373 (September 1972)

Milton, D., Milton, N. and Schurmann, F. (eds.) *People's China* (New York, Vintage Books, 1974)

Munro, D. 'The Chinese View of Alienation', *CQ* 59 (July-September 1974)

Myrdal, J. and Kessle, G. *China: The Revolution Continued* (Harmondsworth, Penguin Books, 1973)

Nathan, A. 'Policy Oscillations in the People's Republic of China: A Critique', *CQ* 68 (December 1976)

Nee, V. *The Cultural Revolution at Peking University*, (New York, Monthly Review Press, 1969)

Nelsen, H. 'Military Forces in the Cultural Revolution', *CQ* 51 (July-September 1972)

—— 'Military Bureaucracy in the Cultural Revolution', *Asian Survey*, Vol.14, No.4 (April 1974)

Nissen, B. 'The World Bank: A Political Institution', *Pacific Research and World Empire Telegram* (September-October 1971)

Oglesby C. and Schaull, R. *Containment and Change: Two Dissenting Views of American Foreign Policy* (New York, MacMillan, 1967)

Oksenberg, M. 'The Political Groups, Political Participation and Communication', in Wei (ed.) 1972

O'Leary, G. 'Ultra-leftism and Lin Piao', *Journal of Contemporary Asia*, Vol.4, No.2 (1974)

Parish, W. 'Factions in Chinese Military Politics', *CQ* 56 (October-December 1973)

Payer, C. *The Debt Trap: The IMF and the World Bank* (Harmondsworth Penguin Books, 1974)

Peck, J. 'Why China Turned West', *Socialist Register*, 1972

PFLP *Eighth National Congress of the Communist Party of China* (1956) Vol.1

—— *The Polemic on the General Line of the International Communist Movement* (1965)

—— *The Struggle Between the Two Roads in the Chinese Countryside* (1968)

—— *The Ninth National Congress of the Communist Party of China Documents* (1969)

—— *The Tenth National Congress of the Communist Party of China Documents* (1973)

—— *Selected Articles Criticizing Lin Piao and Confucius*, Vol.1, (1974)

—— *Documents of the First Session of the Fourth National People's Congress of the People's Republic of China* (1975)

Perkins, D. 'An Economic Re-appraisal', *Problems of Communism*, Vol.22, No.3 (May-June 1973)

Pfeffer, R. 'Mao and Marx in the Marxist Leninist Tradition: A Critique of the China Field and a Contribution to a Preliminary Reappraisal', *Modern China*, Vol.2, No.4 (October 1976)

Powell, R. 'The Party, the Government and the Gun', *Asian Survey,*
     Vol.10, No.6 (June 1970)
—— 'The Military and the Struggle for Power in China', *Current History,*
     Vol.63, No.373 (September 1972)
'A Progressive Labor Party Member', 'China Takes the Capitalist Road',
     Workers International Newsletter, Vol.1, No.1 (1973)
Pusey, J. *Wu Han: Attacking the Present through the Past* (Cambridge
     Mass., Harvard University Press, 1969)
Qishi Niandai Zazhi she *Liumei Huayi Xuezhe Chongfang Zhongguo
     Guangan Ji, (A Collection of Observations by Chinese-American
     Scholars Revisiting China)* (Hong Kong, 1974 presumed)
Ransom, D. 'The Berkeley Mafia and the Indonesian Massacre',
     Ramparts (October 1970)
Rawski, T. 'Recent Trends in the Chinese Economy', *CQ* 53 (January-
     March 1973)
Rhee, T. 'Sino-Soviet Military Conflict and the Global Balance of Power',
     The World Today, Vol.26, No.1 (January 1970)
Rice, E. 'The Sino-U.S. Detente: How Durable?', *Asian Survey,* Vol.13,
     No.9 (September 1973)
—— *Mao's Way* (Berkeley, University of Calinfornia Press, 1974)
Richman, B. *A Firsthand Study of Industrial Management in Communist
     China* (Los Angeles, University of California, Graduate School of
     Business, Division of Research, 1967)
—— *Industrial Society in Communist China* (New York, Random House,
     1969)
Riskin, C. 'Small Industry and the Chinese Model of Development',
     CQ 46, (April-June 1971)
Robinson, J. *The Cultural Revolution in China* (Harmondsworth, Penguin
     Books, 1969)
—— *Economic Management in China: 1972* (London, Anglo-Chinese
     Educational Institute, 1972)
Robinson, T. 'The Wuhan Incident: Local Strife and Provincial
     Rebellion during the Cultural Revolution', *CQ* 47 (July-September
     1971)
—— (ed.), *The Cultural Revolution in China* (Berkeley, University of
     California Press, 1971)
—— 'China in 1973: Renewed Leftism Threatens the New Course',
     Asian Survey, Vol.14, No.1 (January 1974)
Rosenberg, N. 'Neglected Dimensions in the Analysis of Economic
     Change', *Bulletin of the Oxford University Institute of Economics
     and Statistics,* Vol.26, No.1 (February 1964)

Rossanda, R. 'Mao's Marxism', *Socialist Register,* 1971

Salisbury, H. *To Peking and Beyond: A Report on the New Asia* (London Arrow Books, 1973)

Scalapino, R. 'China and the Balance of Power', *Foreign Affairs,* Vol.52, No.2 (January 1974)

Schram, S. 'Mao Tse-tung and the Theory of Permanent Revolution', *CQ* 46 (April-June 1971)

—— (ed.), *Authority, Participation and Cultural Change in China* (Cambridge University Press, 1973)

—— 'The Cultural Revolution in Historical Perspective', in Schram (ed.), 1973

—— (ed.), *Mao Tse-tung Unrehearsed* (Harmondsworth, Penguin Books, 1974)

—— ' Some Reflections on the Pfeffer-Walder "Revolution" in China Studies', *Modern China,* Vol.3, No.2 (April 1977)

Schurmann, H. 'China's "New Economic Policy" – Transition or Beginning', *CQ* 17 (January-March 1964)

—— *Ideology and Organization in Communist China* (Berkeley, University of California Press, 1966)

—— and Schell, O., *China Readings 3: Communist China* (Harmondsworth, Penguin Books, 1968)

Schwartz, B. 'The Essence of Marxism Revisisted', *Modern China,* Vol.2, No.4 (October 1976)

Selden, M. *The Yenan Way in Revolutionary China* (Cambridge Mass., Harvard University Press, 1971)

—— (ed.), *Re-making Asia: Essays on the American Uses of Power,* (New York, Pantheon, 1974)

Sigurdson, J. 'Rural Industry – A Traveller's View', *CQ* 50 (April-June 1972)

—— 'Rural Industry and the Internal Transfer of Technology', in Schram (ed.) 1973

Sims, S. 'The New Role of the Military', *Problems of Communism,* Vol.18, No.6 (November-December 1969)

Smil, V. 'Energy in China: Achievements and Prospects', *CQ* 65, (January 1976)

Snow, E. *The Long Revolution* (New York, Random House, 1971 and Harmondsworth, Penguin Books, 1974)

Solomon, R. *Mao's Revolution and the Chinese Political Culture:* (Berkeley, University of California Press, 1971)

Stalin, J. *Economic Problems of Socialism in the USSR* 1952 (PFLP, 1972)

Starr, J. 'Conceptual Foundations of Mao Tse-tung's Theory of
    Continuous Revolution', *Asian Survey,* Vol.11, No.6 (1971)
—— 'From the 10th Party Congress to the Premiership of Hua
    Kuo-feng: the Significance of the Colour of the Cat', *CQ* 67
    (September 1976)
State Statistical Bureau *Ten Great Years – Statistics on Economic
    and Cultural Achievements of the People's Republic of China*
    (PFLP, 1960)
Stone, I. 'Nixon's War Gamble and Why it Won't Work', *New York
    Review of Books,* Vol.18, No.10 (1 June 1972)
Sweezy, P. and Bettelheim C. *On the Transition to Socialism* (New
    York, Monthly Review Press, 1971)
Tang, A. 'Policy and Performance in Agriculture', in Eckstein,
    Galenson and Liu (eds.) 1968
Teng T'o (pseud. Ma Nan-t'un) *Yanshan Yehua* (Beijing Chubanshe,
    1963)
Terrill, R. *800,000,000, The Real China* (New York, Delta Books,
    1971)
Ting Wang (ed.) *Li Yizhe Dazibao* (Hong Kong, Mingbao Yuekan
    Chubanshe, 1976)
Townsend, J. *Political Participation in Communist China* (Berkeley,
    University of California Press, 1967)
Tsang Chiu-sam *Society Schools and Progress in China* Oxford,
    Pergamon Press, 1968)
Union Research Institute *The Case of P'eng Teh-huai* (Hong Kong,
    1968)
—— *Documents of the Chinese Communist Party Central
    Committee,* Vol.1 (Hong Kong, 1971)
U.S. Congress, Joint Economic Committee *China: A Reassessment
    of the Economy. A Compendium of Papers Submitted to the
    Joint Economic Committee, Congress of the US* (Washington DC,
    US Government Printing Office, 1975)
Wakeman, F. 'A Response', *Modern China,* Vol.3, No.2 (April 1977)
Walder, A. 'Marxism, Maoism and Social Change', *Modern China,*
    Vol.3, No.1 (January 1977) and Vol.3, No.2 (April 1977)
Walker K. *Planning in Chinese Agriculture: Socialisation and the
    Private Sector 1956-1962* (London, Frank Cass, 1965)
——Organisation of Agricultural Production', in Eckstein, Galenson
    and Liu (eds.) 1968
Waller, D. *The Government and Politics of Communist China* (London,
    Hutchinson, 1970)

Watson, A. 'A Revolution to Touch Men's Souls: The Family, Interpersonal Relations and Daily Life', in Schram (ed.) 1973

Wei Yung (ed.) *Communist China: A System-functional Reader* (Columbus, Ohio, Merrill, 1972)

Wertheim, W. 'Suharto and the Untung Coup — The Missing Link', *Journal of Contemporary Asia,* Vol.1, No.2 (1971)

Whalen, R. *Catch the Falling Flag: A Republican's Challenge to his Party* (Boston, Houghton Mifflin, 1972)

Wheelwright E. and McFarlane B. *The Chinese Road to Socialism* (New York, Monthly Review Press, 1970)

Whiting, A. 'The Sino-American Detente: Genesis and Prospects', in Wilson (ed.) 1973

Whitson, W. 'The Field Army in Chinese Communist Military Politics', *CQ* 37 (January-March 1969)

Wich, R. 'The Tenth Party Congress: The Power Structure and the Succession Question', *CQ* 58 (April-June 1974)

Wilson, D. 'The Role of the People's Liberation Army in the Cultural Revolution', in Australian National University, Department of Far Eastern History, *Papers on Far Eastern History,* No.3 (March 1971)

Wilson, I. (ed.) *China and the World Community* (Sydney, Angus and Robertson, 1973)

Winckler, E. 'Policy Oscillations in the People's Republic of China: A Reply', *CQ* 68 (December 1976)

Wu Yuan-li 'The Economics of Mainland China's Agriculture: Some Aspects of Measurement, Interpretation and Evaluation', in Buck, Dawson and Wu (eds.) 1966

Yahuda M. 'Chinese Conceptions of their Role in the World', *Political Quarterly,* Vol.45, No.1 (1974)

Yunnan Renmin Chubanshe *Ba Xin Dangzhang zuowei Jixu Geming de Zuoyouming lai Xue,* (*Study the New Party Constitution as an Instruction on Continuous Revolution*) (Kunming, 1970)

CONTRIBUTORS

Bill Brugger is Senior Lecturer in Politics at the Flinders University of South Australia. He formerly worked at the Peking Second Foreign Languages Institute (1964-6) and the Contemporary China Institute, School of Oriental and African Studies, University of London (1968-71). He is the author of *Democracy and Organisation in the Chinese Industrial Enterprise 1948-53* (1976), *Contemporary China* (1977) and a number of articles. He last visited China in 1976.

Sylvia Chan is Lecturer in Chinese at the Centre for Asian Studies, Adelaide University. She lived in Peking from 1951-72. She formerly worked at Peking Teachers' College (1961-72). She has translated a number of English language works into Chinese and has worked on a dictionary and several English language texts books published in China.

Joseph (Yu-shek) Cheng is Assistant Lecturer in Government at the Chinese University of Hong Kong. He formerly worked at the University of the South Pacific, Fiji. He has published articles on Chinese politics and International Relations and is currently completing a PhD thesis on Sino-Japanese relations at the Flinders University of South Australia. He visisted China in 1975.

Greg O'Leary is Lecturer in Sociology at Adelaide College of Advanced Education. He formerly worked at Adelaide University where he completed a PhD on Chinese foreign policy. He is the author of several articles on China and International Relations. He visisted China in 1976.

Andrew Watson is Lecturer in Chinese at the Centre for Asian Studies, Adelaide University. He formerly worked at the Sian Foreign Languages Institute (1965-7) and Glasgow University (1968-74). He is the author of *Living in China* (1975) and a number of articles. He has edited and translated *Transport in Transition: The Evolution of Traditional Shipping in China* (1972) and Mao Tsetung, *Economic and Financial Problems* (forthcoming). He last visisted China in 1976.

Dennis Woodward is Tutor in Politics at the Flinders University of South Australia. His research is concerned with the period between the Ninth and Tenth Party Congresses, with particular emphasis on the rural areas of China. He is currently working with Graham Young on a study of 'the theory of continuous revolution'. He has published articles on Australian and Chinese politics. He visited China in December 1975/January 1976.

Graham Young is Tutor in Politics at the Flinders University of South Australia. His research is concerned with the Chinese Communist Party, particularly the rebuilding of the Party after the Cultural Revolution. He is also collaborating with Dennis Woodward in a study of 'the theory of continuous revolution'. He visited China in 1975.

INDEX

accounting
   industrial 189
   level of agricultural 19, 138, 154,
      159, 163, 166-7, 256
administrative streamlining 18
Africa 211, 213, 215, 221, 239
agriculture
   as the foundation 127
   capitalist tendencies in 16-17,
      20, 23, 160-4
   colleges 105
   electrification of 133-5
   factionalism in 29
   ultra-leftism in 13, 158-9, 265
   see also communes, land reform,
      rural organisation, Socialist
      Education Movement, state
      farms, Tachai production
      brigade, tractor stations
Albania 96, 234
alienation 19
   of Party from masses 38, 47-52
anarchism 51, 54, 46, 62-3, 66, 138,
   162, 175, 179-83, 193, 198,
   256, 275
Andors, S 172
Angola 204
Anshan Iron and Steel Corporation
   23, 130
   Constitution 23, 189
art and literature 26-7, 108, 113,
   258, 270

Ball, G. 215
Bandaranaike, S. 86
Bangladesh 203
Bastid, M. 155
Baum, R. 153-5
Ben Bella, A. 215
Bennett, G. 90
Bettelheim, C. 24, 173-4, 195
bonuses 149, 176, 193-7
'bourgeois right' 118, 121, 167,
   262-3, 265
Brezhnev, L. 203, 243
Britain 217, 220, 229, 243
bureaucratism 15, 42, 57, 103,
   106, 157, 182, 187

cadres
   as capitalists 27
   as leadership type 15, 18, 37, 54-5,
      60, 65, 130, 135, 162, 171-2,
      175, 187, 191, 197, 271
   May Seventh schools 93, 209, 257
   military 31, 56
   new and old 31, 55-6, 59, 62, 75,
      184, 257
   participation in manual labour
      23, 55, 98, 138, 177, 182,
      191, 268
   rehabilitation of 54-5, 88, 209, 253, 270
capital accumulation 135-6
'capitalist road', top persons in
   authority taking the 27, 38,
   45, 54, 97, 123, 267, 273
Central China 128, 147
   Hunan 82, 129, 132-4, 257
   Hupei 129, 131
   Kiangsi 132, 134, 148
chairmanship of the People's
   Republic 20, 80, 87, 270
Changchun Automobile Works 61,
   193, 195-6
Chang Ch'un-ch'iao 111, 258, 261-2
Chang Kuo-t'ao .59
Chang, P. 88
Chang T'ieh-sheng 116-7, 120
Chao K'ai 266
Chao Kang 135 |
Chao Kao 258
Ch'en Po-ta 80, 220, 223
Ch'en Tu-hsiu 63
Ch'en Yi 204
Cheng Wei-shan 80
Chiang Ch'ing 113, 257, 266
Chiang Kai-shek 228
Ch'iao Kuan-hua 233, 236
Ch'in dynasty 258-9
   first emperor of 258-62
Ch'i Pen-yu 95
Ch'iu Hui-tso 80
Chou En-lai 88, 111, 114, 120,
   134, 148, 180, 220, 222, 235,
   237-42, 254-5, 257-60, 262-3,
   266-7, 270
Chou Jung-hsin 121, 264

293